AMERICAN LITERATURE AND AMERICAN IDENTITY

American Literature and American Identity addresses the crucial issue of identity formation, especially national identity, in influential works of American literature. Patrick Colm Hogan uses techniques of cognitive and affective science to examine the complex and often highly ambivalent treatment of American identity in works by Melville, Cooper, Sedgwick, Apess, Stowe, Jacobs, Douglass, Hawthorne, Poe, and Murray. Hogan focuses on the issue of how authors imagined American identity—specifically as universal democratic egalitarianism—in the face of the nation's clear and often brutal inequalities of race and sex. In the course of this study, Hogan advances our understanding of nationalism in general, American identity in particular, and the widely read literary works he examines.

Patrick Colm Hogan is a Board of Trustees Distinguished Professor in the Department of English and the Program in Cognitive Science at the University of Connecticut, U.S.A.

AMERICAN LITERATURE AND AMERICAN IDENTITY

A Cognitive Cultural Study from the Revolution through the Civil War

Patrick Colm Hogan

LONDON AND NEW YORK

First published 2020
by Routledge
2 Park Square, Milton Park, Abingdon, Oxon OX14 4RN

and by Routledge
52 Vanderbilt Avenue, New York, NY 10017

Routledge is an imprint of the Taylor & Francis Group, an informa business

© 2020 Patrick Colm Hogan

The right of Patrick Colm Hogan to be identified as the author of this work has been asserted by him in accordance with sections 77 and 78 of the Copyright, Designs and Patents Act 1988.

All rights reserved. No part of this book may be reprinted or reproduced or utilised in any form or by any electronic, mechanical, or other means, now known or hereafter invented, including photocopying and recording, or in any information storage or retrieval system, without permission in writing from the publishers.

Trademark notice: Product or corporate names may be trademarks or registered trademarks, and are used only for identification and explanation without intent to infringe.

British Library Cataloguing in Publication Data
A catalogue record for this book is available from the British Library.

Library of Congress Cataloging-in-Publication Data
A catalog record has been requested for this book.

ISBN: 978-0-367-47380-8 (hbk)
ISBN: 978-0-367-47379-2 (pbk)
ISBN: 978-1-003-03521-3 (ebk)

Typeset in Bembo
by Taylor & Francis Books

To the memory of Leslie Fiedler (1917–2003)

CONTENTS

List of figures	ix
Acknowledgments	x
A note on usage	xi

Introduction: The complex ambivalence of being us	1
1 What is identity? And what is American?	19
2 *The Last of the Mohicans*: Senility and love in a new nation	42
3 *Hope Leslie*: Critique, defiance, and ambivalence	58
4 William Apess: A Native American writes back	73
5 *Uncle Tom's Cabin*: The childhood model and delegitimating U.S nationalism	83
6 Harriet Jacobs, women's friendship, and antinationalism	98
7 Frederick Douglass, manhood, and the lost home	110
8 *The Scarlet Letter*: Sexuality, sin, and spiritual realization	123
9 Poe's "The Black Cat": An allegory of misogyny	142
10 Judith Sargent Murray: Women's virtue and the equality of the sexes	148

11 *Moby Dick*: Interracial romance beyond the nation   161

Afterword: In place of a premature conclusion   176

References   *184*
Index   *196*

FIGURES

9.1 *Desire and Misogyny.* 144

ACKNOWLEDGMENTS

The manuscript benefited significantly from the thoughtful comments of two anonymous referees. I myself benefited from the kind encouragement of my colleague, Wayne Franklin, and from his comments on an earlier version of the chapter on Cooper. Polly Dodson of Routledge was the ideal editor for this manuscript, and I am very grateful for her work. And Zoe Meyer, also of Routledge, was repeatedly helpful as usual.

My greatest debt here, as always, is to Lalita Pandit Hogan, who—from the time we were graduate students—urged me to read American literature more systematically and attentively. I finally listened (as usual, much after I should have). Lalita also introduced me to Leslie Fiedler as an author and as a person.

A NOTE ON USAGE

In recent years, a number of writers have objected to the use of "American" to refer to the people or properties of the United States rather than to the entirety of the people or properties of the Americas. I cannot bring myself to see this as a significant issue. The U.S. has certainly been imperialistic, both in the Americas and elsewhere. However, I doubt that the use of "American" has anything to do with that. There is simply not much else in the name "United States of America" to use in forming a felicitous word for citizens or properties ("Uniteans," "Statesers"?). There is, of course, no such problem with "America," for which one can usually substitute "U.S." However, in some cases, the tone is not right if one says "U.S.," which is likely to suggest an emphasis on legal or governmental aspects of the nation rather than, say, cultural aspects of the nation. Imagine the opening of Allen Ginsberg's famous poem not as "America I've given you all and now I'm nothing" but instead as "United States I've given you all and now I'm nothing." Moreover, it does not seem particularly plausible to claim that this use of "America" makes some sort of claim for the entire hemisphere; in American English, we use "America" only for the U.S., referring collectively to the two continents as "the Americas."

INTRODUCTION

The complex ambivalence of being us

Waking from (dogmatic) slumbers

I remember Rip van Winkle from when I was a child. In cartoons, he was a comic fellow who slept for 20 years and woke up to find the world transformed. My parents used to call me "Rip van Winkle" when I would oversleep. My guess is that the joke was neither original nor uncommon. It was, to my mind, a tall tale, a hyperbolic farce, attributed to a man—Diedrich Knickerbocker—named after goofy-looking pants. I unreflectively assumed that it was patriotic, celebrating the new nation that appears in its second half.[1]

As if I were Rip himself, I woke up one day to find myself assigned to teach early American literature. I protested that I was not really an expert in the field. Our kindly Associate Department Head reassured me. He also pointed out that, enrollment trends being what they were, I was more needed there than elsewhere. So, I was teaching "Rip van Winkle."

When I first reread the prefatory material, I felt confirmed in my assumptions about nationalism. "The Author's Account of Himself," pseudonymously penned by Geoffrey Crayon, celebrates the physical beauty of the nation—"on no country have the charms of nature been more prodigally lavished" (Irving 2017: 27) and "never need an American look beyond his own country for the sublime and beautiful of natural scenery" (28). It goes on to parody the Comte de Buffon and his view that the natural environment of America produced a degenerating effect, dwarfing Americans relative to their European cousins (see 28, n.4). When Crayon speaks of the "swelling magnitude of many English travellers" in the New World (28), the irony is obvious. That "swelling magnitude" is not a measure of their physique or intellect but of their egotism, inasmuch as they gaze with ludicrous disdain on the colonials.

Of course, these hints of nationalist enthusiasm did not prevent "Rip Van Winkle" from being a tall tale as well. Crayon cites Knickerbocker as proof of the veracity of Knickerbocker's story, which is not unlike Sarah Huckabee Sanders quoting Donald Trump as evidence of the truth of a story told by Donald Trump. He does, however, offer further support for the general esteem in which the fictional Knickerbocker was held by the people. Just as some national leaders have their profiles in bas-relief on national currency, Knickerbocker became a hero for bakers, "who have gone so far as to imprint his likeness on their new year cakes" (29).[2]

But I soon began to realize that this is not simply a matter of wit. Irving embeds an entirely untrustworthy narrator (Knickerbocker) in another untrustworthy narrator (Crayon), with the pseudonymous character of the latter possibly suggesting the unreliability of the author himself. The ironic distance is only enhanced by the fact that Crayon misidentifies the likely source of the story while denying that it has any source at all (see Levine 2017: 40, n.5). But what could be the point of extending the authorial distance so greatly that it appears impossible to identify anything that Irving himself might wish to assert thematically? Perhaps it is all a matter of extreme playfulness. Alternatively, cases of this sort sometimes suggest an authorial desire for plausible deniability.

I began to get a sense of what that deniability might involve when I read further in the story, and kept in mind the fact that support for the American Revolution was not as universal as we (Americans) commonly imagine. Estimates vary, but it seems that about 50% colonists supported independence; 15–20% opposed it, and 30–35% would not commit. Persecution of loyalists was significant, and the Revolutionary War produced "at least 60,000" refugee loyalists within a short period in 1782–1783 (Jansen 2018: 495, my translation). The population of the new country was about 2.5 million in 1776.[3] That is over a 2% refugee rate—the equivalent of almost 8 million refugees, given today's population of about 329 million.[4] The story concerns the great and unpredictable changes that took place between the 1760s and the 1780s, changes that U.S. nationalists celebrate.[5] Irving seems to take a more critical view.[6] But, given the antipathy nationalists tend to feel toward anyone who seems to question national devotion—as depicted in the story through people's hostility toward loyalists—it would perhaps have been imprudent for Irving to be too overt about that critical view (even if his attitude falls far short of loyalism and merely suggests a degree of critical distance from the revolution, and even given that he was writing at a different time).

If we read the story with these complex, diverse, and changeable attitudes toward nationalism in mind, we may begin to interpret the story a bit differently. In the third paragraph, Irving (2017: 30) describes Rip as "a simple good natured fellow" living "while the country was yet a province of Great Britain." He descended from Dutch colonists of some renown. This begins to suggest a possibly heroic story of the new nation. But we soon learn that Rip had "an insuperable aversion to all kinds of profitable labour" (31), which outraged his wife, who harassed him continually about his lack of industry. Rip spent his time playing with the children and engaging in philosophical discussions with friends. He was, in short, the antithesis of what an American was supposed to be: industrious. As J. Hector St. John de Crèvecoeur (1981: 67) has his American farmer explain in "Letter III: What Is an American?": "We [i.e., Americans] are all animated with the spirit of an industry which is unfettered and unrestrained, because each person works for himself."

On the other hand, while Rip's fecklessness is particularly noteworthy, it hardly seems to be the case that his companions are putting their shoulders to the wheel. Those who did not see industry as a dominant feature of actually existing Americans nonetheless viewed it as a norm—perhaps like Rip's wife. For example, Nancy Isenberg (2016: 82) explains that Paine "was thoroughly convinced that independence would eliminate idleness" (Mrs. Winkle chastises Rip specifically for "idleness" [Irving 2017: 32]). Paine was far from the only nationalist leader who admonished the people to be industrious. As Isenberg (2016: 64) notes, "Benjamin Franklin was obsessed with idleness." Moreover, "industry" was one of the 13 virtues he stressed as fundamental. In his autobiography, he lists it as virtue number six, adjuring his readers: "Lose no time; be always employed in something useful; cut off all unnecessary actions" (Franklin 1910). That and the fourth-named virtue, "resolution"—"Resolve to perform what you ought; perform without fail what you resolve"—combine to foster a very un-Winklean work ethic. In a way, Rip's unproductive sociability is a direct affront to the paradigmatic American; he is the photographic negative of the revolutionary ideal. When he returns to "the skirts of the village" (Irving 2017: 36), his wife is gone and the new, revolutionary society has taken her place. He escapes both hard labor and chastisement only because of his age. But the philosophical—perhaps un-American—life lived by Rip and his companions (much to the distress of Mrs. Winkle) is gone. In connection with this, it is important to recall that Rip's aversion was specifically to "profitable labour"—work that produced money. Is that, then, what the new nation sought and, perhaps, delivered—profit?

Well, not exactly. When Rip arrives, he finds his "house gone to decay" with a "half-starved dog" (36). The philosophers' inn is no more, and a "rickety wooden building stood in its place" (36). The new structure is in a state of ill repair. Windows are broken and patched up with bits of old clothing. Instead of a proper sign, we read the legend, painted over the door, "The Union Hotel" (37). At the risk of stating the obvious, Irving is taking up the standard metaphor of the nation as a building. Here, it is a ramshackle one, poor and risking collapse. This in part reflects the economic and political condition of the new Union. As Edward Baptist (2016: 4) explains, after the revolution "the weak federal government was buried in debts owed to creditors all over the nation and Europe." Economically and politically, "chaos ruled: thirteen different states had thirteen different trade policies, currencies, and court systems" (8). In many places, "farmers … couldn't pay debts or taxes," but "debt relief" risked bringing "economic disaster for creditors" (8–9; see also Grumer 1970: 22). To all appearances, this is not an improvement, but a decline from the quaint (prerevolutionary) inn. The irony is only enhanced when we learn that, instead of the active though profit-challenged Winkle, the man in charge of the new Union is Doolittle—presumably because he will do little, unlike Rip, who did a lot, though not for profit.

The most thematically significant part of the story comes next. We had learned earlier that the inn had "a rubicund portrait of his majesty George the Third" (Irving 2017: 32). Now, looking at the hotel, he spies "the ruby face of King George" (37). But, there is something strange. His clothing and headgear are different, and the portrait is captioned "GENERAL WASHINGTON" (37). The scene can be read in two ways, allowing for plausible deniability. It may be interpreted as simply manifesting Rip's misunderstanding, which is what it does reflect within the story. But it also suggests that the author, assisted by the coincidence of names, may be connecting the new, democratic leadership with old forms of aristocracy. Howard Zinn (2015: 85) writes that Washington "was the richest man in America." Carl Degler comments that "no new social class came to power through the door of the American revolution. The men who engineered the revolt were largely members of the colonial ruling class" (qtd. in Zinn 2015: 85). Isenberg (2016: 98) points out that "under the administration of George Washington, the Federalists established a 'Republican Court,' with rules of protocol, displays of genteel etiquette, and formal weekly ... visits by ... the national elite." Moreover, "around the president emerged a cult of adulation that imitated certain aspects of royal pageantry." In keeping with this, in 1789 "Vice President John Adams proposed before the Senate that the president required a more daunting title, such as 'Majesty.'"

The hint of some sympathy with loyalism may lead us back to the first moments of Rip's return. Feeling rejected by the animal he takes to be his dog, he thinks that this is an "unkind cut" (Irving 2017: 36). The words allude to a famous passage in Shakespeare's *Julius Caesar*, when Marc Antony points to a gash where (he claims) Brutus stabbed Caesar and labels it the "unkindest cut" (III.ii.177). *Julius Caesar* is not a monarchical play. It involves clear criticisms of the triumvirate that rules Rome after the assassination. However, it is also not a revolutionary play. The conspirators are as problematic as the royalists. We might infer that Irving's story presents a similar attitude toward the contesting parties in the revolution.

The story continues as we learn just what "Union" means in this context. Leaving aside Rip's conflict with his wife, the community of Rip's village appears to have lived in relative peace and harmony before the revolution.[7] Now, however, Rip is immediately asked to take sides in a sharp social division between Federalists and Democrats. The implication is that the Union is less unified than the pre-Union society was. A still sharper and more dangerously antagonistic—and even violent—division follows, when Rip—believing that he is saying nothing controversial or even political—characterizes himself as "a loyal subject of the King" (37). The mob immediately becomes agitated. They denounce him as "a spy!," then implicitly recall the tens of thousands who had fled, calling him "a refugee!" and crying out that he be driven away—not accepted into the community, but chased farther from his home to live in what would presumably be perpetual exile (37). From the mob's perspective, he is nothing but a "culprit" (38), though there is no reason to believe that he has done anything wrong.

When the hysteria dies down, Rip asks about his friends. One appears to have died a natural death. One has achieved fame and fortune due to the revolution. One died in the war. The results, then, are mixed, but the negative appears predominant. It hardly seems that the election of Van Bummel to Congress compensates for the death of Dutcher. One may think that Dutcher gave his life willingly. But that is unclear. The revolutionaries practiced conscription, even though forced military service was one of the complaints they had against the British (Zinn 2015: 79).

Rip then cries out that Rip van Winkle is now unknown. Those crowded around him point to a "lazy" (Irving 2017: 38) lay-about in the vicinity. It is Rip's son. Evidently, Paine's prediction about the revolutionary end of idleness was overly optimistic.[8] The resemblance is so great that Rip suffers identity confusion. Or, rather, that is what happens literally in the story. The thematic point is different and concerns the society at large. Rip is speaking for at least many people in the Union when he despairingly exclaims: "Every thing's changed, and I'm changed, and I can't tell what's my name, or who I am!" (38). The story imagines the revolution, not as freeing people to express their true identity, stifled by the British, but as changing them—or at least their conditions and their "name" ("British" to "American")—without any clear sense of what their new identity might be. Establishing that identity is the task of nation-building and the task of much early American literature.

The story concludes with Rip understanding that "the country had thrown off the yoke of old England" and "instead of being a subject of his Majesty, George the Third, he was now a free citizen of the United States" (40). The phrasing seems positive. Surely, throwing off a yoke is good, as is being "free" rather than "subject." But the previous events make the statement at least questionable. The prerevolutionary peace of the village hardly seems like a yoke. More significantly, since "Rip was no politician," the "changes of states and empires made but little impression on him" (40). There were profound consequences for the life of the new King George (Washington) and that of Congressman Van Bummel. But the change for ordinary people was, perhaps, insignificant.

Rereading this story, and examining it in detail, led me to think more systematically about the importance of nation-building in early American literature, particularly about the importance of cultivating a sense of personal identification with the new nation. It also led me to recognize that there is much greater ideological complexity than I had previously imagined in the project of national identity formation. "Rip van Winkle" initially looks to be a straightforward story. It seems highly comic, with little seriousness of purpose. What seriousness it has appears—on a superficial reading—to follow standard national ideology, affirming the rejection of the English yoke for American freedom. But even the slightest attention to its details shows that it is a far more ambiguous and ambivalent work. As I read or reread more early American literature, I found that thematic and emotional complexity over and over again.

Why American identity?

My previous writings on identity have suggested that—like many other aspects of human cognition and emotion—it is complicated and variable. Ingroups and outgroups change, sometimes radically, with life-and-death consequences. I have written about this in many contexts—even when treating major American writers, such as Stowe, Douglass, and Whitman. But I have never considered the issue in relation to American identity and American nation-building in particular—despite the very broad political relevance of American identity and, perhaps more surprisingly, despite its narrow personal relevance to myself.

I take it that the economic and military position of the United States over the last century makes it clear why U.S. national identification is politically consequential all over the world. In contrast, its personal relevance may seem insignificant. Or maybe not, since personal relevance bears on each of us, if in variable ways with diverse outcomes. It is perhaps worth dwelling briefly on my own case, since it illustrates the general point and is certainly the instance I know best. It may also serve to partially contextualize the analyses that follow.

For a long while, I assumed that American identity did not really affect me. Of course, being raised in the United States and living here mean that my habits, knowledge, and particular interests and skills are to some degree shaped by specifically American practices. I am reminded of this in banal (but consequential) ways when I cross the road in countries that drive on the left, for example. Moreover, I have great admiration for some aspects of American society, such as the valuing of civil liberties. But I have great admiration for some aspects of Indian, Chinese, French, Danish, and other societies as well. More significantly, I have little sympathy for identity categories of any sort—including national identity categories. But, if I am honest with myself, I have to acknowledge that I feel categorically "American" in some contexts. For example, I gave a talk at Nanjing University in Nanjing, China, a few years ago. At the dinner afterward, one of the guests raised a toast to the speaker's country. "To America," he said, then, quoting Mao Zedong: "First, friendship. Then, competition."[9] Though I liked Nanjing enormously and generally felt quite at home there, I suddenly felt very American and very non-Chinese. Of course, this was a special context, a context in which I was identified as "Other" by one of my hosts. But the fact that my relation to American identity is complex, contextually variable, and ambivalent does not make it unreal. Indeed, my example illustrates some of the central issues with identity. It may begin to suggest why identity is so easy to foster in short, antagonistic bursts and also why it is difficult to sustain in the way necessary for nation-building.

Does this mean that I turned to American identity and American literature because I have become more accepting of nationalism? Well, no; it does not. On returning from China, I actually wanted to teach Chinese literature more frequently along with literary theory. However, declining enrollments (at least in my classes) led to my placement in American literature survey courses. But I would not have pursued this project had the literature not appealed to me deeply as well at both an intellectual and an emotional level. Moreover, in reading literary works produced in the first century of U.S. independence, I was struck by the degree to which many writers were, consciously or unconsciously, devoted to nation-building. Fredric Jameson (1986: 70) famously remarked that "all third-world texts are necessarily ... to be read as ... national allegories." The claim is wildly overstated. However, it does correctly suggest that, in the context of a new nation, we might expect a good deal of the national literature to treat the nation or nation-building—particularly through cultivating or at least addressing national identification—whether it does so metaphorically ("as ... allegory") or literally. Early U.S. literature (as well as some prerevolutionary literature) shows this tendency.

Some preliminary comments on national identification and subnational division

One recurring problem for nation-building is overcoming rival forms of identification. These may be transnational or subnational. Transnational identifications might involve, say, religion or language. For example, in 1947 the partition of British India created two new nations—India and Pakistan—along with a complex set of sub- and transnational identities. Consider, for example, religion and transnational identification. Indian Hindus did not have much of a religious community outside of India. But Indian Muslims did. Pakistani Hindus, like Indian Muslims, had religious affiliations with a large population outside their nation. It may seem that the situation of Pakistani Muslims was parallel to that of Indian Hindus. But it was not, or not quite, because there was a large body of Muslims outside both Pakistan and India in the worldwide Muslim *ummah* or community, though there are complications here due to Shia and Sunni differences and other divisions internal to Islam. Of course, not all such complications of national identity are religious. For example, staying with the same region, we find transnational issues of language in East Pakistan, which was not Urdu-speaking, but Bangla-speaking, like Indian Bengal—a difference that was part of the reason for its eventual secession as Bangladesh.

Subnational divisions often reflect transnational ones. Indeed, outside of war, transnational commonalities often have practical consequences primarily as subnational divisions. Thus, the dissolution of one national union due to subnational divisions rarely leads to a subsequent transnational unification. Bangladesh separated from Pakistan, but it did not become part of (the Indian state of) Bengal. Indeed, this seems to be one of the reasons why the Kashmir crisis is so intractable. The regional superpowers—India and Pakistan—are not allowing Kashmiris the choice of independence. The only alternatives that anyone appears to consider are remaining with India, despite the subnational division based on majority religion, or uniting with Pakistan, simply because the majority's Islamic faith gives them a transnational connection. The reasons for this general state of affairs are clear, at least on the surface. A transnational connection does afford people an alternative identity category. For example, "Muslim" affords Kashmiris an alternative identity, rather than "Indian." However, that is a bare possibility. It would require nation-building efforts to make that alternative identification more deep and enduring—and more specific—as an identification with Pakistan.

Reading early U.S. literature, I found the concerns with nationhood that one would expect, which are often the same sorts of concerns found in the more recent nations that form the subject of the field of postcolonial studies today.[10] Of course, the most striking continuities were with the "settler colonies," the lands where the colonizers sought to displace and replace the indigenous population rather than govern and exploit it as they would in "occupation" (or "exploitation"[11]) colonies. Australia and New Zealand are the standard cases, with South Africa and Rhodesia/Zimbabwe being to some extent intermediate. (Israel/Palestine is a still more recent case of the same general sort; the plantation of Northern Ireland from England and Scotland is an earlier—seventeenth-century—instance.)

Some aspects of settler colonization in the prehistory and history of the United States have been analyzed valuably by Roxanne Dunbar-Ortiz (2014). She focuses on the ways in which settler colonies seek to take ownership of the land itself by driving the indigenous population off the land, commonly through genocide. This is undoubtedly the most important and execrable part of settler colonialism—loss of human life. Dunbar-Ortiz and other Native American writers are also deeply concerned with the damage to Native American cultures, another issue of obvious importance. My intellectual concern in the following pages is with identity or identification, the ways in which people categorize and conceptualize themselves and others.

As I will discuss at greater length in the following chapter, in describing and explaining such identification it is crucial that we do not confuse some very different phenomena that happen to share the name "identity." Most fundamentally, we need to distinguish between *practical identity* and *categorial identity*. Practical identity is the sum of our propensities and capacities—our interests, skills, aspirations, emotional inclinations, beliefs, and everything else that underlies and enables our engagement with the world, prominently our interactions with other people. That part of our practical identity that is shared distinctively with some group defines the *practical culture* of that group. For example, in language the phonology, morphological principles, syntactic rules, vocabulary, and other capacities that enable my speaking, listening, writing, and reading constitute my linguistic practical identity. The overlap across all individuals who communicate fluently through this sort of practical identity defines the English language: it is part of the practical, linguistic culture of English speakers.

Categorial identities are, fundamentally, labels—the tags we put on ourselves and on others that name putative essences. Just as we name species of animals, we name pseudospecies of people—white and black, American and Chinese, Catholic and Protestant, and so forth. The common assumption is that some categorial identities align with cultures, which are themselves relatively uniform. For example, "Christian" names a group of people who share certain beliefs, attitudes, skills, forms of knowledge, and so forth. Put differently, according to this common view there are real identities of groups; these real identities manifest themselves in (relatively) uniform cultures; and the real identities and uniform cultures are named in a set of species-like labels. But, in fact, things are not like this at all.

A great deal of research in social, cognitive, and affective psychology indicates that identity categories establish assumptions about group connection that need not have any basis in practical identity. This is true even in cases where practical considerations would seem to be so forceful as to completely overrule such assumptions. For example, people may consider themselves Chinese speakers even though they cannot communicate at all with one another. ("Dialects" of Chinese are best defined, linguistically, as distinct languages.) A Christian mystic, an Absolute Monistic Hindu, and a Muslim Sufi may share more significant beliefs and attitudes (thus greater practical identity) with one another than with more mainstream Christians, Hindus, and Muslims—or the religious leadership of these groups—respectively (a point made by Ashis Nandy and colleagues [1998: 51–52], among others). Nonetheless, they may each identify categorially with their socially standard religious label, leading them to take different sides in a religious riot. This category-guided commitment results from the fact that categorial identification defines "ingroups" and "outgroups," naming supposed essences segregating "us" from "them." The "cultures" associated with such groups are not real but aspirational; as Citrin and Sears (2014: 79) point out, "identities have normative content." Members of a religious, national, or other ingroup do not automatically share the same beliefs, attitudes, skills, and so on. Their practical identities vary. In consequence, the practical culture of the ingroup is not uniform. That is why the ingroup hierarchy (e.g., the nationalist political leadership) is continually working to inculcate cultural practices and to police cultural deviations.

Before going on, I will give one brief illustration. I suspect that the majority of students in my American literature class would self-identify as Christian (if in a relatively broad and often nondenominational sense). However, I asked them recently to think of a story involving Jesus and a judgment regarding a woman who had committed adultery. Only one person in the class had any clue—and she said: "The Ten Commandments!" I recounted the story of the woman caught in adultery, ending with the often-quoted words: "He that is without sin among you, let him first cast a stone at her" (John 8:7, KJV). Only one person in the class said that the story and the quotation were at all familiar. It seems clear that any categorial identification they do share does not grow from their shared practical identity regarding the life and teachings of Jesus. On the other hand, Christian religious leaders would almost certainly advocate the acquisition of such shared practical identity as a norm.

Subnational identitification in America

Like any country, the United States has its range of subnational divisions. These include region (as de Crèvecoeur's [1981: 73] American farmer remarks, in addition to the "general characteristics" of the nation as a whole, "each province has its own"), religion (think of the issue about John F. Kennedy being a Catholic), and many others. However, two types of division within the polity have arguably been the most psychologically important—sex and race.[12] These will therefore be the central focus of the following chapters.

As to the former, even in an age of genderqueer activism and sex reassignment surgery, sex remains a deeply important part of a person's self-concept (roughly, how one understands oneself) and of one's "socially attributed identity" (how one is understood by other people). It has also been central to the economic and political organization of almost all societies. Indeed, contemporary struggles over sex and gender identity, far from contradicting this centrality, often manifest it strikingly. This is clearly the case with most sex reassignment surgeries, as transgender men and women seek to conform their anatomy to their most important identifications. Genderqueer activism can be seen as important precisely because sex and gender identifications are in fact so pervasive. Presumably, this depth and pervasiveness are due in large measure to the obvious role of sex difference in reproduction and its historical centrality in organizing aspects of familial life (e.g., due to nursing). (Note that I am not claiming that reproductive differences between men and women in any way justify the subsequent development of sex hierarchies, just that the reproductive difference seems to be the principal reason for the importance of sex in a wide range of societies.)

The *national* relevance of this division is indicated by the fact that women were generally excluded from the democratic structure of U.S. society until 1920. This disenfranchisement of half the population was of great importance to many writers and activists who had committed themselves to the project of nation-building, working to foster a sense of unity and identity of the people. The male–female division was important in this project for two reasons. First, the new nation needed to set aside old antagonisms in order for everyone to contribute to the common work of forming the new society. Having men and women at odds with one another would not serve this practical unification. Perhaps even more significantly, the self-concept of the new nation—thus, people's idea of what makes them Americans—was, as we will discuss, bound up with ideals of democracy and equality. For this reason, writers interested in American identity had to address such problematic cases as the treatment of women. As Sheila Skemp (2009: 69) notes, "the American Revolution had momentarily disrupted traditional notions of gender identity. Its emphasis on universal natural rights had led some to question old constructions of gender and to call for a new paradigm upon which to build human relationships."

As to race, from the revolutionary period onward racial divisions have had a destructive prominence in U.S. nationalism, fracturing national unity along two axes: first, that between Europeans and Amerindians; and second, that between Europeans and Africans. (Obviously, other divisions followed, as with the recent demonizing of Muslims and Latinx people. However, these first two have been foundational and enduring for American national identification.) In the former case, the settlers engaged in the usual practices of settler colonialism, taking the land and killing the people who tried to prevent them from taking the land. As Dunbar-Ortiz (2014: 8) points out, "settler colonialism, as an institution or system, requires violence or the threat of violence to attain its goals. People do not hand over their land, resources, children, and futures without a fight, and that fight is met with violence."

The second case is historically more unusual, though it ended up characterizing many places in the "New World." This was not a matter of driving native people off the land and taking the land (settler colonialism) or setting up an administrative structure to extract value from the labor of the native population (occupation/exploitation colonialism). Nor was it a matter of demanding tax payments from a conquered region (the earlier, tributary model). It involved taking possession of people and using them as mobile instruments of labor in slavery. It was painfully obvious that this posed practical and ideological problems for the new nation, problems of ongoing, violent, internal conflict and problems of principle.

These racial divisions became particularly important concerns for American authors who were developing a popular sense of American identity. They took up a number of recurring techniques to address and respond to these divisions, as did writers on sex hierarchies. Some of these techniques have been isolated by earlier critics and theorists of American literature. For example, I will pay a good deal of attention to the interracial romance of characters in early American literature, in some degree following the insights of Leslie Fiedler. However, one contention of the following pages is that such recurring patterns may be more accurately described and more effectively explained by drawing on recent research in cognitive and affective science and social psychology rather than on psychoanalysis (as in Fiedler's case) or on structuralist and deconstructive approaches, which have been influential in recent decades.[13]

What about class?

Before going on to outline more fully what I will be treating in the following chapters, I should briefly remark on why I am not treating class as an identity division crucial to nation-building. It is not at all because I consider socioeconomic status to be unimportant. Indeed, I consider it to be the most consequential subnational division. Colonial conflict is not, fundamentally, cultural. It is fundamentally a matter of material interests, such as land or resources. But it is often *culturalized*, conceived of, or rationalized in terms of culture. Thus, settler colonialism in the Americas was a matter of gaining control over the land. However, invasion and appropriation were justified by reference to a series of cultural claims. These included legal assertions that migratory peoples had no rights to land that they had not settled and developed (see, for example, Cronon 1987: 13–14 on the colonists' claims about "civil right of ownership" requiring the inhabitants to reside on and "improve" the land). They also extended to religious allegations that Native American belief and ritual had a Satanic provenance and demonic affiliations (see, for example, Dunbar-Ortiz 2014 on the idea that the land was "controlled by the devil" [36] and needed to be freed from "evil" [48]). Thus, colonialism is likely to give rise to antagonism about culture. But that antagonism is a sort of secondary elaboration of the primary antagonism, which is, again, material.

Moreover, the point is not confined to colonialism. In many respects, the problems of women and non-whites in the United States are a matter of class. I do not mean that women have the status of factory workers or peasants or that they take part in the same sort of work (though, obviously, they sometimes do). I mean, rather, that much of the disability suffered by women has derived from their reduced earning potential, their dependence on the income of their husbands, and related economic disadvantages. In this respect, even a wealthy woman may share some features of her situation with impoverished classes. Similarly, the disabilities suffered by racial minorities are pervasively a matter of ownership of the means of production or of place in the relations of production.

However, despite its high functionality, class has not had the widespread and continuing *psychological* importance of race or sex (or sexual identity, which I will also touch on). In the first chapter, I will consider some variables that affect the degree to which we are likely to identify ourselves or others with a particular category. One such variable is salience. Unlike some nations, class in the United States does not tend to be highly salient due to, say, speech (which we are more inclined to see as a function of region or race). Another variable is "opposability," the degree to which the category organizes society into an ingroup and one or perhaps two outgroups. But class in the United States is not generally viewed as opposable in this identification-fostering way. Marxist analysis limits the number of classes by reference to people's locations in productive processes and to ownership of the means of production. In the United States, however, class tends to be defined in terms of income, which varies continuously. For Marx, Jones may be a worker and Smith a capitalist. But in the usual American view, Jones is part of the minutely hierarchized middle class. While Smith may be "upper class," his/her income is continuous with that of Jones, since there are people with incomes at every level between them. (It is no accident that recent class-conscious politics in the United States has relied on a binary opposition between "the one percent" and the rest of us.)

The preceding point is related to the most important aspect of class ideology in the United States. A key element of the egalitarian self-concept of Americans is that equality is not equality of income or wealth, but equality of opportunity. Equality of opportunity means that everyone is capable of succeeding materially in life. The possibilities for one's future are not limited by one's birth (as, say, a commoner). They are constrained only by the limitations of one's enterprise and talent. Thus, it is a crucial part of U.S. national ideology that in the United States economic class is not—or at least need not be—*enduring*. (The durability of an identity category is another key factor in fostering a sense of group identification; on these and other variables affecting group identification, see chapter two of Hogan 2018, *Understanding Nationalism*.) It is in one's power to change one's economic class. Of course, not all writers accept this view. Indeed, it is mistaken. As James Gilligan (2001: 44–45) points out, "social mobility is actually less likely in the U.S. than in the supposedly more rigid social structures of Europe and the U.K." Gilligan concludes that a range of "features of U.S. society" operate "to maximize the gap between aspiration and attainment." Far from pervading American life, Horatio Algers are less common here than elsewhere. Even so, the misconception of unimpeded social mobility is widespread, and is part of the reason why class has not typically been a key category in building or contesting American nationhood. In the following pages, I will therefore not take up socioeconomic class beyond occasional references to points where issues of class appear particularly consequential for understanding the psychology of U.S. national identification.

What follows

Chapter 1 begins with a theoretical overview of identity, drawing on recent work in cognitive and affective science and social psychology.[14] After treating general points about social identity, it turns to the most important recurring features in the American self-concept—specifically, the view of America as embodying the ideal of universal, democratic egalitarianism. From here, it considers the way that this self-concept was radically and obtrusively at odds with the actual social conditions of the nation. The discrepancy between America and the idea of America appears with particular force in relation to the status and treatment of Native Americans, African Americans, and women. The chapter goes on to consider some of the ways in which Americans from dominant groups (thus European Americans and American men) thought about and emotionally reacted to race- and sex-defined outgroups and some of the ways in which authors tried to respond to race and gender biases with their consequences for national identity. For example, one recurring technique, recognized initially (with some significant differences) by Leslie Fiedler, is the attempt to address racial divisions on the individual level through interracial attachment bonding (often romantic love). Literature does not deal with generalities, but with particulars. It does not treat demographic patterns, but individual feelings and actions. By representing interracial romantic love, a writer may directly oppose the forms of individual antagonism and/or disgust that give emotional force to racial divisions, including of course those inside the nation. Another technique discussed in this chapter is the recurring use of two cognitive domains—age and animacy—to provide cognitive models for thinking about and responding to outgroup members.

The following chapters treat the three outgroups just mentioned. Chapters 2 through 4 consider the status of Native Americans; Chapters 5 through 7 take up African Americans; and Chapters 8 through 10 consider gender relations. In each case, I have sought to represent a range of authorial perspectives, including both the hegemonic groups (European Americans and American men) and the disenfranchised groups (Native Americans, African Americans, and women). Chapter 11, the final chapter, examines Melville's *Moby Dick* in part as an internationalist criticism of a wide range of racial divisions, the range being signaled by Queequeg's ambiguous racial and cultural affiliations; this chapter also touches on sexual preference in relation to American egalitarianism.

More exactly, Chapter 2 turns to James Fenimore Cooper's enormously influential novel, *The Last of the Mohicans*. Though widely condemned for its treatment of Amerindians as a vanishing race, the novel is, I argue, relatively progressive on the whole. Indeed, Cooper's development of interracial bonding—both in friendship and, even more, in heterosexual romance—is deeply opposed to some common racist attitudes of the time. The novel is not without ambiguity and ambivalence, however. Cooper tacitly criticizes the most common cognitive models used to demean Native Americans, but he also employs versions of those models, if often in less harmful forms.

Chapter 3 takes up Catharine Maria Sedgwick's *Hope Leslie*, a novel that was unjustly forgotten for many years, until it was rediscovered by scholars seeking to restore works by women to their rightful place in literary history. Sedgwick's novel presents an account of the relations between European Americans and Native Americans that is, in certain respects, more accurate and uncompromising in its representation of European American crimes than other novels of the period. At the same time, Sedgwick does not idealize Native Americans. The novel also takes up gender issues bearing on both European and indigenous women. As with Cooper, we find in Sedgwick many common techniques, including interracial romance, though the latter seems to be developed with less conviction in Sedgwick than in Cooper. Sedgwick's representation of racial and ethnic relations in this context is, however, complicated for readers today by her clear advocacy of Christianizing the Amerindians.

The final chapter on Native Americans, Chapter 4, turns to William Apess, an early Anglophone Amerindian writer. He takes up many of the same techniques used by Cooper and Sedgwick to respond to hegemonic views about Amerindians. For example, he deftly guides his readers to shift their perspective from European to Native American. However, there are also some differences. Perhaps surprisingly, Apess is more insistently Christian in his arguments. More predictably, he is aware of Native Americans as readers of his work, and therefore does not write solely for whites. Finally, though he is more ambivalent about interracial love, he does attend to attachment bonds more broadly, stressing the consequences of racism and colonial conflict for what we would call attachment security.

The first chapter treating African Americans, Chapter 5, examines Harriet Beecher Stowe's *Uncle Tom's Cabin*, another work that is often viewed as racist. The condemnation of Stowe's novel is both understandable and (partially) mistaken. It is understandable because Stowe does take up a childhood model to characterize Africans. However, she complicates that model and develops its implications in ways that lead to antiracist conclusions. Moreover, unusually for the writers considered here, Stowe challenges—perhaps even rejects—U.S. nationalism and American identity itself when faced with slavery's terrible negation of universal, democratic egalitarianism.[15]

One striking aspect of Stowe's novel is its harsh criticism of the interracial romance as a putative antithesis to racial antagonism. This point is developed systematically, and with a perhaps even clearer feminist orientation, in Harriet Jacobs's *Incidents in the Life of a Slave Girl*, which is examined in Chapter 6. Jacobs unflinchingly represents the exploitation and interpersonal cruelty that were an almost inevitable part of interracial sexual relations under slavery. Only at the end of the memoir does Jacobs come to represent interracial bonding as an important part of racial reconciliation. That bonding, however, is in the form of female friendship, not romance. Jacobs also takes up and extends Stowe's evaluation of U.S. nationalism, developing what is probably the sharpest criticism of the United States of all the writers discussed in this book.

The final chapter on African Americans, Chapter 7, considers Frederick Douglass's autobiographies, paying particular attention to his third and final retelling of his life. It argues that there were, in effect, two Frederick Douglasses. The first, familiar Douglass was the vigorously masculine, confrontational, muscular opponent of slavery and critic of the United States. The other Frederick Douglass, however, was the adult version of a vulnerable child, suffering from the insecurities of early attachment loss and longing for full integration into the America that had rejected him and people like him. If Jacobs is the most antinationalist writer considered in these pages, Frederick Douglass is arguably her opposite and counterpart, the most patriotic American.

With Chapter 8, the book turns to gender relations, first considering Nathaniel Hawthorne's *The Scarlet Letter*. Hawthorne does not appear to be concerned focally with nationalism. Rather, his main interests appear to be spiritual and moral. However, these topics are inseparable from social and political life in Hawthorne's conception; as such, they require attention to the nation. Nonetheless, the different concerns stressed by Hawthorne give his novel a distinctive orientation. He treats gender issues by way of treating ethics and religion. Specifically, a central ethical precept suggested by *The Scarlet Letter* is the necessity of self-criticism as the antidote to the fundamental sin of spiritual pride. It is crucial that this is *self*-criticism, not criticism of others. Fundamentally, the sexual asymmetry of patriarchal society means that men more readily escape self-criticism—or, as in the case of Dimmesdale, risk succumbing to the excess self-criticism of spiritual despair when they are wrongly exonerated of sinfulness. In either case, the result is the spiritual degradation of men. Hawthorne develops the consequences of the sexual double standard and its unexpected spiritual consequences through the course of the novel. In the end, he suggests a radical restructuring of society that rejects this double standard in part through the work of (female) prophetesses adumbrated by Anne Hutchinson and Hester Prynne—thus, a society that could perhaps begin to be truly universal and egalitarian.

Chapter 9 considers Edger Allen Poe's story "The Black Cat" as an allegory for misogyny and male violence. I chose this story and this reading for two reasons. First, it seemed to me a valid but highly unexpected interpretation of the work. My hope is that other readers will agree with its validity, not only because I would like them to agree with me, but also because the validity is necessary for my second, more important reason. That second reason is that Poe's story suggests the ubiquity of concerns about the social implications of gender hierarchy. It is clear that a number of authors take up the debilitating consequences of patriarchy. Of the authors covered here, this is true not only of Hawthorne, but of Sedgwick, Stowe, and Jacobs as well. But the suggestion of "The Black Cat" is that gender hierarchies—and the injustice of those hierarchies—may be more pervasive sources of discontent (whether due to anger or guilt) than we often imagine.

Chapter 10 turns to Judith Sargent Murray, the author of the important 1790 tract "On the Equality of the Sexes," considering two of her plays, which were written only a few years later. The first of these plays, *Virtue Triumphant*, appears to take up Murray's feminist ideas in a way directly relevant to American identity. Specifically, it addresses the equality of men and women in marriage. However, the play is equivocal on the nature of such equality, which is developed somewhat ambiguously in terms of social class. The play also presents us with some gender stereotypes, though this is complicated by the suggestion that an androgynous combination of putatively masculine and feminine traits is both preferable and possible. The second play, *The Traveller Returned*, deals more explicitly with national identity in representing—and criticizing—early governmental structures of the revolutionary United States. On the one hand, Murray appears to accept patriarchal structures in her representation of the relations between male and female characters. However, the structure of the play points to something else. Specifically, Murray is clearly critical of the suspicion and intrusive policing of citizens by the new nation's Committees of Safety. These, in turn, are directly paralleled with the suspicion and intrusive policing of wives by husbands. She thereby hints that relations between the sexes need to be reconsidered if the nation is to achieve any reasonable level of equality and personal freedom, another key norm of the predominant American self-concept.

Finally, Chapter 11 considers Herman Melville's *Moby Dick*, examining Melville's treatment of Ishmael and Queequeg. In criticizing racial and ethnic biases, both cognitive and affective, Melville draws on several techniques familiar from the previous chapters, prominently including the development of interracial romance. Since the romance involves two men, this allows Melville to take up (albeit somewhat indirectly) the problem of national norms in relation to sexual preference as well, an obviously key area in practical identity and one that has had increasing significance for social identity definition in the United States in recent decades. Melville also develops the important topic of individualism and touches on the nature and function of the state. Perhaps most significantly, Melville presents a portrait of interracial reconciliation that is multiracial and multicultural—indeed, global. In connection with this, he suggests a sort of internationalism, which is arguably the logical culmination of American identity as universal, democratic egalitarianism. It is for this reason that I have placed this chapter last.

The book concludes with a brief afterword, explaining (as is perhaps obvious) that a great deal more work needs to be done before we can begin to reach any definite conclusions about American identity or its relation to American literature. Among other things, the present volume is not in any sense a survey of American literature. It is, rather, an attempt to isolate some significant patterns in the literary treatment of U.S. identity in roughly the first century of national independence.[16] I have sought to isolate these patterns by paying careful, detailed attention to a limited number of works by influential writers and by integrating into my analysis theoretical and empirical insights drawn from cognitive science, affective science, and social psychology. This method necessarily sacrifices breadth of coverage for at least what I hope is depth of understanding. The loss of breadth undoubtedly means that the picture I paint of American identity leaves out many types of identification (and rejection of identification) expressed and experienced by Americans. However, my hope is that it provides a fuller comprehension of the strong currents of identification (and disidentification) on which it focuses its attention.

More exactly, if the book is at all successful, it should do three things. First, it should provide readers with a fuller understanding of the techniques of identity development generally. In this way, it is part of cognitive and affective science. Second, it should expand their knowledge of major concerns and techniques of specifically U.S. national identity, especially in relation to subnational divisions. In this way, it is part of cultural studies. Finally, it should develop their comprehension of and response to the particular works that it discusses. In this way, it is part of literary criticism. The second and third goals of the book—regarding U.S. national identity and the its relation to American literature in the first century after independence—may be further specified through the following basic points: (1) universal, democratic egalitarianism is a central norm for American society, as it is held as such a norm by a wide range of people who identify as American; (2) this norm is clearly, indeed obtrusively, violated by race- and sex-based hierarchies; (3) a great deal of American literature is dedicated to responding to this contradiction; (4) the violations of universal, democratic egalitarianism have psychological components that can be precisely described and systematically explained by principles drawn from cognitive and affective science; and (5) the cognitive and emotional complexity of the literary works treating the problems of race and sex—complexity that includes authorial inconsistencies in thought and ambivalence in emotional response—may be illuminatingly interpreted by way of cognitive and affective science, including by way of such subfields as cognitive and affective narratology.

Notes

1 This is a common assumption about the story. My students, for example, take it for granted that Irving criticizes the tyrannical Mrs. Winkle in parallel with the similarly tyrannical English monarch. The idea is not confined to my students. Leslie Fiedler (1992: 339) writes that Rip has "slept away the life of the shrew who bullied him, as well as that of George III, who had oppressed his country."
2 In an earlier version of this introduction, I added my own fictional testimony to the following effect: "As Jefferson Quill, D.D., attested some half-century after the publication: 'Even now, in some small, family-owned shops no more than an hour's carriage ride from Hartford or Springfield, one might find the proprietor passing out samples of Christmas cookies to the children of patrons. Sculpted onto the crusty surface of these treats is an image that some say is the Savior, but that the bakers insist is the revered figure of Knickerbocker, who bore a striking resemblance to the Galilean.'" However, this so confused and distressed one of the readers of the manuscript that I felt it was necessary to remove the passage.
3 According to the estimate of the U.S. Census Bureau (https://www.census.gov/news room/facts-for-features/2016/cb16-ff13.html [accessed 17 May 2019]).
4 On the current U.S. population, see the data from the U.S. Census Bureau (https://www.census.gov/en.html [accessed 17 May 2019]).
5 Rebecca Grumer (1970: 17, 16) points out that "loyalty and pride in being part of the ... British Empire" were very high "in the early 1760s" and that "it was not until after 1763 that the American colonials began to question their loyalty to the British Empire." As John Murrin (1987: 339) notes, before 1764 "virtually none" of the colonists "embrace[d] a national destiny" for America.
6 As Sarah Wyman (2010: 216) puts it, Irving "implicitly questions the value of the American Revolution." George Putnam (1917: 254) makes the more limited, but related, claim that Irving "was able to free himself from the local feeling of antagonism toward the ancient enemy Great Britain."
7 Unsurprisingly, critics have recognized the general themes of lost community and equivocal liberty in the story (see, e.g., Anderson 2000 for a careful and influential reading).
8 As was the revolutionaries' "plan" for "peace forever," which was affirmed in "Common Sense," which was published in 1775 (Paine 1969: 68).
9 The slogan appears to have been used initially to mean that competition should be placed behind friendship; see Andrews (2016) on the saying "friendship first and competition second." As one writer at the time summarized the point, "friendship is more important than competition" (qtd. in Fan and Lu 2013: 61). However, my host at least appeared to mean that first our nations should be friendly, then, they should compete (e.g., in intellectual pursuits).
10 In many ways, the present study involves concerns of colonialism and its aftermath (hence, the allusion in the title of Chapter 4 to Bill Ashcroft and colleagues' (2002) influential book on postcolonial literature). However, it is different from dominant strands of postcolonial studies not only in focusing on the United States, but also in drawing on empirically grounded work in cognitive and affective science and social psychology, rather than on poststructuralist conjecture or psychoanalysis. For an overview of common psychological

approaches in postcolonial studies, see Ward (2007); for examples of mainstream postcolonial analyses of American literature, see Madsen (2015).

11 See Rothermund (2006: 211).

12 As Michael Moon and Cathy Davidson (1995: 1) write, in a slightly different context, "race and gender challenge nationalist paradigms."

13 In the following pages, I am confining myself to a psychological approach, as identity formation is a psychological process. But this is not to imply that social and historical approaches are irrelevant. They are deeply important and illuminating (when done well—a qualification that obviously applies to psychological approaches also). Ideally, sociohistorical and psychological accounts should be integrated. But there is no space for that in the present volume. In addition, it would require an author with far broader knowledge than I have.

14 Surprisingly, there has been only a limited amount of work on American literature that is based on cognitive or affective science. In Latinx literary studies, the pioneer in this area is Frederick Aldama (2009). Others have followed in Aldama's footsteps, including Christopher González (2017), Patrick Hamilton (2011), Doug Bush (2019), and Stephanie Fetta (2018). Outside Latinx studies, Alexa Weik von Mossner has made very important contributions to a wider range of topics in American literature. But Weik von Mossner has focused on rather different topics—the environment, in one case (*Affective Ecologies*, 2017), and U.S. authors' internationalism in the other (*Cosmopolitan Minds*, 2014). The latter topic, developed in her *Cosmopolitan Minds*, is a fitting counterpart to the present study in focusing on works that are not best understood in relation to the issue of national identity, except insofar as they set it aside. The book that is perhaps closest to the present volume in spirit is Mark Bracher's (2013) valuable *Literature and Social Justice*. As with Weik von Mossner's books, Bracher's text has a different focus—in this case, social justice. However, social justice is central to the topics of racism and sexism, thus to the discrepancy between American ideals and actual social life in the United States. In keeping with this, many of Bracher's analyses are related to those presented in the following pages. When the following analyses touch directly on social justice, the connections between the works become particularly clear. For example, when treating autonomy and essentialism in Wright's *Native Son*, Bracher may be seen as in some ways extending and deepening the idea of stereotype explanation as discussed here (though it would be anachronistic to put it that way). In consequence, Bracher's text and the present volume are complementary books that could, I believe, be read together very productively.

15 For unclear reasons, some readers balk at "universalism" in this statement. It merely means that the democratic and egalitarian principles apply to everyone, not to some elite ingroup. It is the same sense of "universal" as characterizes, for example, Frederick Douglass's antislavery work. As John Michael (2008: 201) explains, "Frederick Douglass made his literary career and fashioned his public identity by championing the universality of America's abstract principles against the specificity of its racist failings." Douglass "appealed for racial liberation by opting for the universal in the form of those principles of equality and justice that are especially dear to Americans and peculiarly central to the nation's identity. These universal principles offer no defensible grounds for exclusion or privilege and should make the inequities of the color line and of imperialism unacceptable to America and its peoples" (Michael 2008: 220). Moreover, despite the bizarre view of many Humanities professors that universalism is somehow oppressive, group oppression is always antiuniversalist. It is, for example, the putative *differences* between Europeans and Africans that were invoked to justify race-based slavery, not their common humanity. Conversely, as Sam McFarland discusses at length, there is extensive evidence that identification with all humanity—a form of universalism—is an important source of pro-social behavior (e.g., working to save Jews during the Holocaust [see McFarland 2017: 632]). Of course, this universalism must ultimately transcend nation as well—even if the nation in question proclaims universalism as a great value.

16 I plan a separate volume on the subsequent century or so.

1

WHAT IS IDENTITY? AND WHAT IS AMERICAN?

What is identity?

Identity is an ambiguous concept. The term "identity" is used in a wide variety of ways, and discussions of identity are often befuddled by promiscuous shifts among these meanings. I will begin with three, crucially different senses of "identity." The first is *what I am*; the second is *how I conceive of myself*; and the third is *how others conceive of me*. All of these senses need further clarification. But their fundamental difference should be intuitively evident. For the first (*what I am*), I will sometimes use the term "self." However, this word is often used ambiguously as well. Therefore, rather than "self," I will more often than not take up the phrase "practical identity"[1] in referring to identity in the sense of *what I am*. By *practical identity*, I mean the entire complex of one's cognitive and affective properties. The phrase is designed to emphasize one's capacities and dispositions—thus, what one is capable of thinking or doing physically, what goals one has, what emotional responses one is likely to have in different circumstances (including one's ambivalences and contradictions), and so on. For example, it is part of my practical identity that I am able to speak English fluently, but not Irish. It is also part of my practical identity that I would like to read Mandarin fluently, and that I make periodic, ineffectual efforts at learning that language.

As to the second meaning of "identity," I will follow the common practice and refer to *the way I conceive of myself* as my "self-concept." However, I will emphasize *categorial identity* as a key component of self-concept. To understand categorial identity, we need to understand the way that categorization operates more generally in the human mind. We identify targets by several means. To some extent, we identify targets as individuals (e.g., I might identify a particular barking quadruped as my neighbor's dog, Spot). However, we also identify targets by their membership in certain classes of things (e.g., as *a dog*). The most important classifications of targets give what we tacitly conceive of as essences, definitive features. Such classifications serve to orient our understanding and response. For example, with animate targets the crucial level of categorization is commonly that of species, which predicts behavior bearing on our self-interest. We categorize a particular target as a bear and therefore expect predatory behavior, and we have a fear response. Individual information tends to displace group information; thus, I may fear an unknown dog, but be perfectly at ease with Spot.

Categorial identity is sometimes referred to as "pseudospeciation," since it in effect serves to identify groups of humans as if they were species. Specifically, categorial identities are social classifications that serve to predict the behavior of other people relative to one's own self-interest and that serve to orient one's emotional response toward those people. The emotional orientation is called "interpersonal stance"; this comprises the general set of principles that govern our motivational response to the target. Part of *interpersonal stance* is one's response to the target's emotions. If my interpersonal stance toward Jones is *parallel*, I will feel empathy with him, suffering over his grief. If my interpersonal stance is *complementary* (e.g., fearful or antagonistic), I might feel *Schadenfreude* over his grief. Part of interpersonal stance is one's response to the behavior of the target. If I feel affectionate trust, then I am likely to feel happy if Smith approaches me. If I feel fear, however, I may recoil at her advance.

The pseudospeciation of identity categorization defines *ingroups* and *outgroups*. Ingroups are sets of people with whom one shares a categorial identity. Prominent identity categories today include nation (e.g., American), race (e.g., white or black), ethnicity, and religion. Probably the most pervasive and fundamental, but also most complex, identity categories are sex (thus male and female) and gender (e.g., masculine and feminine). Outgroups are the sets of people against whom one's ingroup identity is defined. There is a tendency for us to narrow identity group oppositions to one or two primary outgroups. In some cases, this is largely taken care of by the nature of the groups themselves. For example, despite intersexing, the evolution of bisexual reproduction largely defines sex in such a way as to yield one primary outgroup for each ingroup (male for female and vice-versa). In contrast, the black–white racial opposition in the United States is more obviously produced by biologically arbitrary divisions.

A great deal of social psychological research shows that ingroup–outgroup divisions are very easy to create and have a consistent set of consequences. The simple act of arbitrarily dividing people into categories (e.g., by the penultimate digit of their social security numbers) can serve to create identity oppositions. Such oppositions entail a series of orientations, including interpersonal stances and cognitive and evaluative biases. For example, people tend to judge members of an ingroup more hard-working and better-looking than members of outgroups, even when the group divisions are arbitrary and ad hoc, which is to say, created solely for the purposes of the study (see Duckitt 1992: 68–69; see also Hirschfeld 1996: 1). Research on longer-standing identity-group divisions (e.g., by race) indicate that we are more likely to adopt a parallel interpersonal stance toward ingroup members and an antipathetic interpersonal stance toward outgroup members (see the research reported in Gazzaniga 2011: 164 and Hein et al. 2010: 155; see also Hess 2009: 253–254), that we tend to interpret the behavior of outgroup members as more hostile (see Kunda 1999: 347 and Sapolsky 2017: 85), and that we generally follow different cognitive and affective principles in responding to ingroups and outgroups.

Again, it is easy to establish ingroup identifications. However, making one group division functional will typically involve rendering other group divisions relatively and temporarily dysfunctional. For instance, bringing to mind shared religion may mute outgrouping based on ethnicity. In this way, group identifications may be sometimes surprisingly unstable. On the other hand, it is clear that some categorizations are more stable than others. For example, it takes experimental design to make some categories define ingroups (e.g., having an even number as the penultimate digit of one's social security number). In contrast, sex categorization seems to arise pretty easily on its own. In any case, variability in categorial identification often leads to conflicts in group definition. For example, in a dispute between the United States and Russia, U.S. citizens from Russia or of Russian ancestry may differ in the degree to which they see themselves primarily as American or primarily as Russian. In cases such as this, social activists who wish to stress one identity category are faced with the problem of just how to foster their preferred sorts of categorization (e.g., an American president in conflict with Russia may wish to consider how he or she might foster an American identification among Russian Americans). As should be clear by now, the main concerns of the present book—the reconciliation of subnational divisions by race and sex in the United States—are an instance of this problem.

In *Understanding Nationalism* (Hogan 2009), I argue that some identity categories tend to supersede others based on a specifiable set of properties. These properties include salience, durability, functionality, affectivity, and opposability.[2] Salience is simply the degree to which a given category is immediately noticeable, the degree to which it forces itself on our attention. Religion is for the most part not salient in the United States, since there are few perceptual clues as to most people's religious affiliation. Sex, in contrast, tends to be highly salient. Durability is the degree to which a category may change. State residence could serve as an identity category in some cases, but it is changeable in a way that sex or even nationality is not (e.g., it is much easier for Jane to move to a different state than it is for her to become biologically male). Functionality is the degree to which a category has consequences for the distribution of goods or services in a society. Affectivity is the degree to which a given category elicits emotional response. Finally, opposability is the extent to which a category allows a two-way (or, at most, three-way) opposition. For example, the regional division of the United States into North and South has greater opposability than the division into states. The identity category of, say, "Connecticut resident" is in part dissipated due to its contrast with 49 other state identity categories (though it may become more opposable in a given context—say, a sports rivalry between two state universities).

Before going on to say more about categorial identity, I should return to the opening division among the senses of identity—*what I am; how I conceive of myself;* and *how others conceive of me*. I have been speaking of categorial identity as if it is solely a matter of self-concept (thus, how I conceive of myself). However, one's categorial identity is, in the great majority of cases, first of all a matter of other people's attribution. A child does not simply decide that he or she is a boy or girl. He or she finds that other people refer to him or her as a boy or a girl, put him or her together with groups of boys or girls, and so on. On the other hand, sometimes self-concept diverges from social categorization, as when a transgender woman identifies as female, while society generally identifies her as male. In national identification, a person of Middle Eastern ancestry might fully identify as American but be explicitly or implicitly classed as "foreign"—indeed, as a member of a primary, antagonistic outgroup—by many other Americans.

These discrepancies between self-identification and social attribution lead us to another important conceptual distinction and an associated empirical point. As to the former, the definition of an identity category is typically very minimal and is often entirely distinct from the set of norms that accompany a category. As to the empirical point, I suspect that many people assume that identity is, first of all, a matter of shared inclinations, beliefs, or practices. In other words, I suspect that many people assume that categorial identification reflects shared practical identity. For example, by this common assumption Americans share a lived culture; that lived culture, as a series of shared practices, is possible because the practical identities of Americans overlap extensively and distinctively. (The overlap is distinctive insofar as it is not shared by other groups; sets of shared features do not define one as American if they are shared by all humans or by all Western democracies, for example.[3]) That overlap of practical identities, then, is taken to define the essence that is named by the national identity category, which is "American."

Of course, it is the case that groups that share a category commonly share distinctive features of practical identity as well. However, the causal sequence—though complex—operates almost entirely in the opposite direction. Children are socialized into being boys or girls because they are socially categorized as boys and girls through minimal "inclusion criteria" (usually, external genitalia). Similarly, it is because Jones is born in the United States and labeled "American" that he is brought up as an American. The same point holds for religion (one is raised into the practical identity of being Catholic because one is labeled "Catholic" due to one's parentage and baptism); race and ethnicity (one is raised as, say, Jewish because one is socially categorized as Jewish due to maternal descent)—and so on.

Thus, shared categorial identity does not simply rest on a prior, shared practical identity. Rather, shared categorial identity is typically based on some minimal definition. However, identity groups regularly aspire to establish a culture, and thus an extensive and distinctive overlap in practical identity. That aspiration, in turn, commonly involves a set of norms. The fulfillment of those norms is often taken to separate the "real" members of an identity group from those that are members "in name only." For example, being an American might be minimally defined by fulfilling requirements for citizenship. However, we are all likely to take "American" to name a rather more robust set of properties. To take an extreme example, few people would be willing to call Doe a "real American" if she was working as a spy for another country. This is a case in which a definitional ingroup member betrays fundamental norms and thereby earns the scorn of other ingroup members. A different sort of example may be drawn from American nativists—for example, the Know-Nothings of the mid-nineteenth century—who tended to think of real Americans as Protestant, thus not Catholic (as Leonard and Parmet [1971] discuss at length); today, nativists might be willing to include Catholics (or even Jews), but not

Muslims. As the example of nativism suggests, some members of a group may consider the minimal definition for the group to be overly inclusive, insofar as it encompasses people who violate putatively fundamental norms of the group (e.g., by not being Protestant). In practice, then, the basic social definition of identity groups (e.g., the social definition of "American" in terms of U.S. citizenship) may be at odds with the categorial attributions or identifications accepted by particular individuals. This may, in turn, lead some Americans (e.g., nativists) to outgroup other Americans, even when the latter are definitionally part of the national ingroup.

These points lead us back to the topic of subnational divisions. Again, practical identity principally follows categorial identification (and not the other way around). For example, in the vast majority of cases, a person has the beliefs and practices of, say, Catholicism—thus, Catholic culture or practical identity—because he or she was categorized as Catholic at birth, and thereafter socialized as Catholic. Even converts most often come to identify with the category before they have assimilated much of Catholic practical identity. Indeed, that categorial identification motivates them through the process of acquiring the practical identity. Moreover, social attributions, individual self-concepts, and group norms may all diverge considerably (as we see, for instance, in transgendering). In consequence, there are likely to be fault lines—both categorial and practical—that divide any identity group. In the case of a national identity group, we refer to these divisions as "subnational." National identification may also be troubled by another sort of disalignment. In that case, individuals may favor identity categories that are larger, that are not confined to the nation. As to practical identity, the problem in that case is that the shared features of practical identity are not distinctive. For example, universalism (which affirms that the key features of individual practical identity are shared by people across cultures) is generally internationalist. These forms of expansive inclusiveness are termed "transnational." (Marxist internationalism is a prominent example.)

As these points indicate, national unity is not already given in a shared culture that is simply recognized with a label at the time of a declaration of independence. Rather, national unity has to be fostered in a process of nation-building. That nation-building is, precisely, an operation on categorial and practical identity, an operation in which citizens are encouraged to favor the national identity category (not a subnational or transnational alternative) and in which they are "acculturated" in such a way as to produce a distinctive overlap of practical identities in keeping with the norms of the national identity category. In the case of the United States, a critical problem for nation-building—a problem treated extensively in the fiction, drama, and poetry of the new nation—was (and still is) just how to respond to the subnational divisions based on race and sex. To understand the centrality of these issues for U.S. identity, we will need to consider some of the distinctive features of the U.S. self-concept as that is understood by many Americans.

What is a (real) American?

Needless to say, American ingroup definition has all the usual properties that characterize national (and other) ingroups. For example, the sense of broad, ingroup superiority is clear. Thus, in Letter III ("What Is an American?") of *Letters from an American Farmer*, J. Hector St. John de Crèvecoeur (1981: 67) has his farmer write that "we are the most perfect society now existing in the world." When commentators refer to "American exceptionalism," they seem to imply that there is something exceptional about this. But, in considering America an exception to a broader pattern, Americans are simply doing what ingroup members always do.

On the other hand, ingroups form in particular conditions and with unique histories. Those conditions and histories lead to different specifications of general principles. Thus, the way Americans imagine U.S. exceptionalism is, in part, distinctive. But even that needs to be qualified. Ingroup distinctiveness tends to follow a common pattern. Key features derive from the same general categories—distinctiveness of language, place, ethnicity, religion, history, and/or social and political structure. Moreover, in all these cases, distinctiveness tends to be formulated principally in opposition to one prominent outgroup (or sometimes two prominent outgroups). In the first years of the United States, this prominent outgroup was England. This, of course, changed. For example, during the Cold War the main national outgroup was the Soviet Union. Nonetheless, in each case the opposition was bound up with the definition of ingroup distinctiveness.

Consider language. One important part of American national distinctiveness was the American dialect, the way of speaking—and, indeed, way of spelling—that differentiated Americans from the English.[4] It is worth stressing that this is not a pre-given difference in practical identity. Certainly, there were different ways of speaking—different pronunciations, preferred idioms, etc.—in the United States and England. But there was diversity within each nation and overlap between the nations. A specifically American form of English was in part real, but in part created (e.g., by decisions about spelling), and in part simply imagined. The creation of an American dialect was in some ways a task assigned to such novelists as Mark Twain and such poets as Walt Whitman. Whitman characterized American English as involving "native idiomatic words" that are "of the national blood" (qtd. in Ayeres 1921: 569). In connection with these points, the development of a specifically American English has been a particular concern in American literary study, and the reason why at times writers could be taken to task for writing in an idiom that was putatively British rather than American.[5] (Indeed, "after the Revolution" some "enthusiastic patriots ... advocated the abrogation of English in 'these States' and the invention and adoption of a new language" [Trent et al. 1917: vi].)

The claim of and attempt to form a distinctive language are connected with the claim of and attempt to form a distinctive literary tradition. Much influential work in American literary study has been devoted to the task of defining a specifically American literary tradition, often in contrast with a British tradition. Indeed, in the not too distant past a book on literature and American identity would almost certainly have undertaken the project of defining American literary distinctiveness. An influential example from the middle of the last century is Richard Chase's *The American Novel and Its Tradition*, which claims that there is a "radical divergence" between English and American literary traditions (Chase 1957: 3). To make this case,

Chase often relies on vague and impressionistic claims that are difficult to evaluate. For instance, he maintains that "the English novel" is marked by "great practical sanity." In contrast, "the American imagination" is characterized by "radical forms of alienation, contradiction, and disorder" (1957: 2). Thus, he takes up the great Romantic opposition between, in Friedrich Nietzsche's (1968) terms, the Apollonian and the Dionysian. In keeping with Romantic tendencies, he favors the former; in keeping with nationalist tendencies, he identifies his national tradition with the preferred (Dionysian) alternative. But the distinction is so abstract and metaphorical that it is hard to imagine any nation or literary tradition that, through the selective use of examples, could not be argued to be either Apollonian or Dionysian, depending on one's preference. This equivocal quality is unsurprising. Identity definition is largely vacuous, a mere matter of categorizing us as us and them as them and then asserting the uniqueness of the *us*. That assertion of uniqueness is likely to require a degree of obscurity, since the people—and the literary works—of one's ingroup commonly differ as much among themselves as they differ from members of one's outgroups. (Of course, none of this prevents Chase from being an astute and illuminating critic of individual works.)

A special feature of *national* ingroups is their stress on place, specifically on the land. The land is central to the definition of the nation, since the national ingroup is a group connected with a particular national territory. This has direct, literal consequences, as when Americans celebrate the extent and diversity of the land (in implicit contrast with the more limited landscape of England). The point was perhaps particularly important at the time of U.S. independence due to the widespread theory that group identity was shaped by physical features of the place.[6] The idea was advanced influentially by de Buffon (Georges-Louis Leclerc), who did not think highly of the effects of American landscapes on Americans (as we saw in discussing Washington Irving in the Introduction). For this reason, in *Notes on the State of Virginia* (1787) Thomas Jefferson set out to refute the view that the environment in North America has a degenerative impact on the inhabitants.[7]

In the United States probably the most consequential aspect of the place was its specific form of organization. Nations generally define national space in terms of centrality, with the capital being particularly definitive of the nation, while thinly populated, rural areas may be imagined as more peripheral. The U.S. capital was, of course, significant. But one part of the periphery became equally important—indeed, more important—in the imagination of American nationhood. That is the frontier. As Jedediah Britton-Purdy (2019: 27) notes, "as early as the days of Thomas Jefferson, official American mythmakers cast the United States as a frontier nation, one defined by its sense of the boundless possibilities." Rebecca Grumer (1970: 31–32) explains that the "presence of a vast area of almost free and sparsely settled land" was a key geographical factor "in establishing the meaning of America." The significance of the frontier has been widely discussed and there is no need to treat it in detail here. However, it is worth reminding ourselves of its practical and metaphorical implications. The idea of the frontier facilitated Americans' view of their nation as "a process of endless becoming and ceaseless unfurling" (Grandin 2019: 3). Of course, that process was a matter of conquest. But it was commonly viewed by European Americans as simply extending the United States into areas that were not part of any other nation, lands that were not owned. Moreover, despite the fact that this expansion was possible due only to the involvement of national armed forces, it was regularly construed as a matter of individuals staking out lands for themselves. Thus, as imagined, the frontier combined individualism with national expansion. Moreover, contrary to fact, the expansion was viewed as natural growth, not as imperial conquest. In part as a result of this self-understanding, Americans have been able to conceive of their nation-state as distinctively nonimperial and as perhaps uniquely reconciling individual freedom and initiative with national advancement. Greg Grandin (2019: 1) summarizes the "Frontier Thesis," which is that "the expansion of settlement across a frontier of 'free land' created a uniquely American form of political equality, a vibrant, forward-looking individualism."[8]

American nationalists also drew on the standard metaphors or models for the relations between the national landscape and its citizens, giving them particular inflections (in the way other nations have done). The most common metaphor linking the citizens to the land is the metaphor of people as plants with their roots in the national soil. As commonly developed, this metaphor suggests a long-standing, ancestral connection with a particular place. In other words, one's "rootedness" is one's familial and ethnic connection with the land. This use of the metaphor, however, would have been problematic for European Americans, since they lacked that connection with the land. In consequence, they developed the metaphor in a way that incorporated and justified immigration. For example, de Crèvecoeur (1981: 69) has his American farmer write that "in Europe they were as so many useless plants, wanting vegetative mold and refreshing showers; they withered, and were mowed down by want, hunger, and war; but now by the power of transplantation, like all other plants they have taken root and flourished."

The national property of "transplantation" is related to the ethnic diversity of the new nation. Another distinctive feature of America's self-concept is that it is not ethnically homogenous. It is, in some degree, multiethnic—"a mixture" or "promiscuous breed," including "English, Scotch, Irish, French, Dutch, Germans, and Swedes," a "strange mixture of blood, which you will find in no other country" (de Crèvecoeur 1981: 68, 69). In keeping with this, it is the product of diverse cultures. Of course, not everyone agreed on just how multiethnic the nation might be. Nor did all citizens concur on the nature and extent of cultural mixing. English and North European Protestants were largely acceptable even to "nativists." However, immigrants from Catholic Europe were much more likely to be seen as an illegitimate ethnic addition. Even de Crèvecoeur's (1981: 85) American farmer takes a dim view of the drunken, quarrelsome Irish, whom he contrasts with the more Americanly "industrious" Scotch. Once the Irish and others from this category became established, the exclusionary response shifted to Asians or to Muslims. But there were always advocates of more inclusive notions of Americanness. Moreover, even the nativists were to some extent multiethnic. Similar points apply to cultural traditions. Indeed, a wide range of writers have accepted not only multiple European subcultures but also Amerindian traditions—and, subsequently, African traditions—as part of American national culture,[9] sometimes identifying a key part of our difference from England as the result of these interactions and influences.[10]

The (limited) ethnic diversity of the new nation was connected with its (limited) religious diversity. Crucially, the religious quality of the U.S. national self-concept was fundamentally nonconformist. It was vehemently opposed to an official church, an opposition most famously codified in the doctrine of the separation of church and state. However, the precise nature of religious belief and practice in the new nation was complex and contested. For some, the new nation must accept all religions. For others, multireligiosity stopped when it came to Catholics. In many respects, American practical identity has been shaped by Puritanism—either positively (through the influence of Puritan modes of thought) or negatively (by reactions against Puritanism).[11] This is true not only for religious belief proper, but also for areas governed by religion, such as views of sexuality. More generally, American self-concepts and selves have been partially formed by the development of and conflicts among the many religious tendencies in American society. Moreover, this religious ferment has helped foster at least a superficial valuing of nonconformism. Of course, in practice, Americans are as conformist as anyone else. Indeed, Alexis de Tocqueville (2002: 292) famously went so far as to write that "I know no country in which there is so little true independence of mind and freedom of discussion as in America." And, as John Murrin (1987: 335) points out (referring to an earlier period), "in New England, except for Rhode Island, Old World dissent became New World establishment." But the ideology of U.S. nationalism, thus Americans' national self-concept, often includes some sense that "doing your own thing" is a moral and social value to be admired and cultivated. We like to think of ourselves as exemplary instances of Henry David Thoreau's (1906: 358–359) "man [who] does not keep pace with his companions ... because he hears a different drummer" and "step[s] to the music which he hears, however measured or far away."

This valuing of individual independence of thought and action is connected with a historical distinction of the United States. It began as a country by a revolution, the throwing off of the old government and the establishment a radically new society. That beginning gave Americans reasons to value and celebrate revolution. As with nonconformism, the celebration of revolution is largely a matter of lip service only. In its foreign policy, for example, the United States has supported revolution only to the degree that it is perceived to serve U.S. interests (or, more properly, the interests of some of its elite sectors). Our celebration of revolution in practice involves little more than considering it high praise to call a new styling gel or advertising technique "revolutionary." Nonetheless, the valuing of revolution—the sudden repudiation of the old and its replacement by the new—is part of the national self-concept, at least for many people.

To a great extent, these various putative differentiae are consequential as extensions of the fundamental, sociopolitical distinctiveness of the United States. That distinctiveness is its democratic egalitarianism. In contrast particularly with England, the United States had no king and no aristocracy. It could therefore see itself as a meritocratic system in which any inequality was the result not of birth but of success in competition. As de Crèvecoeur's (1981: 67) American farmer puts it: "Here are no aristocratic families, no courts, no kings." One result of this view has been that the American self-concept largely ignores class. As Nancy Isenberg (2016: 1) notes, in "popular American history ... It is as though in separating from Great Britain, the United States somehow magically escaped the bonds of class." It is democratic by the same token, in that the government serves merely to represent the will of the people, not the interests of some hereditary rulers.

This central idea of America is clear in what is arguably the United States's definitive founding document, the 1776 Declaration of Independence, specifically in its often-quoted early assertion, "We hold these Truths to be self-evident, that all Men are created equal, that they are endowed by their Creator with certain unalienable Rights, that among these are Life, Liberty and the pursuit of happiness. That to secure these Rights, Governments are instituted among Men, deriving their just Powers from the Consent of the Governed." The phrase regarding "the Consent of the Governed" and the reference to "Liberty" address the repudiation of tyranny (developed at length in the rest of the document). The positive side of this repudiation is democracy. The democratic rejection of tyranny is affirmed as an "unalienable Right," a "self-evident" "Truth" that is fundamental and non-negotiable. It applies to "all"; thus, it is universal. Finally, it is rationally justified by the "self-evident" "Truth" that all are "created equal." Thus, the fundamental character of American identity, as set out in the opening sentences of the Declaration of Independence, is the formal principle that America asserts and upholds *universal, democratic egalitarianism*. In addition, this formal principle enables "the pursuit of happiness." (I take it that "Life" is simply the condition for the other rights and does not add anything substantive to the enumeration.) The pursuit of happiness is a secular and mundane goal (contrast a document that affirmed the guarantee of "Life, Liberty, and the pursuit of grace" or "Life, Liberty, and the pursuit of moral self-improvement"). It is also an individual goal. It may well be that the best way for each of us to be happy individually is for us to cooperate in developing a mutually beneficial society. But the point of saying that "all" have the "unalienable Right" to "the pursuit of happiness" is precisely that no individual can be denied the right to pursue happiness, because the happiness of the monarch or the aristocracy—or even the collective society—takes precedence. (For example, the principle should suggest that African Americans cannot be denied the right to pursue happiness even if that deprivation would make the European American majority happy.)

One result of this is that the United States comes to adopt a sort of super-exceptionalism. Moreover, paradoxical as it may at first sound, the United States is exceptional in its exceptionalness precisely because of what it shares with every outgroup. Specifically, in being democratic and egalitarian, the United States is the ideal toward which every other national group strives and the exemplar that shows such groups that reaching the ideal is possible. The United States, then, is unique precisely in its universality. As Thomas Paine (1969: 23) put it in "Common Sense," "the cause of America is in great measure the cause of all Mankind." Grumer (1970: 30–31) explains that it was a "[p]opular belief" that America was destined to stand "as the example of free government to the rest of mankind."

In short, the core of America's national self-concept is that it is democratic, egalitarian, and universal. Of course, there are other aspects of American life that have been consequential for American self-understanding, such as the idea of the frontier. But America's growth at the frontier, as well as its religious diversity, its nonconformity, its revolutionary break with the past—even American speech, apparently free from the prestige hierarchy of the Queen's English—all these features of American identity derive their value from the democratic, egalitarian, and universal nature of American society.

But, of course, there is something obtrusively wrong with this picture—indeed, there are many things wrong with this picture. As Geoff Ward (2002: 29) points out, for example, the Declaration of Independence is marked by "the glaring omission of a major section of the citizenry from equality and the pursuit of happiness." Most obviously, this was a slaveholding society, in which hundreds of thousands of people were property with no political voice and no social standing.[12] Americans' claims to democracy, equality, and universality hardly applied to its slaves. As James Tallmadge exhorted in 1819 (qtd. in Grumer 1970: 301): "You boast of the freedom of your Constitution and your laws … and yet you have slaves in your country." This contradiction between asserted ideals and actual practices sometimes appears with stunning, stark irony. For example, writing in December 1776, Paine (1969: 75) condemns British "tyranny" as enforcing a form of "slavery." He goes on to explain that this is "impious" because "so unlimited a power can belong only to GOD." The point is a reasonable one (given Christian beliefs), but it hardly applies uniquely to the British side in the conflict. I should note that this was not hypocritical on Paine's part, as he supported the abolition of slavery as well (see his *African Slavery in America*). But the argument that the British were acting like slave-masters was not confined to abolitionists; indeed, Samuel Johnson went so far as to say that one "hear[s] the loudest yelps for liberty among the drivers of negroes" (qtd. in Ortiz 2018: 15). I personally do not see how anyone can read the Declaration of Independence without feeling that it is not only deeply inspiring in its initial assertions of universal, democratic egalitarianism, but also deeply hypocritical in blaming the British for infringements of "unalienable Rights" that are trivial in comparison with the colonists' treatment of slaves.[13]

Moreover, the problem is not confined to African Americans. In addition to slavery, the United States was a society founded upon conquering land, taking it from Amerindians—"merciless Indian savages," as they are called in the Declaration—and driving them off that land.[14] The massive loss of Amerindian lives, the imposition of European legal ideas, and the dismissal of Amerindian claims and practices all make assertions of universal, democratic egalitarianism sound almost parodic. The point is no less obvious with respect to women, who were almost entirely barred from politics and who were largely excluded from the profit-generating part of the economy.[15]

Citrin and Sears (2014: 80) see American identity as having two main alternative formulations, "two normative prototypes," "cosmopolitan liberalism" and "nativism." The former "emphasizes commitment to egalitarian democratic political values and individualism," while the latter "holds that only people with certain ethnic characteristics can become acculturated to American values" (2014: 80). Similarly, Carroll Smith-Rosenberg (2010: 465) writes that, "throughout our history ... two visions of the United States have attracted and challenged us. The first imagines America as a country in which diversity, equality, and inalienable political rights are celebrated. The second refers to the United States' dark history as a white man's republic, jealously guarding its borders, suspicious of any who would darken its racial heritage." These do not seem to me to be equal alternatives in most cases. Rather, the universal, democratic egalitarianism appears to be the standard way of understanding American identity, and the ethnic particularism appears to be a response to the obvious contradiction between the ideal and the reality, a rationalization of discriminatory structures through cognitive and affective ideologies. The rationalization often relies on a view of ethnic and religious groups as differing in their cultural (or, in some cases, racial) openness to universal, democratic egalitarianism. Citrin and Sears (2014: 81) suggest as much when they refer to writers such as Samuel Huntington. They explain that Huntington recognizes the centrality to America of "values of equal treatment, economic self-reliance, and political participation." Nonetheless, "Huntington argues that America's common culture rests on the values of the Anglo-Protestant ethnic 'core.'" Thus, they indicate that, for Huntington, Anglo-Protestantism is important precisely because it putatively fosters democratic egalitarianism. So, even Huntington assumes that universal, democratic egalitarianism is the fundamental American identity principle. In contrast with Huntington's ethno-religious particularism, however, "Americans define national identity far more often in terms of ... the vote, civil liberties, equal opportunity, and individualism" (Citrin and Sears 2014: 83), rather than ethnicity and/or Christianity.

Thus, it seems most plausible to conclude that universal, democratic egalitarianism —along with individualism—is the usual, national self-concept of Americans as such (i.e., as Americans, rather than as members of any other identity group). Of course, this view is not shared by everyone, and even those who do share this view differ in precise definition and emphasis. Even so, this appears to be the most standard understanding of what it means to be American. Given this minimal or basic self-concept, the obvious contradiction with real social conditions in the United States is almost impossible to ignore. Responses to this contradiction may be broadly organized into two tendencies. Nativists rationalize the violation of democratic, egalitarian, universalist norms usually by reference to deficiencies in the outgroup. Non-nativists—"cosmopolitan liberals," in Citrin and Sears's (2014) terminology—seek to reconcile the subnational groups in some way, thereby bringing practice into greater conformity with principle.

In the case of Native Americans, for example, we find in Benjamin Franklin a sensitive and humane politician of the cosmopolitan liberal orientation. Franklin (1910: 462) takes up the simple technique of imagining the perspective of outgroup members. Thus, he notes in his "Remarks": "Savages we call them, because their manners differ from ours, which we think the perfection of civility"; and yet "they think the same of theirs." Indeed, adverting to what I am calling *practical identity*, Franklin sees reason to prefer Amerindian customs. He explains that Native

Americans welcome and help strangers. In contrast, Europeans ask for payment for any hospitality and, if an Amerindian visitor has no recognized currency, reviles the unmoneyed traveler with such execrations as: "Get out, you Indian dog" (Franklin 1910: 466). To take another instance, Judith Sargent Murray's (2017) 1790 "On the Equality of the Sexes," a revised version of a piece first written eleven years earlier, takes up the question of women's place in the new nation, and there were many, including men, who sympathized with her views, seeing the second-class status of women as unjustifiable.

Whether one did or did not hold what we would consider progressive views on race and sex hierarchies, they were a problem. Again, the new nation wanted to see itself as democratic, egalitarian, and universal. But it was very difficult to maintain this view in the face of African slavery, the dispossession of Native Americans, and the disenfranchisement of women. One result was that efforts at nation-building routinely took up these problems. Among such efforts, we find the work of politicians, journalists, historians, and a range of other writers and activists. One of the most prominent groups in nation-building consisted of literary authors—novelists, playwrights, short-story writers, poets. Imaginative literature is one of the most emotionally effective ways of addressing the nature of and possibilities for a nation, and American authors certainly took up this task. But the results were not always the sorts of nationalist appeals that some treatments of American literature might suggest—whether patriotic treatments celebrating the national commitments of American authors or revisionist studies that criticize those commitments. In fact, American writers commonly treated the topic of American identity with cognitive complexity and emotional ambivalence, as we already saw in the case of Irving.

In connection with the last point, I should say what I mean by "efforts at nation-building." I do not primarily have in mind verbally articulated decisions to write or do something that would develop people's sense of national identification or make their practical identities converge. I am referring, rather, to a process that is typically much less self-conscious. It is largely a matter of feeling that certain sorts of themes (themes that critics might categorize as national) are important and engaging, thus natural topics for literary treatment; that certain developments of those topics (developments that a critic may identify as fostering national identification) seem to the author to produce a literary effect that he or she feels is good and apt, and so on. Of course, authors also make self-conscious decisions about national identity in their works. The point is that a novel, play, story, or poem may deal with nation-building even when the author does not settle explicitly on doing so.

Attitudes toward outgroups

In the next section, I will outline some of the main ways in which American authors have sought to deal with what we might identify as the *central problem of American identity—the fundamental incompatibility between the social structure of American society and the core beliefs of the American self-concept*. This contradiction is basically an issue of reconciling identity categories. That problem, in turn, derives from the ways in which we—not only Americans, but everyone—think and feel about outgroups and ingroups. I therefore address those prior concerns in the present section.[16]

To consider outgrouping with any clarity, it is important to begin with some distinctions. In the case of men's outgrouping of women, a fundamental distinction is roughly captured by the terms "patriarchy," "sexism," and "misogyny." The terms are used somewhat differently by different speakers, but we may systematize the distinction they mark in the following way. *Patriarchy* is a social and political system that makes goods and opportunities available to men and women in partially different and ultimately nonmeritocratic ways to the overall benefit of men. I say "ultimately nonmeritocratic" because women may be trained in ways that do not suit them for particular occupations (e.g., if they are not taught mathematics). The selection of men for those occupations may be meritocratic, but the greater suitability of men at that point does not itself rest on superior merit, only superior education. I say "overall benefit," since patriarchy typically offers some benefits to women (e.g., exemption from military draft).

Though the distinctions among *patriarchy*, *sexism*, and *misogyny* are formulated for one particular ingroup–outgroup relation, they point us to parallel distinctions in other types of identity group relations. Unfortunately, the terminology in these cases is even less clear. Even so, *patriarchy* has an approximate parallel in the word *discrimination*, though the latter stresses individual behavior rather than social behavior. Thus, we may say that there is a racially discriminatory sociopolitical system that makes goods and opportunities available to European Americans and African Americans in partially different and ultimately nonmeritocratic ways to the overall benefit of European Americans. There is a related but not identical system bearing on Native Americans, and so on. We may then refer to individual instances of nonmeritocratic apportionment of goods and/or opportunities as race-based discrimination, sex-based discrimination, and so on.

Discriminatory systems serve the broad interests of the dominant group while maintaining some sort of social equilibrium that allows the systems to continue functioning. One key component of such systems, a component that contributes crucially to their functionality, is ideology. Ideology serves to rationalize the system. When operating perfectly, it convinces people in the system that the system is indeed meritocratic, at least on the whole and with only limited exceptions. This discourages disprivileged groups from rebelling against the system, since they are putatively getting what they merit anyway. Meritocratic ideology also makes it easier for dominant groups to avoid whatever empathy and associated self-recrimination they might otherwise experience. (The same benefits operate in the other direction for any areas of social and political life in which the dominated group might have some relative advantage. For example, patriarchy in medicine may have given women some advantages, on the whole, in entering nursing.) In the case of male–female relations, this ideology is called "sexism"; in the case of white–black and European–Native-American relations, we may refer to it as "cognitive racial bias."

I refer to the preceding as *cognitive* biases because it is important to distinguish the emotional component of ingroup–outgroup relations explicitly. In male–female identity categorization, this emotional component, at least in one of its forms, is called "misogyny."[17] The term, *misogyny*, refers narrowly to the hatred of women. However, emotional attitudes toward outgroups—including the attitudes of men toward women—vary considerably, even when those attitudes are consistent with cognitive bias and are functionally supportive of the discriminatory system (patriarchy). For example, men may pity women for their putative incapacities. It would therefore be more appropriate to refer to *affective bias*, which may be sex-based, race-based, and so on. The key feature of affective bias is that it involves a nonparallel interpersonal stance. When we view someone as an outgroup member, we do not engage in effortful empathy, imagining how we would feel in their situation, shifting the relevant variables (e.g., reimagining ourselves with their aspirations or interests). Rather, our response to such outgroup members may be antipathetic, condescending, or otherwise divergent from their experience. This leads not to sympathy and symhedonia, but to *Schadenfreude*, demeaning pity, envy, or indifference. (In contrast, our interpersonal stance toward people we identify as members of ingroups is, again, usually parallel.)

Cognitive biases regarding outgroups often take the form of stereotypes, standardized beliefs about particular groups (e.g., women or Africans). I take it that stereotypes are widely familiar. A perhaps less-familiar component of cognitive bias is *cognitive modeling*, the use of broad "source domains"—systems of semantically interrelated concepts—for thinking about outgroups. As, for example, Ashis Nandy (1983) has indicated, we face a cognitive problem when we try to think of some group of humans as inferior. Insofar as we share a species definition with outgroup members, it would seem that we are in some way equal. One way of guiding our thought is to model the ingroup–outgroup relation on some other hierarchy. In *The Culture of Conformism* (Hogan 2001), I argue that there are a few models that tend to recur with great frequency in this context.

The first modeling domain is what I refer to as "animacy" (loosely following one use of the term in linguistics). This model places humans in the central position, nonhuman animals in a subhuman position, and spirits (e.g., angels and devils) in a superhuman position. It is obvious that we often model outgroups on animals. It may seem that we do not put them in the superhuman position. But that is wrong. We actually do this routinely. Satan is probably the most common model for an outgroup that is thought of as being hostile, possessing a keen intelligence for deception and seduction, and having the power to destroy us as a group. (A prominent example of demonic modeling may be found in Nazi ideas about Jews.) As is well known, sexist ideology often characterizes one set of women—perhaps "true" women (cf. "real" Americans)—as angels, thus (among other things) superior to the sorts of concern that would require equal treatment with men.

Another widespread modeling domain is that of *age grades*. In this case, the ingroup is mapped onto the middle position of *adult*. Outgroups are then mapped onto *children* or *the aged*. The assimilation of outgroups to children is probably obvious enough that it requires no elaboration. The assimilation of "Others" to the aged is less common but still frequent enough. As with the superhuman in animacy, the aged may be divided into two groups with opposite evaluations, roughly *the wise* and *the senile*. As Ashis Nandy (1983) discusses, the British often viewed the people and culture of India in terms of aged models (though the theoretical framework in which he discusses this modeling is different).

Nandy's work also suggests that male–female outgrouping has a special place in this conceptual system. Sex-based cognitive bias commonly draws on these two domains. Other forms of cognitive bias (e.g., race-based cognitive bias) draw not only on age and animacy models, but also on the model of men and women. For example, Nandy (1983) points out that British imperialists often viewed colonized populations as particularly feminine (see the first chapter of *The Intimate Enemy*). In this way, sex relations are often paradigmatic for other types of outgroup modeling and cognitive bias.

Finally, it is important to make a few comments on the emotions associated with identity. Of course, any emotion can occur in relation to identity concerns. But I want to emphasize here a limited number of emotions, which seem to be particularly significant for categorial identity. The first of these is pride. Pride is, in effect, the default emotion for one's relation to an identity category. Whatever one's group identification, one begins by viewing members of one's group more positively than others. Again, in comparison with outgroup members, one sees ingroup members as harder-working, better-looking, and so forth.

There are two emotions that are likely to displace pride. The first is shame. This emotion results from a sense of ingroup inferiority conveyed particularly by the disgust or contempt—or, in some cases, condescension and pity—that one senses from outgroup members. For obvious reasons, shame is particularly likely to develop among members of a socially dominated group. When the contempt from the outgroup is seen as justified (due to ingroup inferiority), shame is likely to develop into paralyzing despair. Especially when viewed as unjust, shame is likely to trigger rage and violence (see Waller 2011: 295). But rage itself may dwindle into despair, insofar as one feels that the bias, and thus the discriminatory sociopolitical system, are unalterable (see Waller 2011: 255).

While the dominated group is more likely to find group pride disrupted by shame, the dominant group may find group pride troubled by guilt. By *guilt* here, I mean a sympathetic response to the suffering of others combined with a sense of a personal obligation to help relieve that suffering due to a feeling of partial responsibility for it. Thus, in the late 1960s many Americans found their pride in being American disturbed by a sense of the pain caused by the U.S. military in Southeast Asia. Guilt tends to inspire attempts at reparation or at the very least the discontinuation of ongoing harm (e.g., the ending of the Vietnam War).

In the new nation, there were numerous sources of possible shame or guilt with respect to national and subnational identity categories. These included the following. In the revolutionary period and the early years of the new nation, Americans often felt anger against England as a dominating outgroup. However, as Irving's story (i.e., "Rip van Winkle") suggests, this could be combined with guilt over disloyalty and violence against the English,[18] either as members of an encompassing ingroup or due to an empathic response not qualified by identity categories. Leslie Fiedler (1992: 202) refers to this as "the sense of guilt felt by Americans over the Revolution against the mother country."

More directly relevant to our concerns, European Americans could feel anger over the raids and kidnappings perpetrated by Amerindians against Europeans (as recounted, for example, in captivity narratives). But they could also feel guilt over the theft of Amerindian land and the genocidal effects of European colonization, which ultimately reduced the Native American population from 100 million to 10 million (Dunbar-Ortiz 2014: 40). Thus, Fiedler (1992: 202) mentions "the expropriation of the Indians" as another source of "guilt felt by Americans." Conversely, Native Americans could feel shame and rage or despair over the events leading to this outcome. For example, as Peter Mancall (1995: 8), among others, has argued, it does not appear plausible to attribute Native American alcoholism simply to some putative genetic predisposition; rather, "Indians drank at least in part because the world they knew was eroding around them"—or, perhaps more accurately, because they suffered from a feeling of helplessness in the face of unwanted change, a sense of despair over never being able to do anything to halt or alter the course of this change.

The shame, rage, and despair inspired in African American slaves is too obvious to require comment; so too are the feelings fostered by the history of subsequent discriminatory sociopolitical systems in the United States. Antagonism could be provoked in whites by black resistance to white domination. But human sympathy for African Americans suffering exploitation, disenfranchisement, discrimination, and brutality or murder could and did also inspire feelings of guilt and attempts at reparation by European Americans. At the same time, one risk of sympathetic responses is that they may intermingle with outgrouping and lead to patronizing pity. This may in turn foster a sense of shame and either resentment or withdrawal (or both) among African Americans.

Finally, women—like African Americans or Native Americans—certainly often heard their husbands, fathers, or brothers proclaiming the universal, democratic equality of the new nation. Hearing this, many could not help but feel demeaned and angry over the exclusion of themselves and their entire half of the population from political and social equality. Moreover, unlike the experience of African Americans and Native Americans, this sense of exclusion was regularly part of women's closest human relations, linking them with personal betrayal as well. On the other hand, in part due to this proximity some men could not help but see the injustice of the patriarchal system embedded in a democracy with aspirations toward universal equality. Moreover, some men inevitably felt empathy and guilt over particular mistreatments of women (often their own mothers, sisters, wives, or daughters, though also acquaintances and even strangers), such as the trial and execution of supposed witches.

Literature against subnational identity biases

Thus, with respect to each group the contradictions between national self-concept and actual sociopolitical conditions and their history were often salient and emotionally consequential. In some cases, the emotions drove a deeper wedge between the subnational identity groups. This occurred perhaps most obviously on the side of the dominated people—Amerindians, African Americans, and women. But those emotions also involved conciliatory feelings, including sentiments of remorse encouraging reparation. Ultimately, the anger of the oppressed and the reparative remorse of the oppressors required changes in the discriminatory sociopolitical system—including, for example, political enfranchisement. But a crucial part of changing discriminatory practices is changing emotional and cognitive biases. Many authors of novels, stories, plays, and poems self-consciously or unselfconsciously crafted works that responded to cognitive misunderstandings and nonparallel interpersonal stances. It was rare for an author to set aside dominant biases entirely. But it was common for authors to recognize problems with standard ways of thinking about and emotionally responding to subnational identity categories. These authors repeatedly—if most often inconsistently—developed ways of responding to these biases and thereby responding to subnational divisions.

Authors' responses to bias were of course guided in part by the ways in which they envisioned their readership. An author writing for a white readership and seeking to change their interpersonal stance toward nonwhites needed to inhibit his or her readers' inclinations toward anger, disgust, and contempt. This posed difficulties. The obvious way of opposing anger was by cultivating compassion—and, indeed, compassion is crucial for limiting identity-group opposition. But the risk of compassion is that it will combine with an underestimation of the outgroup—through, for example, the use of a childhood model—and thereby lead to humiliating pity.

Authors often sought to avoid the cognitive bias of demeaning outgroups through one of two methods. The first was idealization and the fostering of admiration. If we are inclined to see an outgroup as inferior, praising members of the outgroup as superior would appear to be a suitable and effective response—as it is. But it has risks also. In suggesting that women are not bestial, an author may shift them into the angelic model; in removing Native Americans from the category of children, an author may end up characterizing them as wise elders. In both cases, the outgroup remains an outgroup and subject to cognitive and affective biases. As Dovidio and colleagues (2017: 271) note, modern forms of "racism can reflect the expression of more positive feelings toward Blacks than toward Whites."

The other common way of confronting models that harm outgroups is no less problematic. This involves taking up the usual model and either explaining or elevating it. For example, one could argue that Richard Wright's portrait of Bigger Thomas in *Native Son* broadly conforms to the stereotype of a violent, perhaps even animal-like ("subhuman," as James Baldwin [1955: 41] puts it) black man. Rather than repudiating the stereotype in this case, Wright seeks to explain what happened to Bigger that produced this bestial outcome. The difficulty with this approach is obvious. Readers may leave the book with their stereotypes reinforced, and thus with their biases enhanced, despite the explanation. By "elevating" the model, I mean treating the model as if it should be admired and privileged. Thus, for example, Stowe often represents African Americans as childlike. However, she represents this childlike quality as superior to the adult attitudes of European Americans. The risk here is, of course, the same—that readers will leave the book with their biases strengthened. (On the other hand, even these cases are complicated by the fact that, in certain contexts, some biases may have positive consequences. For example, if Stowe managed to shift some readers from thinking about Africans as animals to thinking about them as children, that may have had beneficial effects on their response to the Fugitive Slave Act. The latter may have seemed reasonable regarding animals, but cruel with respect to children.)

Authors treated not only the feelings of superiority or disdain and anger toward sub-national outgroups. They also treated European Americans' fear and disgust, arguably the two most profoundly divisive emotions separating identity groups. Perhaps the main way in which European American authors responded to the fear and disgust of racial outgrouping is through the motif of *interracial romance*. The combination of sexual desire and attachment bonding that characterizes romantic love involves the most thorough repudiation of disgust and distrust. As such, the romantic love of whites and blacks or European Americans and Native Americans often serves to express the most thoroughgoing rejection of subnational, interracial antipathy. It also appears in a more moderated form—the form of attachment bonding without sexual desire—in the common motif of interracial friendship. On the other hand, such friendship often has sexual overtones (or more than overtones). I will pay particular attention to this motif in the following chapters.

In isolating and focusing on interracial romance, I have been inspired by the work of Leslie Fiedler (1992: 353), who beautifully expressed the aspirations and limitations of this motif when he wrote of "a society in which, momentarily, the irreparable breach between black and white seems healed by love." Though Fiedler could not have known this at the time, the motif is not merely a recurring dream in fiction. As Dovidio and colleagues (2017: 283) explain, citing empirical research, the "power of cross-group friendships and romantic relationships to combat bias" is "well-documented" (on the former, see also Poteat and Birkett 2017: 377). In keeping with this conclusion, Sheryll Cashin (2017: 134, 5–6) points out that "a study of whites married to blacks and other people of color … documented increased understanding of racism." She explains that she does "not claim that every interracial relationship automatically confers such" benefits, but "many do, leading us on an arc toward less emotional segregation." Indeed, Dovidio and colleagues (2017: 284) connect the theme with our central concerns in this book when they explain that "cross-group friendships and intimate relationships … can promote positive intergroup attitudes as well as egalitarian norms." In this way, interracial bonding in friendship or romance may concretely diminish racism and contribute—in an admittedly limited way—to the advancement of egalitarian ideals.

As will become clear, however, I disagree with most details of Fiedler's account. Fiedler famously argued that American literature is pervaded by the theme of "innocent" (or nonsexual) homoerotic male bonding across races. Thus, he sees this bonding as insistently nonheterosexual and even bound up with a flight from women's society. In this, I believe he is mistaken. First, the motif appears importantly in a range of heterosexual relations. Second, the flight from female society seems to me far rarer in U.S. literature than Fiedler imagines; indeed, most of the works where he believes this to be a motivating factor (e.g., *Moby Dick*) appear to me to have little to do with fleeing female society in particular (as opposed to mainstream society more generally). Third, when the romance is between two men or two women, it is not necessarily nonsexual. Finally, Fiedler develops this motif in a psychoanalytic context that is quite different from the present treatment of the motif as a specific response to one emotional component of subnational division and associated national guilt (or anxiety, in some cases). Nonetheless, my sensitivity to interracial romance was conditioned by Fiedler's challenging and often deeply insightful analyses of U.S. literature.

Returning to the motif of interracial romance itself, I should note that "romance" here definitely does not mean sexual desire alone. Interracial sexual desire tends to be exploitative and even brutal when not accompanied by attachment bonds. In consequence, authors often represent interracial lust as one of the cruelest expressions of an oppressive system. The brutality of interracial lust is treated by both white and non-white authors. But it is almost certainly more prominent in the works of the latter. This is one of the ways in which writings by authors from dominated groups tend to differ from writings by authors from dominant groups.

There are, of course, other differences as well. For example, it may be the case that "subaltern" authors are more inclined to cultivate respect for their ingroup without idealizing it, developing more "three-dimensional" black, Amerindian, or female characters.[19] On the other hand, the most crucial differences seem to be a matter of the target readership. Works appealing to Native American or African American readers have a different function than works appealing only to European American readers, though the techniques authors use overlap in the two cases. Specifically, in parallel with European Americans, many Native Americans and African Americans undoubtedly feel antipathy toward racial outgroups, prominently including European Americans. However, the most pressing needs of such dominated groups are likely to involve overcoming shame and despair. Thus, the task of authors addressing nonwhite readers is often not, first of all, a matter of diminishing fear or anger, or of fostering compassion or a sense of guilt. The task of such authors is more urgently a matter of inspiring pride and a sense of agency, a feeling of confidence. This may work against national reconciliation, and it often involves the enhancement of subnational divisions rather than their dissipation. In connection with this, authors addressing subaltern readers are less likely to focus on intergroup connections, concentrating instead on the internal relations of the dominated identity group. This, in turn, is less likely to entail a critique of intergroup disgust and distrust. Indeed, it can often lead authors to reject not only interracial lust but even interracial romance as a response to subnational identity conflict.

The preceding points apply in some degree to the subnational division between women and men as well. For example, writers treating cognitive and affective bias based on sex (thus sexism and misogyny in the broad sense of the term) work to shift the interpersonal stance of men and the cognitive models they commonly impose on women; alternatively, when addressing women, they may seek to foster a sense of empowerment over and against feelings of helplessness.[20] However, there are evident complications bearing on the motif of intergroup romance. The most obvious point is that there is no taboo on the romantic involvement between men and women. Thus, romantic love alone is unlikely to be seen by anyone as responding to cognitive and affective bias in this case. More generally, men and women, though partially segregated, interact much more fully than do other identity groups. In consequence, individual men and women are more likely to suspend outgroup categorization with individual response. Thus, John might routinely think of Jane principally as Jane (this particular person), rather than as a (generic) woman. (On the displacement of stereotypes by individuating information, see Holland et al. 1986: 215.) On the other hand, outgrouping can easily reassert itself even in these cases. Moreover, authors can and do at times give special importance to romantic love in treating sex-based bias. Such love cannot by itself stand as a repudiation of sexism or even some forms of misogyny. It may, however, be used to intensify the reader's emotional response (e.g., by making a male lover's sexism an act of personal betrayal, thereby possibly enhancing our empathic response to the woman's situation) or to highlight the injustice of patriarchy and its violation of universal, egalitarian principles (e.g., in separating lovers).

Conclusion

Identity is a complex concept, or rather set of concepts. Within this set, several distinctions are crucial, including that between categorial identity and practical identity. Nation-building requires the cultivation of both, thus people's shared self-categorization and their shared capacities and propensities (collectively, their shared culture). American identity is complex as well. Fundamentally, it involves a view of the United States as democratic and egalitarian. As such, it is both different (in rejecting other nations' feudal systems) and universal (in providing a model that serves every ordinary person everywhere). But, of course, the United States is not and has never been universal in its democratic practices, and it is not and has never been fully egalitarian. Particularly critical discrepancies may be found in race and sex, thus the status and treatment of Native Americans, African Americans, and women. In each case, from the time of the nation's founding, systematic discriminatory practices have been a part of the political and economic system, nonparallel interpersonal stances have skewed emotional responses to in- and outgroups, and cognitive biases have undervalued the capacities of the disenfranchised. The cognitive biases were in part given shape and emotional force by appeal to the common cognitive models of animacy and age. To some extent, writers succumbed to these prejudices. But to some extent, they challenged them. For example, a number of writers sought to oppose fear of and disgust at outgroups; one prominent means of opposing these divisive and often violence-rationalizing emotions was through the sympathetic depiction of interracial romance.

Notes

1 My use of this phrase is different from that of Christine Korsgaard (1996: 101), which I came upon after I had already adopted the phrase in treating postcolonial literature, culture, and tradition (see Hogan 2000: 322).
2 Readers familiar with Samuel Huntington's book on American identity, *Who Are We?*, will recognize that he too is attentive to "the importance that Americans attribute to

their national identity compared to their many other identities" (Huntington 2004: xv). However, Huntington refers to such hierarchization of identities as "salience," thereby seeming to suggest that salience is the only relevant variable.

3   This necessity of difference for identity goes at least some way toward explaining the fetishization of putative cultural difference by humanists; it is part of an affirmation of distinctive, categorial identities forming ingroups and outgroups. It is more difficult to explain why the affirmation of difference—which is foundational for all types of racism—is viewed by so many humanists as antiracist.

4   Rebecca Grumer (1970: 255) notes that "Noah Webster ... proposed changing American spelling to give it a distinctly nationalistic flavor."

5   On national identity and language, see, for example, Kerkering (2003: 126–127). The mention of national linguistic idiom brings up an important tension in the conception of group identity. It is a function of the difference between category norms and practical identities. On the one hand, certain aspects of practical identity are supposed to be the, so to speak, natural expression of any given member of the group. For example, speaking American English is supposed to be a result of one's American identity. On the other hand, those and other aspects practical identity in fact vary among members of the group. Thus, speaking or writing "American" has to be encouraged, sometimes even coerced. I will not be focusing on the presumption that features of practical identity are a direct manifestation of categorial identity, in part because it is so obviously wrong. On the other hand, as John Kerkering (2003: 29) points out, using a different terminology and with different theoretical presuppositions, features of a literary work need not be "indexical of either nation or race" (i.e., they do not need to directly manifest national or racial identity) for "the belief in their indexicality to be consequential."

6   The idea is related to the common metaphor of people as plants (on the latter, see Lakoff and Turner 1989). As de Crèvecoeur (1981: 71) puts it, "men are like plants; the goodness and flavor of the fruit proceeds from the peculiar soil and exposition in which they grow."

7   See Levine (2017: 28, n.4). Jefferson's text is available online at https://www.thefederalist papers.org/wp-content/uploads/2012/12/Thomas-Jefferson-Notes-On-The-State-Of-Vir ginia.pdf (accessed 9 December 2019).

8   Due to the particular focus of this book, I will make only occasional reference to the idea of the frontier. In addition to Grandin, readers interested in this topic and its relation to American identity may wish to consult Slotkin (1994) and Sundquist (1995).

9   See, for example, the Wikipedia entry on "Culture of the United States" (accessed 17 May 2019) for an instance of such a view. (I take Wikipedia to be an apt source here not for its scholarly claims but for its place in the broader intellectual and popular imagination, which is important for this point.)

10 As should be clear, I do not find common culture—thus shared practical identity—to be crucial to national identification. Rather, I take it that categorial identity is generally what is at issue. Moreover, despite the focus of this book, I am not an advocate for the United States or any other ingroup (even though, in spite of my self-conscious evaluations, I sometimes do feel ingroup national identification with America, as the present analysis would lead us to expect). Nonetheless, I have cultural preferences and generally favor diversity or pluralism in cultural influences. All this puts me at odds with a writer such as Huntington (2004: xvi, xvii), who sees culture as central and who writes as a "patriot," maintaining that "Americans should recommit themselves to ... Anglo-Protestant culture, traditions, and values." On the other hand, I do believe that there should be enough uniformity in practical identity to sustain a general commitment to universal, democratic egalitarianism (even as we disagree on precisely what that entails). I am also deeply uncomfortable with the alignment of cultures with ethnicities or races. Insofar as a cultural practice is valuable, it is in principle valuable for anyone, not merely for people who have some putative ancestral connection with it.

11 The point is not confined to the early America. As Emory Elliott (2001: xi) noted, "the complex question of the connections between the culture of the Modern United States and the world of seventeenth-century Puritan New England remains at the center of the ongoing search for a national identity."

12 Almost 700,000, according to the 1790 census (see Nielsen 2013: 42, drawing on figures from the U.S. Census Bureau).
13 As one of the readers for this book pointed out, in addition to the types of ambiguity discussed at the outset of this chapter, "American identity" is ambiguous, as "it can refer to either the characteristics of the US nation-state or to an individual's self-categorization as, and investment in being, an American." Again, when one identifies with a group, one typically adopts a set of norms, by which one evaluates oneself and the group as a whole. This is why, for example, people can feel guilt over actions performed by their group (e.g., their nation-state), even when they had nothing to do with the actions themselves. Thus, a person's sense of himself or herself as an American is often inseparable from a norm of universal, democratic egalitarianism. But that norm is all too obviously at odds with many practices of the identity group, prominently including the official and unofficial characteristics of the nation-state as indicated in the preceding paragraph.
14 I should perhaps note at the outset that I do not romanticize Native American society, contrasting a noble Indian with a degraded European. I take it that people generally behave very badly toward outgroups and they tend toward brutality in military conflict. Both the Europeans and the Amerindians were often "merciless ... savages," though of course in any particular conflict one side may be significantly more brutal than the other (and one subgroup may be significantly more humane than another—witness, for instance, Quakers in the European community). The main overarching difference is simply the obvious one—that the Native Americans had a prior claim to the land and that in consequence the Europeans were the initial and repeated aggressors. Moreover, the devastation of the Native American population by European diseases along with some other factors eventually gave Europeans a decided advantage in the conflict, and as a group's power and impunity grow, its willingness to behave cruelly commonly grows as well. Put simply, in violent conflicts those with greater power tend to cause more harm. This too was largely the case in the history of European–Amerindian conflicts.
15 Grumer (1970: 37) too stresses sex and race, writing that "women, the black slaves, and the Indians had almost no part in" the "vision" of America as "a society based on ... liberty and equality." There were, of course, other disenfranchised groups, such as many of the disabled (see, e.g., Nielsen 2013: 49–77).
16 I will focus on denigratory outgrouping, though many of the same consequences (e.g., hiring discrimination) follow from ingroup favoritism, which is in some ways more dangerous, as it is widely considered innocuous or even laudable. Thus, Marilynn Brewer (2017: 93–94) observes that "Whites who consider themselves low in prejudice make a conscious effort to suppress negative affective reactions to Black stimuli, but show no suppression of differential positive affect toward White stimuli. Apparently, this more subtle ingroup positivity is not consciously recognized as a form of prejudice." John Dovidio and colleagues (2017: 274) explain that "more liberal individuals display less explicit prejudice on self-report measures but show pro-White implicit racial bias at levels equal to those of conservatives."
17 As I mentioned above, different people use these terms somewhat differently. For example, Martha Nussbaum uses "sexism" more or less as I do, but combines misogyny and patriarchy. Thus, in *The Monarchy of Fear*, she defines misogyny as "an enforcement strategy, a type of virulent hatred and hatred-behavior aimed at keeping women 'in their place'" (Nussbaum 2018: 15).
18 As in the case of Major André, which we will touch on in connection with Judith Sargent Murray's writings.
19 I should stress that this is not at all to say that dominated groups never stereotype members of their own category; they do. Nor is it to say that dominant category authors never develop three-dimensional outgroup characters; they do, too.
20 On the emotionally deleterious consequences of feeling helpless—but also on the socially harmful effects of some strategies for feeling empowered—see the fourth chapter of Nussbaum's (2018) *The Monarchy of Fear*.

2

THE LAST OF THE MOHICANS

Senility and love in a new nation

James Fenimore Cooper's *Last of the Mohicans* (1826) is a clear but also complex instance of the sorts of identity development outlined in the preceding chapter. In this book, Cooper sets out in part to address the subnational division between European Americans and Native Americans. To do this, he draws on the sorts of techniques and models we have been considering. The result is, unsurprisingly, mixed. To some extent, the novel takes dominant forms of identity opposition and substitutes less aggressive or less antagonistic forms. For example, Rebecca Grumer (1970: 139, 151) writes that "the typical view of the Indian in this period" is represented by Hugh Brackenridge, who referred to them as "animals," as did many others. Leslie Fiedler (1992: 160) characterizes Charles Brockden Brown's representation of Amerindians (in his 1799 novel, *Edgar Huntly*) in the same terms, writing that "his red men are … treated essentially as animals, living extensions of the threat of wilderness." Cooper may suggest that they are, rather, assimilable to the aged. This may still leave them in some degree inferior to European Americans, but not so inferior as animals, thus not justifiably subjected to anything like the same degree of mistreatment. Think, for example, of what you would feel justified in doing to a rat in your home versus how you would feel justified in treating Grandpa. In keeping with this topic, "the majority of Americans in the early nineteenth century thought that 'the only good Indian was a dead Indian'" (Grumer 1970: 141).

Cooper's novel is, then, an instance of a general, cognitive tendency that is common in ideological critique. Following a range of Marxist theorists, we may identify *dominant ideologies* that rationalize and sustain specific policies that themselves serve to reproduce nonmeritocratic hierarchies—fundamentally, hierarchies of economic class, but incidentally other hierarchies (e.g., racial hierarchies) that contribute to the stability of the class system (e.g., by fragmenting the working class along racial lines). We may distinguish these from encompassing *problematics*, larger sets of options that are socially available to critics of dominant ideology and that still function to maintain social stratification. Put differently, problematics comprise constraints on what can be questioned or challenged and how it might be questioned or challenged.[1] Problematics, in this sense, limit what mainstream social critics are likely to say about a set of social conditions or behaviors. For example, the U.S. war in Vietnam involved particular policies. Mainstream critics might criticize the war—thus depart from the dominant ideology—while still sustaining the set of ideas and attitudes that undergirded the broader set of policy goals. More exactly, Noam Chomsky and others have argued that during the Vietnam War mainstream analysis of the war began with the official position—in our terms, the dominant ideology—that it was a benevolent act of support for the people of Vietnam (Herman and Chomsky 2002). Mainstream critics of the war might insist that it was too costly, that it was unwinnable, or that it was based on a misunderstanding of the Vietnamese people. In our terms, these alternatives defined a problematic for treating the war. The extreme view within this problematic would involve the admission that, on some occasions, there were local war crimes committed by U.S. troops. This problematic excluded a critique of the war as a fundamentally imperialist invasion of another country involving pervasive war crimes (see, for example, Herman and Chomsky 2002: 169–252). As such, the criticisms allowed by the problematic served to rationalize and sustain an encompassing imperialist project that on the whole served the interests of American capital (at least in principle and in the short term).

The standard account of dominant ideologies and problematics concerns literal claims or beliefs (about political acts, economic practices, and the like). But the same ideas apply no less to models and metaphors. The sorts of metaphors that commonly serve to conceptualize outgroups may readily form problematics. Thus, critics of one form of outgroup modeling are likely to bolster their criticism by drawing on alternatives from the same metaphor domain or by shifting to another standard domain. This is arguably what Cooper does at those points where he assimilates Native Americans to the elderly. He takes up an option from the problematic of outgroup models, which is to say, a model that is not unique to his novel but part of a set of common ways of thinking about and responding to outgroups.

As the cases of Vietnam and Cooper both illustrate, none of this should be taken to suggest that there are no differences in the problematic or that the differences are inconsequential. Differences between the "conservative" and "liberal" alternatives—for example, those supporting and opposing the Vietnam War—are often quite significant. They could make the difference between death and life for large numbers of people. The same point holds for Cooper's use of the model of old age.

Moreover, Cooper—like most of the authors we will be considering—is more complex and contextual than this indicates. He responds to the outgrouping of Native Americans and the associated subnational division with techniques other than a shift to a more liberal version of the problematic. Another practice that challenges dominant ideologies also partially revises the problematic itself. This involves altering the way in which the problematic is mapped onto the world. In this case, it is a matter of just how ingroups and outgroups are selected and organized. This too is ideologically equivocal. One deleterious model for Native Americans—or any outgroup in times of violent conflict—is demons. Using this model regularly facilitates severe, often brutal mistreatment. But Cooper, so to speak, "dehomogenizes" the outgroup, distinguishing different subgroups of Native Americans. Characterizing any such group as animalistic or demonic is, of course, potentially extremely harmful. Even so, such differentiation within the outgroup to some degree challenges the dominant ideological identification of all Native Americans as an outgroup. Moreover, at points, Cooper makes it clear that "outgroups" are ingroups for their own members and may well see "us" as an outgroup, as when Magua animalizes Europeans, exclaiming that "the palefaces are dogs!" (2014: 383). Readers might simply dismiss this as demonic error on the part of Magua or other Native Americans with similar views. However, they may also take it, perhaps more plausibly in this case, to indicate that we all outgroup others in much the same, universally invalid ways.

As noted in Chapter 1, another technique for partially reconciling subnational identity groups is the explanation of stereotypes. This in some respects remains within the dominant problematic and often the dominant ideology. As such, it is a risky choice for resolving dilemmas of national identification, as it is quite possible that one might reinforce at least the categories of the dominant problematic, even if one is proposing a very different reason for the categorization. To recur to an earlier example, when in *Native Son* Richard Wright seeks to explain why an African American man might turn into a rapist and murderer, there is a real risk that he will enhance the likelihood of readers viewing African American men as rapists and murderers. On the other hand, this approach does diverge from the dominant problematic in that it accounts for the stereotype not by appealing to the nature of African American men, but rather by suggesting that anyone placed in particular social circumstances would be likely to behave in similar ways. Cooper too takes up this approach specifically in relation to his primary villain, Magua.

Indeed, there is a further aspect of Cooper's technique here that is worth noting. Magua may be viewed a sort of Satanic figure who, like John Milton's Satan, is developed with a degree of romantic sympathy. In other words, there is not only an explanation of Magua's cruel behavior, but a degree of admiration for his vigor and perseverance, even as he acts in ways that we cannot condone. On the other hand, this Romantic Satanism is, at best, only hinted at in the course of the novel. (It is taken up more clearly and systematically in Michael Mann's 1992 film, however.)

Most significantly, Cooper also seeks to alter the interpersonal stance of his readers by developing stories of interracial attachment bonding. (Needless to say, he would not have phrased it in this manner.) As Grumer (1970: 140) explains, popular writers of the period suggested that "there was no possibility that the two races [Amerindian and European] could ever mingle in society or even live peacefully." Cooper's novel repudiates this view prominently through the friendship between Hawkeye and Chingachgook and through the (somewhat understated but significant) romantic bond between Uncas and Cora. The latter is particularly striking in light of such comments as that of Timothy Flint (author of the 1833 *Indian Wars of the West*) that "a union with" Indians is "as incompatible as with animals of another nature" (qtd. in Grumer 1970: 151). This seems to be the very center of Cooper's project, as stressed in the closing pages of the work.

Thus, like most of the other books we will be considering, *The Last of the Mohicans* is complex and to a degree contradictory in its treatment of race. But this does not mean that no attitudes or ideas are more predominant than others. To my mind, the book is more about changing interpersonal stances than about shifting from one aspect of the dominant problematic to another (as perhaps the title, and the final words of the novel, might suggest).

Though Cooper's novel is consistent with many other works in its complexity and ambiguity, it is of unusual significance in its treatment of interracial relations. This is due to its status and influence. Doris Sommer has gone so far as to call *The Last of the Mohicans* the "founding text for America" (qtd. in Cooper 2014). Similarly, Hugh MacDougall (2014) asserts that "for many, it is—and for almost two centuries has been—the quintessentially American book."[2] Roxanne Dunbar-Ortiz (2014: 103)characterizes it, disapprovingly, as "the official US origin story." Herman Melville identified Cooper as "our national novelist" (qtd. in Dunbar-Ortiz 2014: 103). The point is not confined to the interior of the nation. Fiedler (1992: 181) comments that "in all likelihood *The Last of the Mohicans* has been throughout the world the most widely read of all American novels." Its influence has been extended through adaptations and revisions in other media as well.

Age and ethnic trajectory

Most interpreters, including the most critical, probably agree that Cooper's novel is not racist in a crude and obvious way. However, some hold Cooper responsible for perpetuating some less obvious but still harmful forms of racial ideology. One recent political criticism of Cooper's novel focuses on its attitude toward the supposed disappearance of the Mohicans. Richard Hutson (2005) explains that "Cooper's novel supported an important sentiment in the United States, referred to by the anthropologist Renato Rosaldo as 'imperialist nostalgia.'" In this view, the nostalgic imperialists mourn the loss of Native American peoples and cultures, thus, in Rosaldo's words, "the very forms of life they intentionally altered or destroyed" (qtd. in Hutson 2005). Hutson explains that this allows them to "accept the vanishing" of Native America "in a spirit of innocence." This is, according to Rosaldo, a "peculiar kind of nostalgia … where people mourn the passing of what they themselves have transformed." Hutson goes on to say that in Cooper's novel "vanishing is the Indians' destiny."

This is certainly a problem, though the nature of the problem is not entirely clear. For example, I have Kashmiri Hindu friends who firmly believe that the fate of Kashmiri Hindu culture is that it will be lost forever as the dominant Muslim culture of the valley becomes pervasive. This is certainly pessimistic on their part. But it is not evidence that they are outgrouping Hindus—quite the contrary, in fact. Moreover, it is not even clear from this particular novel that Cooper anticipates the disappearance of Native Americans generally—only the group that he esteems, the Mohicans.

In fact, however, I believe there is something to this objection. In crudely material terms, the idea of Amerindian disappearance serves to legitimate the European American appropriation of frontier land—a hugely important aspect of American life and self-understanding at the time. As Grumer (1970: 137) explains, colonial settlers went west to establish themselves as farmers on inexpensive but fertile land. This required "removal of the Indian tribes." That removal was partially concealed and partially rendered inevitable by the dissemination of the idea that at least some—and perhaps all—Native American cultures and peoples were moribund.

In addition, at a conceptual level, the impending disappearance of an outgroup may be bound up with an age-based model for the group. The "death" of a group is commonly modeled on the death of an individual. As such, it is often connected with an imagination of the group as in some degree fallen into the decline of old age (relative to the robust, young adulthood of the ingroup). Take the converse case. I have considered elsewhere—and will discuss again in Chapter 5—how Harriet Beecher Stowe uses different childhood models to think about African Americans.[3] This is certainly problematic. But it prepares the way for Stowe's (2003: 129) contention that the future of the world—that is, the spiritual future, the only future that is important for Stowe—lies in the hands of Africans; they "will exhibit the highest form of ... *Christian life*." As a race still in their childhood, they have the greatest future ahead of them. What lies ahead for Europeans is only the degeneration of physical and mental capacities in senescence.

Ashis Nandy (1983) argues that, while Europeans commonly assimilated Africans to children, they at least sometimes drew on models of old age for Asians. Though Nandy was focusing on South Asian Indians, the same point would apply to East Asians in at least some cases. In connection with this point, it is worth noting that, in his "Introduction" to *The Last of the Mohicans*, Cooper (2014: 1) connects Native American speech and poetry with "Oriental" tendencies. Moreover, he characterizes their language as like "the Chinese" and "different from ... the African." The point is limited, but it is consistent with one tendency in European ideology—the modeling of Native Americans, like some Asians, on both the "wise elder" and the "senile aged."

In any case, it is clear that Cooper does, at points, assimilate Native Americans to the old. The point is particularly clear in the case of the Delaware sage, Tamenund. When the European American heroes face him, Cora appeals to his "wisdom," addressing him as "Just and venerable Delaware" (2014: 344). She pleads for mercy. But Tamenund, the repository of Delaware wisdom, has declined into senility and can barely converse coherently, lost as he is in fragmentary reminiscences, which may not even be real memories. Cora tries to recall important events and conditions, but his mind wanders. The "patriarch," lost in his "vast age," replies vaguely: "I remember that when a laughing boy ... I stood upon the sands of the seashore, and saw a big canoe with wings whiter than the swan's, and wider than many eagles, come from the rising sun." Cora tries to coax his recollection: "Nay, nay; I speak not of a time so very distant, but of favor shown to thy kindred by one of mine, within the memory of thy youngest warrior." It is no use. She cannot make him remember. "I speak of a thing of yesterday. Surely, surely, you forget it not," she insists, desperately. All the bewildered old man can reply is: "It was but yesterday ... that the children of the Lenape were masters of the world" (345). The sage of the Delawares has gone far into his dotage. Cora can do nothing to draw him out of the fog of confusion and forgetfulness.

Of course, Cooper does not say that there are no young Native Americans or that Native Americans are, generally, suffering from dementia. But he does characterize the repository of their wisdom as lost in the mist of age. The suggestion would appear to be that the people are, in some sense, old as a race and a culture. That aged condition would seem to point toward the immanence of death as well. It does not seem accidental that the novel ends with the image of death. Nor does it seem accidental that this death is announced by Tamenund and is associated with traditional Native American wisdom. Specifically, in the final words of the novel Tamenund laments that he has seen "the last warrior of the wise race of the Mohicans" (397). And, yet, even this is complicated and ambiguous, for Tamenund has also said that "the time of the Red Men has not yet come again" (397), a phrase that suggests a cycle of social dominance that returns after the apparently final phase of old age and death.

Nonstandard stereotyping

But, again, there are other ways in which Cooper's use of standard models is complicated and serves to challenge dominant ideology and even aspects of the encompassing problematic surrounding relations between Europeans and Native Americans. One important part of this is his refusal to characterize Native Americans as a single, uniform race. Cooper's ethnic generalizations are more fine-grained. As any reader of the novel is aware, the depiction comes roughly to an identification of Hurons as bad, Mohicans as good, and Delawares as potentially good but confused. (Indeed, the aging and decline that characterize Native Americans in the novel may be confined to the good Native Americans. It is the Delawares who are associated with senility and the Mohicans who die out.) Of course, any such ethnic generalization is wrong and racist. The point is that Cooper's treatment of Native American ethnicities does not support the broad denigration of Native Americans found among many European Americans. MacDougall (2014) points out that, at the time the novel was published, "most Americans still probably held the view, later attributed to General Philip Sheridan, that 'the only good Indian is a dead Indian.'" This is not a view in any way suggested by the novel.

In some cases, the characterizations of the Native American ethnicities are literal. Thus, Hawkeye insists that Hurons "are a thievish race ... you can never make anything of them but skulks and vagabonds" (2014: 36; I take it that the racism of such a statement is too obvious to require elaboration). He contrasts these supposed traits of the Hurons with the "honesty" of Delawares and Mohicans (36). On the other hand, most characterizations of these groups draw on the models outlined above. The Hurons and associated outgroup ethnicities—broadly speaking, those that are enemies of the British-American ingroup—are particularly imagined in terms of the most demeaning and antagonistic models, those of animals and demons. Thus, we find them assimilated to "beasts of prey" (44) in their threat to our heroes and their ingroup. They are "dogs" (275) and more than once "reptiles" (145, 218, 227), thus, in the anthropocentric hierarchy of animals, less than dogs. One is a "cunning varmint" (79); others are "wily sarpents" (83). The supposedly deceitful character of some vermin, and the cleverness of serpents in particular, is a function of the link between these categories and Satan, who in the biblical story of the fall of humankind appeared in the form of a serpent. Indeed, the Native Americans with whom our heroes find themselves most at odds are repeatedly characterized as "sarpents" (45, 78, 83, 221).[4]

The association of enemy Native Americans with the demonic model is not confined to the implications of their serpent-like wiliness. Of course, their putative capacity to deceive is important. They are "cunning ... devils" (2014: 45). But their demonic quality is not confined to deceit. It is closely related to demonic rebellion against God, who is rightly worshiped by Christians. Thus, a Huron cry of success sounds "as if fifty demons were uttering their blasphemies at the fall of some Christian soul" (82), and the exulting Hurons are "children of the devil" (82). Some Native Americans (though also some associated Europeans) engage in "deviltries" (50). One enemy Native American is a "red devil" (44, perhaps leaving space for Africans to be characterized as black devils) and so on through many repetitions of the characterization. (The words "devil" and "demon" appear frequently in the novel, usually in connection with Hurons or related groups.) It is important to note that this characterization was widespread. Writing in the mid-nineteenth century, Henry Schoolcraft explained that Amerindians were commonly viewed as "the very impersonation of evil—a sort of ... demon" (qtd. in Grumer 1970: 154).

Stereotype explanation

In confining both the animal and demonic models to a subset of Native Americans, Cooper does deviate somewhat from the dominant ideology and problematic of European American society at the time. However, the deviation is very limited. It fosters a sense that some Native Americans merit our trust and therefore a parallel interpersonal stance. However, the repeated characterization of many Native Americans as vermin or devils seems, in itself, most likely to strengthen antagonistic attitudes toward Native Americans generally. In this way, both main forms of outgroup modeling in the novel—drawing on the age and animacy domains—seem likely to entail significant harms, with only very limited benefits relative to ideological norms at the time. Stereotype explanation in the novel may be somewhat more progressive.

Specifically, Cooper presents us with a single, elaborated case of a malevolent and deceitful Native American—Magua. Magua embodies almost everything European Americans feared and fantasized about their Amerindian antagonists. He was brave and skillful, but treacherous, deceitful, and savage—obsessed not merely with acquisition, but committed to making other people, white people, suffer. Indeed, this is what makes him Satanic. His behavior is not a matter of rational gain (e.g., acquiring wealth). It is, rather, a purely malevolent cruelty. The key point for our purposes is that Cooper seeks to explain this malevolence. Despite his use of a demonic model, the explanation is not that this is the way Native Americans are. Such behavior is not driven by biology or culture. It is not intrinsic. It is, rather, the product of history, in this case a history in which European Americans are at least partially to blame.

Before going on to the details of this explanation, however, it is important to note two ways in which Magua does not fit the usual stereotype. First, he does not sexually assault Cora. MacDougall (2014) points out that an "almost universally held white myth" maintained that "European women captured by Indians would be raped." But Cooper "notes ... that Native Americans virtually never sexually assaulted their captives."[5] Second, Magua certainly has racist prejudices against Europeans and no concern about their well-being. But his cruelty is not generalized. It is aimed at Munro. Harm done to others is, for him, principally a means of achieving revenge against Munro. In this way, his cruelty—and, by extension, the cruelty of other Native Americans—was not something alien to Europeans. It was a case of the cold hatred that drives the villainous heroes of many revenge narratives in the European tradition.

Magua's story has several elements. The first is that he showed a great susceptibility to alcoholism. He "was born a chief and a warrior." But "his Canada fathers came into the woods and taught him to drink the firewater, and he became a rascal" (2014: 112). Prefiguring now-current attitudes, Magua characterizes his response to "firewater" as what we would call an addiction, something over which he had no control. Having no control meant, for him, having no genuinely free choice. And having no genuinely free choice meant not being fairly subjected to punishment. In telling his story, Magua asks rhetorically: "Was it the fault of [Magua] that his head was not made of rock? Who gave him the firewater? Who made him a villain? 'Twas the palefaces" (112). He goes on: "Is it justice to make evil, and then punish for it? Magua was not himself; it was the firewater that spoke and acted for him!" (113).

But it is not the drunkenness alone that drives Magua's vengeful feelings and acts. These result, rather, from further events that are allowed by the addiction to firewater. In each case, the event inspiring Magua's rage is one of shaming. Alcohol puts Magua in a position where he can be shamed. But some people have to make further decisions and engage in further actions to produce that shame. First, Magua is driven from his home and people (112) and his wife is given to another man (114). This is a terrible humiliation, an expression of public disgust with Magua as a person, and not merely the repudiation of particular acts. Moreover, in Magua's eyes it is unfair, as he was suffering the effects of alcoholism and thus not himself. On the other hand, these punishments at least occur "in the family." He experiences the shame before a group for whom he might be able to have basic trust. Moreover, this is not the group that addicted him to alcohol. In this way, their behavior does not appear hypocritical. Finally, this is a group to which he might aspire to return, a group whose respect he might win back. Indeed, he does win back their respect and plans to return (114).

The second case of shame is very different. It involves dehumanization before outsiders, people Magua could never trust, people whose respect he realizes he could never win. To make matters worse, it is the same class of people—Europeans—who infected him with the sickness of alcoholism in the first place. Specifically, Munro has Magua "tied up before all the pale-faced warriors and whipped like a dog" (113).

Why is shame so important here? One common response to shame is "withdrawal" (Scheff 2011: 455), concealing oneself from the disdainful looks of the community. This response is initially facilitated by Magua's exile. In effect, he is forced to hide, to escape observation. The other common response to shame is rage, often including violent revenge (see Alderdice 2007; Ray et al. 2004; and Scheff and Retzinger 1991). That is why humiliation appears to be one source for terrorist violence (see Stern 2003: 32–62). In contrast with exile, public whipping is a form of shaming that renders self-concealment impossible. The act literally (as well as figuratively) bares one before the community, making it impossible to escape their derision. Again, in this case, the initial act of seduction into addiction and the culminating act of dehumanizing ("like a dog") humiliation are associated with the same group. It is, then, unsurprising that Magua would end up with a broadly racist hatred of whites and a specific focus on Munro as the target for revenge.

I believe Cooper does a good job of explaining one sort of trajectory that could lead a Native American to feel and act on their violent, racist rage. And this is valuable in shifting accounts of outgroup violence from racial or cultural denigration to circumstantial explanations. Magua is demonic not because he is a Huron but because he is human and the experiences of shame (along with the associated hardships of exile, the loss of his family, and so on) have driven him to this condition.[6] However, there is equivocation on Cooper's part. Most important, there is little if anything to blame on Europeans. They did introduce Magua to alcohol. But, first, it was not the same Europeans, or even the same national group of Europeans. Second, they were merely following the same principles that they follow with other Europeans, sharing a form of sociality common in Europe. Third, Munro would presumably have found any Englishman guilty in similar circumstances (though the punishment might have been less). Thus no real blame accrues to the Europeans in the novel. In contrast, Magua—representing Native Americans in general and Hurons in particular—might be faulted by some readers for his initial alcoholism and will certainly be faulted by most readers for his vengeful impulse and his willingness to harm innocents (such as Cora) in pursuit of his revenge.

Critique

But, again, the remodeling and subsequent explanation of stereotypes do not set the limits on Cooper's response to the dominant racial ideology of European Americans regarding Native Americans. Perhaps most significantly, there are points at which Cooper clearly and forcefully rejects that dominant ideology and even the encompassing problematic, articulating the faults in standard ways of thinking about relations between Europeans and non-Europeans and suggesting nonracist alternatives.

Before moving on to this, however, I should note one more implicit way in which *The Last of the Mohicans* challenges standard modes of European American thought about the new nation. The land is full of Native Americans, and the history of the nation is inseparable from their presence, activities, and traditions. As Hutson (2014) puts it, "Cooper is in many ways unique in emphasizing the presence of Native

Americans as a critical factor in the creation of the new nation." This is an important aspect of the novel and contributes to the national sense that part of what is definitive about American identity—part of what distinguishes it from European and specifically English identity—is its integration of European and Native American.

The point is related to the novel's explicit opposition to racism. This is evident from the epigraph "Mislike me not for my complexion,/The shadowed livery of the burnished sun," which directly opposes color prejudice. More exactly, rejecting the demonic model in his "Preface," Cooper (1870: v) praises the ethical thought and action of some Native American groups along with their "moral interest, which was so faithfully and so wonderfully transmitted through their traditions." In keeping with this idea, he points out that good people are found, even if rarely, on both sides of the divide between Europeans and Native Americans. "As bright examples of great qualities are but too uncommon among Christians," he explains, "so are they singular and solitary with the Indians." He then maintains that, due to "the honor of our common nature"—thus our shared, human capacity for moral behavior—"neither" group is "incapable of producing" such moral exemplars (2014: 54–55).

Indeed, in the relations between Native Americans and Europeans, Cooper indicates that the moral balance strongly favors the Native Americans. Thus, he straightforwardly states in the Preface that the Mohicans were "dispossessed by the whites" (1870: v). In keeping with this, early in the novel, he condemns "the cold and selfish policy of the distant monarchs of Europe" (2014: 5). Later, Hawkeye—apparently echoing Cooper's own views—asserts that "it is not to be denied that the evil has been mainly done by men with white skins" (255). Despite this, dominant ideology has stressed and even significantly overstated the crimes of Native Americans, thereby promoting panic and the violence of Europeans against Native Americans. Specifically, there was no "ear in the provinces so deaf as not to have drunk in with avidity the narrative of some fearful tale of midnight murder, in which the natives of the forests were the principal and barbarous actors … the magnifying influence of fear began to set at naught the calculations of reason" (8). One example of this is the idea that Indians raped white women. As already noted, Cooper indicates "that Native Americans virtually never sexually assaulted their captives" (MacDougall 2014).

Finally, it is crucial that Cooper viewed the fundamental equality of peoples as extending to the domain of spirituality. It was a common view at the time that non-Christian peoples, who did not share the Bible and did not worship Jesus, were therefore devotees of Satan, the origin of false gods. Indeed, as already noted, Cooper seems to slip into this view now and again. At many places, however, Cooper adopts the liberal view, which we are likely to see as commonplace today but which was not at all commonplace at the time. Specifically, he has Munro refer to God as "the Being we all worship, under different names," thereby giving Native American religions the same status as Christianity. In keeping with this equivalency, he refers to a future time when all "may assemble around [God's] throne without distinction of sex, or rank, or color" (2014: 394). Hawkeye in a sense goes further in supporting racial egalitarianism. He asserts that "there is but a single ruler of us all, whatever may be the color of the skin" (300). The phrasing, though primarily referring to the skin color of the human devotees, also allows that God may as readily be a "redskin" as a "paleface." In these ways, Cooper explicitly repudiates both moral and spiritual racism (as well as sexism and classism in Munro's comment on "sex" and "rank").

Changing readers' emotions

Alterations in the way European Americans think about Native Americans, including ideological critique focused on cognition, are obviously consequential for social and political action. But they are arguably less significant than altering emotional attitudes—for example, whether European Americans feel fear of or compassion for dispossessed Native Americans. The most fundamental and pervasive element in our attitudes is interpersonal stance, the basic orientation of our response to another person's actions or emotions—thus, whether we are inclined to feel empathy for his or her suffering or rather tend toward *Schadenfreude*. Emotional work bearing on attitudes and interpersonal stance is arguably something that literature does especially well.

The principle way that Cooper fosters a change in interpersonal stance is through his depiction and development of interracial attachment bonding. Again, this is a key means of fostering a reader's benevolent attitude—or, equivalently, parallel interpersonal stance—toward at least some members of the racial outgroup. It is valuable to note here that Cooper may have recognized this strategy self-consciously. In other words, he may not have simply developed it unselfconsciously as part of an intuitive sense of what felt right in composing his novel. I say this because he has the sage Tamenund stress European opposition to miscegenation as an exemplary instance of the immoral attitudes otherwise represented by their greed and sinful pride. Thus, he states that "the palefaces ... claim not only to have the earth, but that the meanest of their color is better than the Sachems of the Red Man." This may seem to be the height of his condemnation. But he goes on to articulate what may be seen as an even more extreme instance of their overweening self-regard: They would never "take a woman to their wigwams whose blood was not of the color of snow" (2014: 346). I take it that the obvious impossibility of blood being the color of snow was intended by Cooper to reinforce the absurdity of white race prejudice, particularly with respect to attachment bonding.

In connection with this, it is worth remarking on one peculiar feature of Cooper's novel before moving on. As many critics have noted, Cooper has Hawkeye repeatedly insist on his pure whiteness, the absence of any Native American ancestry. Similarly, he stresses the aristocratic purity of Chingachgook's ancestry. This has led a number of writers to conclude that "there is a strong suggestion that purity of blood represents for Cooper a superior form of humanity" (in Hutson's [2014] words). This is not entirely clear. One obvious motivation for emphasizing Hawkeye's whiteness is to free him from a racial connection that might be taken to bias his judgment. His sympathies with the Mohicans are more authoritative, given that he has no ancestral self-interest in praising them. As to Chingachgook, an obvious purpose of claiming a pure, aristocratic lineage for a Native American is to foster the sort of admiration that often affects people's attitudes toward royalty, even in a democratic country such as the United States. Giving the Mohicans an aristocracy serves to make them more like Europeans, and might elevate the entire group for some European American readers.

More significantly, Cooper may celebrate purity of blood. But, in doing so, he may have a conception of purity of blood that is far different from that held by most of his characters and readers. We find a suggestion of this when Cora is praised as "of a blood purer and richer than the rest of her nation" (2014: 390). Cora was mulatto—mostly European, but with African ancestry, unashamedly admitted by her father. This case suggests that purity of blood is not a matter of racial background. But what is it, then? One possibility is that it is a function of a romantic bond that overcomes social taboos and affirms a free personal union.

To understand this point, we need to consider a scene between Munro and Duncan. Duncan has just asked for the hand of Munro's daughter. Given the social conventions of the time, Munro assumes that he is referring to the older daughter. But Duncan is referring instead to Alice, the daughter of Munro's second, entirely European wife. Munro refers to Cora's mother as "descended … from that unfortunate class, who are so basely enslaved to administer to the wants of a luxurious people" (2014: 177). The phrasing is, I think, brilliant. It does not even identify Africans as a race. It simple identifies slaves as a group of people who, through misfortune—thus, presumably, through no fault or deficiency of their own—have been enslaved due to the hedonism of their exploiters. It is as unequivocal and unqualified a condemnation of slavery as we could imagine even today.[7] It does not equivocate about the absoluteness of the evil, and suggests an entire lack of race prejudice on Munro's part. It seems reasonable to suggest that this purity of love, with no taint of racism (or, worse still, slaveholding), is what makes Cora's blood "purer" than that of others.

It is worth following out the remainder of this scene. Munro accuses Duncan of asking for Alice's hand due to racial prejudice: "'You scorn to mingle the blood of the Heywards with one so degraded—lovely and virtuous though she be?' fiercely demanded the jealous parent" (2014: 178). This presents us with an exemplary case of interracial parent–child bonding that is made all the more powerful by the fact that Munro's speech suggests that he does not even see it as interracial. Readers at the time could hardly have been unaware that slave-owners often had mixed-race offspring due to raping their female slaves, and that they rarely felt an appropriate attachment bond with those children, whom they regularly treated as mere property. Duncan's response is also powerful, and deeply relevant even today: "'Heaven protect me from a prejudice so unworthy of my reason!' returned Duncan, at the same time conscious of such a feeling, and that as deeply rooted as if it had been ingrafted in his nature" (178). Duncan, like a white liberal today, publicly acknowledges that race prejudice is wrong. Indeed, he vehemently protests against it, indicating that the mere suggestion of prejudice on his part is a terrible insult. But this is all in bad faith. He recoils from the idea of union with a mixed-race woman, even one who is predominantly European. Though the purity of Cora illustrates that such unions are pure, Duncan feels aversion as if they were unnatural. I take it that this is not a criticism of Duncan as an individual, but of the numerous white liberals who pretend to oppose racism while harboring racist attitudes.[8]

But the relation between Munro and his first wife is far from the only or main instance of interracial bonding in the novel. Two are particularly important, as critics have stressed (taking up different theoretical frameworks for discussion of the issue). One is a matter of friendship; the other, romantic love. Both oppose the strong antipathy that most European Americans appear to have felt toward Native Americans at the time.

There are several examples of interracial friendship in the novel. For example, despite the undercurrent of racism in Duncan, he forms a bond with Uncas, explaining that the latter "saved my life … and he has made a friend who never will require to be reminded of the debt he owes." What follows is telling. It is Uncas who approaches Duncan then: "Uncas partly raised his body, and offered his hand to the grasp of Heyward." Cooper continues: "During this act of friendship, the two young men exchanged looks of intelligence which caused Duncan to forget the character and condition of his wild associate" (2014: 78). The language is equivocal. Perhaps Duncan forgets the actual wildness of Uncas, or perhaps what he forgets is his own prejudicial idea that Uncas has such a distinctively wild character and condition.

Of course, as critics such as Fiedler have stressed, the novel's exemplary friendship is that of Hawkeye and Chingachgook. The nature of that friendship becomes fully clear at the end of the book, when Hawkeye weeps with Chingachgook over the death of the latter's son. In despair over Uncas's death, Chingachgook says: "'I am alone—'" But Hawkeye "gaz[es] with a yearning look at … his friend" and "crie[s]": "No, no … . No, Sagamore, not alone" (397). Hawkeye goes on to, in effect, reject his own categorial identity and to assert that he is fundamentally linked not with an ethnic group but with Chingachgook and with Uncas. Moreover, this link is divinely sanctioned. "I have no kin," Hawkeye explains, "and I may also say, like you, no people. He was your son, and a redskin by nature; and it may be that your blood was nearer—but if ever I forget the lad who has so often fought at my side in war, and slept at my side in peace, may He who made us all, whatever may be our color or our gifts, forget me! The boy has left us for a time; but, Sagamore, you are not alone" (397). The vision of Hawkeye and Chingachgook weeping together in grief over the death of Uncas is, for me, one of the most moving expressions of friendship that I know of. Its power is greatly increased when we recall the racial attitudes that probably characterized Cooper's readership at the time the novel was published.

The same points hold still more intensely for romantic love, the intimate union of different races. The exquisite, though understated, case of this is the relationship between Cora and Uncas. From the moment she is introduced, Cora—"the first African American heroine in American literature" (MacDougall 2014)—serves to challenge racist ideology. Directly opposing the view that African appearance is ugly, this mulatta woman has "a countenance that was exquisitely regular and dignified, and surpassingly beautiful" (Cooper 2014: 14–15). The characterization of Cora as "dignified" also runs against the view that Africans lack refinement. Cora challenges racism not only by what she is, but also by what she does and says.

For example, early in the novel she criticizes racial and cultural prejudices, asking "coldly"—thus, with reason rather than animus—"Should we distrust the man because his manners are not our manners, and that his skin is dark!" (17).[9]

Her putative racial difference from Uncas has no effect on her response to him. She is drawn to him, romantically and sexually, asking: "Who that looks at this creature of nature, remembers the shade of his skin!" (55). It is presumably because of Cora—at least in part—that Uncas departs from the social conventions of his society and "acted as attendant to the females, performing all the little offices within his power, with a mixture of dignity and anxious grace" (57–58). This is not to say that Uncas foregoes a more traditional, masculine role as protector. When the enemy is approaching, leading Hawkeye and Chingachgook to escape, Uncas insists that he will stay with the women, though he will not be able to defeat the attackers and is likely to end up dead. Cora insists that he leave, explaining that he would "be the most confidential of my messengers" to her father (86). It seems clear that both Uncas's initial (if foolhardy) commitment to stay and Cora's sense of confidential intimacy with him betray a deep, if unstated, attachment bond.

That bond only becomes explicit when, following the lament for Uncas, the Delaware women eulogize Cora, who has also died. She is identified as "the stranger maiden, who had left the upper earth at a time so near [Uncas's] own departure as to render the will of the Great Spirit too manifest to be disregarded" (Cooper 2014: 389). In short, they interpret the nature and proximity of these deaths as evidence of divine sanction for the love of these two. For both Christians and Delawares, there is presumably no higher authority than God, and the point is that their putative racial difference is in no way germane to the validity of their union. The women go on to envision Uncas and Cora united in the afterlife. They "admonished him to be kind to her" (389), as the reader already knows he will.[10]

I take it that the union of Uncas and Cora is not only permissible in the world of the novel, it is ideal; it is a union created directly by God, not by ordinary mortals. Its ideal quality is bound up with the fact that it integrates European, African, and Native American ancestries. It is an exemplar for the reader's own attachment bonds and, what is more important, for his or her attitude toward people of other races that constitute America.[11]

Conclusion

Cooper is complicated and to some degree ambivalent like all the writers we will be considering. However, the idea that his novel is racist appears to get things exactly backwards. He does draw on age grade models to treat some Native Americans, and he draws on stereotypes in characterizing particular Amerindian groups. However, he is consistent in opposing the dehumanization of Native Americans. He *dehomogenizes* them, both as a group and individually, and he sets out to explain some of the stereotypes he does represent. More significantly, he portrays deep attachment bonds between Europeans and Amerindians, bonds by which he endeavors to foster a parallel interpersonal stance on the part of his readers, rather than the antagonistic stance that was common at the time. As part of this, he indicates that the spirituality of the Amerindians and their ethical principles are not inferior to those of the (ingroup) Europeans and are indeed superior in some instances. It is not even entirely fair to criticize Cooper for writing off Native Americans as a vanished race, as he was one of the few European American writers to emphasize their presence and their importance for the development of American identity.

Notes

1 Here, I take up a term from Louis Althusser and others (see Althusser 2005: 32 and 1971: 47–48 and 51), though I alter the precise meaning in keeping with broader, theoretical differences (roughly, those between structuralism and cognitive science).
2 For a detailed and necessarily more complex overview of Cooper's reception (until roughly the mid-twentieth century), see Dekker and McWilliams (1973).
3 See chapter three of Hogan 2013.
4 There is, however, a complication here in that Chingachgook's name means "big serpent" because "he understands the windings and turnings of human nature, and is silent, and strikes his enemies when they least expect him" (2014: 59). The implication in this case appears to be that a degree of wiliness toward the right ends is necessary in the struggle against evil.
5 This is in keeping with Mary Rowlandson's (1791: 50) comment that, during the time she was held captive by Amerindians, "not one of them ever offered me the least abuse of unchastity to me, in word or action." Some critics have in effect suggested that Cooper presents sexual assault indirectly. For example, Shirley Samuels (1992: 103) sees the Amerindians "drinking blood" as a case of "violent miscegenation." On the other hand, Samuels (1992: 104) does acknowledge that this is "nonsexual miscegenation." In any case, the claim does not appear particularly plausible, given that drinking blood hardly involves anything particularly reminiscent of sexual activity.
6 This argument clearly goes against Jane Tompkins's (1995: 104) view that the opposed judgments by Magua and Munro or Cora are the result of "fundamental and irreconcilable dissimilarities of outlook which are culturally based." My contention here is that the principles are fundamentally the same, with the same egocentric and ingroup biases, along with associated inhibitions on empathy; those biases and inhibitions yield the opposed conclusions. In other words, there is no profound cultural difference here. Indeed, I would say that the sensitive, empathetic interpretation that Tompkins gives of the novel generally suggests this very commonality.
7 This is not to say that Cooper himself was so unequivocal in condemning racism in general or slavery in particular (see Person 2007: 16 for some problematic statements by Cooper on these topics). But this is simply another case of the fact that we are not entirely consistent in our beliefs and attitudes, but alter in different contexts (see Hogan 2013: 113–149 for discussion and empirical evidence for this point). There is also the issue of what counts as racist in a given historical context. Barbara Mann (2007: 157) argues convincingly that Cooper was viewed as a "race traitor" by many of his white contemporaries. As she puts it, "critics attacked Cooper specifically because he challenged the hegemony of racism by depicting people of color in sympathetic ways that upended the racist dogma of the day." Conversely, when critics today "condemn Cooper as ... racist," they "betray their ignorance of what true racists acted and sounded like" at the time (2007: 155).
8 Incomprehensibly to me, some critics take this scene to suggest that, for Cooper, revulsion at other races is natural (see Levine 2016: 142, though see also 141, where

Levine affirms that the "critique" of slavery in this exchange is "bold and prescient"). But the very fact that Munro does not feel such revulsion indicates that it is not natural, as does the phrasing with respect to Duncan—"as if it had been ingrafted in his nature." Cooper thus says that Duncan's feelings were *not* natural and that they were not even *grafted onto* his nature; rather, the (culpable) intensity of Duncan's feelings—despite his rational judgment—was as great *as if* this had been the case. Harry Brown (2008: 141) apparently seeks to bolster the case by citing an early critic of the novel who says that many readers will object to a mulatta heroine. But that is precisely what points toward the *antiracist* function of Cooper's portrait. If Cooper felt the same way, he would not have created Cora.

9 This is an instance of a woman "serv[ing] as the troubling voice of moral conscience," a recurring motif in Cooper (McWilliams 2007: 80). In our terms, Cora exposes and debunks the bias against trusting members of an outgroup (on this bias, see Brewer 2017: 91 and citations therein). Diana Nelson (2007: 130, emphasis in the original) contests this view, claiming that Cora is "flatly *wrong*" in this particular case. Indeed, Nelson points out that her mistake ultimately leads to her death. But she is not wrong at all in refusing to distrust someone for his or her ethnicity. The fact that Magua turns out to have been untrustworthy in no way shows that there was any justification for distrusting him initially.

10 In his magisterial biography of Cooper, Wayne Franklin (2007: 481) summarizes—and criticizes—the common critical view that the deaths of Cora and Uncas represent "a wish that black and red peoples might equally exit the American scene and leave the field to white actors." I am pretty much just baffled by such a reading of the novel. What kind of heartless, racist goon would someone have to be to get to the end of the novel and think not "How tragic that these admirable and appealing characters had to die!," but rather "Well, I'm glad they are out of the way; at least two of the [derogatory epithet for nonwhite people] are dead and there is more room for the Master Race!" To understand the novel this way, we would have to construe the deaths of Cora and Uncas as comic, rather than tragic. A far more nuanced reading may be found in Nina Baym's (1992) treatment of the novel. Baym forcefully criticizes the views of D. H. Lawrence and Leslie Fiedler, showing the esteem in which Cooper holds Cora and the elevation of the Cora–Uncas relationship. However, I believe she too errs, basically in rejecting her own emotional response to their deaths. Baym appears to me to share my feeling that these deaths are deeply tragic (though perhaps redeemed in the novel's world by the promise of an afterlife). But she treats the ending as if it were a practical lesson in how women should behave. Yes, tragedies may have this sort of lesson: "Behave this way and you will come to a bad end!" But, at least as often, their tragic quality comes from a very different sort of lesson: "If society does not change, this is the sort of thing that will happen!" The spiritual celebration of Cora and Uncas's love seems to indicate clearly that their story in Cooper's novel is of the second sort.

11 Wayne Franklin (2007: 482) points out that Amerindians were often opposed to miscegenation and frequently rejected bonds with Africans. This is unsurprising once we recognize that these are all cases of ingroup versus outgroup divisions based on identity categories. It also suggests that the union envisioned by Cooper is important not only in bringing Europeans together with Native Americans and Africans, but in bringing the two non-European groups together as well.

3

HOPE LESLIE

Critique, defiance, and ambivalence

A year after James Fenimore Cooper's *The Last of the Mohicans* appeared, Catharine Maria Sedgwick published *Hope Leslie: or, Early Times in the Massachusetts*. As critics have noted, Sedgwick draws on and in some ways responds to her precursor.[1] For example, in naming her complex Native American heroine "Magawisca," she appears to echo Cooper's villain, Magua. More important for our concerns is the shared attention to criticizing what we would refer to as the "dominant ideology" of subnational racial division, though Sedgwick appears to have been more self-consciously committed to this purpose. Like Cooper (Chapter 2), she is treating the past, but her concern is arguably the present. Thus, early in the novel her narrator asks the question: "How far is the present age in advance of" the past? (2012: 9). This in some degree orients the reader toward considering historical errors of thought and feeling as, so to speak, signposts for current errors of thought and feeling.

In connection with this project, Sedgwick takes up many of the same techniques as Cooper. Thus, we find explicit critique, explanation of stereotypes, attachment bonding across identity categories, and remodeling of outgroups. On the other hand, these often operate differently in Sedgwick than in Cooper. For example, her remodeling does not, in general, involve a shift in the dominant problematic, but a repudiation of the model. A reader does not leave Sedgwick's novel with the impression that, rather than all Native Americans being devils or beasts, the Hurons have something devilish about them while the Delawares are declining into cultural senility. (Of course, this is not Cooper's last word on race; *The Last of the Mohicans* is more ambivalent and complex, as we have seen.) Rather, Sedgwick indicates that the linking of Native Americans with Satan is ludicrous. Perhaps, in Sedgwick's case, then, we might better refer to this as *demodeling* (rather than *remodeling*). In addition, Sedgwick makes more use of irony than Cooper, seeking to distance the reader from racist attitudes.

Sedgwick also adopts somewhat different descriptive and moral perspectives than Cooper, and she does this in a way that is likely to please many readers today. As to her descriptive perspective, she sometimes shifts between focalizing European Americans and focalizing Native Americans. In doing so, she does not, for example, reveal some apparently distinctive duplicity on the part of the latter. Rather, she conveys a parallel between these two identity groups, a parallel that is morally consequential. Part of this parallel is particularly interesting. It shows that Native Americans are not simply pathetic victims of European American power. From the start of the novel, Sedgwick stresses Native American self-affirmation and resistance against European domination.

Sedgwick may also be clearer about the motivational forces driving intergroup antagonism. Anger is obviously essential, and it is central to the revenge plot (as we saw in the case of Magua). Anger provokes antipathy in our interpersonal stance, generating a desire to hurt the target (the other person or group). It often underlies *Schadenfreude*. As Martha Nussbaum (2016: 5) argues compellingly, "anger is always normatively problematic, whether in the personal or public sphere."

Three other emotions are important in the novel as well. Fear too undermines our adoption of a parallel interpersonal stance. It leads us to treat the other person or group as a threat, at least insofar as he or she is acting toward us. Fear leads us to interpret neutral behavior—or even some friendly behavior—as hostile, suggesting danger. It leads us to block empathy and respond self-protectively, either through flight or aggression, often combined with anger in the latter case. Fear is particularly important, as it tends to be more enduring than anger, except in the case of rage derived from shame—which, perhaps surprisingly, Sedgwick (unlike Cooper) does not develop.

Finally, among the divisive emotions, Sedgwick stresses disgust, which is often combined with anger and/or fear to produce hate.[2] As, for example, Nussbaum (2010: xiii) discusses at length, disgust involves "a fundamental refusal of another person's full humanity"; in keeping with this, it may underwrite genocide (see Nussbaum 2001: 347–348 on Nazi anti-Semitism and disgust). As Angela Maitner and colleagues (2017: 117) point out, "disgust is ... uniquely related to a desire to forcefully expel or obliterate" a target. In our terms, it is associated with the most harshly antagonistic forms of group division, including the model of the outgroup as vermin or particularly "low" and dangerous animals, as well as demons. (As already noted, the two are sometimes combined, as in the fusion of Satan and the serpent in the Garden of Eden story; this also occurs in the association of vampires—and thus, in some anti-Semitic discourse, Jews—with devils and plague-carrying rats [see Hogan 2013].) In keeping with these points, disgust aimed at Jews was prominent in the Holocaust. While fear alone might foster the segregation or confinement of targeted persons or groups, disgust tends to encourage a desire to extirpate the dangerously contaminating group.

This is not to say, however, that there is no ambiguity or ambivalence in Sedgwick's novel. There is. It too shifts between great sympathy with Native Americans and an apparently almost panicked representation of the threat they have posed to

European Americans. She even includes—as does Cooper (2014: 196)—the standard image of the outgroup monster taking up an innocent and defenseless infant and then dashing his or her brains out (2012: 39). As in *The Last of the Mohicans*, disgust and fear are overcome most forcefully by love, specifically attachment. Thus, there is intergroup attachment bonding in the novel. However, it is equivocal in the cases of both romantic love and friendship.

Critique

The most straightforward instances of Sedgwick's response to divisive racial ideology are the direct statements explicitly or implicitly opposing the dominant ideology or the dominant problematic, with its functional hierarchization of European Americans and Native Americans. For example, near the start of the book—specifically, with the epigraph to the second chapter—Sedgwick orients the reader toward an egalitarian understanding of Native Americans. The epigraph is a quotation from Roger Williams, the seventeenth-century minister and founder of the Rhode Island colony (for a discussion of Williams's thought and influence, see Barry 2012). It reads: "For the temper of the brain in quick apprehensions and acute judgments, to say no more, the most High and Sovereign God hath not made the Indian inferior to the European" (2012: 8). The sentence not only asserts the intellectual equality of the races, but also gives divine sanction to that equality.

A few pages after this epigraph, Sedgwick has William Fletcher explain that "these Indians possess the same faculties that we do. The girl, just arrived ... hath rare gifts of mind—such as few of God's creatures are endowed with. She is just fifteen; she understands and speaks English perfectly well" (2012: 12). Again, divine authority is given to the claim of equality. Moreover, there is secular authority as well; specifically, Sedgwick adds a footnote giving historical testimony of such a case. The issue of language fluency is an important one. Even today, many Americans appear to think that someone is intellectually inferior if his or her command of English is faulty. If it did not often have harmful consequences, it would be amusing, given the extremely feeble grasp most Americans have of foreign languages. In any case, the point is also illustrated from the other side, when Hope Leslie's sister, Faith, is abducted and raised as a Pequod. She learns Pequod fluently and can stammer out only a few fragments of English (see 129). (This illustrates one of Sedgwick's techniques of criticizing bias by reversing the situation of Native Americans and European Americans.)

Another, more general instance of critique may be found in William Fletcher's account of how Native American war captives were treated by the British: "Some, by a Christian use of money, were redeemed; and others, I blush to say it, for 'it is God's gift that every man should enjoy the good of his own labour,' were sent into slavery in the West Indies" (Sedgwick 2012: 12). Here, Sedgwick adopts the common technique of contrasting genuinely Christian action (freeing the captives through charitable giving of funds) and hypocritical, un-Christian behavior (enslaving the captives). Fletcher goes on to indicate that the Native Americans could also act in a manner consistent with Christian principles. Specifically, he explains that "Monoca, the mother of these children, was noted for the singular dignity and modesty of her demeanor. Many notable instances of her kindness to the white traders are recorded" (12). Lest skeptical readers take such behavior as a mere fiction invented by the author to produce an affecting narrative, here, too, Sedgwick inserts a footnote with supporting historical documentation.

Parallelism of European American and Native American

The linguistic competence (or incompetence) of Faith Leslie is one example of Sedgwick's paralleling European American and Native American behaviors. Another striking case concerns what is perhaps the most common image used to exemplify Native American barbarity—scalping. At one point, Digby enters with a Native American. The latter "untied his pouch and drew from it a piece of dried and shrivelled skin, to which hair, matted together with blood, still adhered. There was an expression of fierce triumph on the countenance of the savage as he surveyed the trophy with a grim smile. A murmur of indignation burst from all present" (2012: 15). At first, this appears to be a gratuitous introduction of "savage" behavior. The senior Fletcher demands "in an angry tone": "Why did you bring that wretch here?" (15), perhaps echoing the modern reader's indignation, though for a different reason (i.e., Fletcher would object to the indecorousness of the intrusion, while a reader might worry that Sedgwick is invoking the image for racist purposes). But Digby explains that "I did but obey Mr. Pynchon, sir. The thing is an abomination to the soul and eye of a Christian, but it has to be taken to Boston for the reward." Like Fletcher, the reader at this point is likely to wonder just what the reward might concern. Digby explains: "The reward, sir, that is in reason expected for the scalp of the Pequod chief" (15). Thus, Sedgwick encourages the reader to activate his or her view of Native Americans as savages who scalp their victims (recalling, for example, Mary Rowlandson's [1791: 11] characterization of scalping as the "manner" of Native Americans). But no sooner does the reader think this than he or she is informed that *the British* have contracted for the assassination of enemy leaders and have stipulated scalping as part of the assassination (to provide evidence of the death and to humiliate and dispirit the enemy). This is not at all fanciful on Sedgwick's part. Colonial governments regularly offered rewards for the scalps of Native Americans, including during the Pequot War (see Dunbar-Ortiz 2014: 64–65).

Another striking case of this sort occurs after Mononotto's attack on Bethel and slaughter of the women and children there. Mononotto takes his two children with him. He removes the English clothing of his son, Oneco, and proclaims: "Thus perish … every mark of the captivity of my children" (Sedgwick 2012: 39). So-called "captivity narratives," in which a European American was abducted by Native Americans, perhaps to be freed by British forces, were common before Sedgwick's novel. When Magawisca and Oneco were captured and brought to Bethel, they were abducted in a way parallel to the way European Americans were sometimes taken into Native American communities. However, the (European) residents of Bethel do not think of it this way. At least some view themselves as generously helping the two young people (see 14). By making them servants (who were, at the time, often little better than slaves; see Zinn 2015: 42–47), they see themselves as offering the children the opportunity for religious salvation. Magawisca and Mononotto have a quite different perspective. This is shown, first, by Magawisca's message to her father: "Tell him his children are servants in the house of his enemies" (16) and subsequently by Mononotto's actions and statement about "captivity." Indeed, they both saw it in just the way European Americans saw the abduction of their own families. Moreover, just like Mononotto, European Americans would not hesitate to attack a Native American village, killing those present, in order to rescue their family members.

This criticism of ideological one-sidedness in captivity narratives occurs in two other contexts, expanding the political reach of the novel. As already noted, European Americans tended to see the captivity of Native Americans as a way of creating good Christians, because the Native Americans grow up to be European in their beliefs and habits. But the story of Faith Leslie shows that this is not due to some superiority of European custom overcoming barbarism. It is simply a matter of being enculturated, just as speaking Pequod is a matter of growing up with Pequod speakers, rather than English speakers. Culturally, Faith Leslie is a Pequod, just as a Pequod raised by European Americans would be European in custom. Indeed, the case may be even better with Faith because she is raised apparently without racist prejudice.[3]

Finally, Sedgwick gives us another case of abduction by a European. This is Sir Philip's attempted abduction of Hope. This is a purely predatory abduction based on Sir Philip's lust, thus wholly unlike Mononotto's capture of Faith or Oneco's later capture of Hope as a bargaining chip to negotiate the release of Faith; the Europeans see themselves as having freed Faith, but the Pequods—including Faith herself—see them as having abducted her. Indeed, Sir Philip's kidnapping of Hope recalls European commonplaces about Native Americans raping European captives. Specifically, Sir Philip intends to appeal to Hope, convincing her to accept him. However, if he fails in this, he will subject her to "stern necessity, which even a woman's will could not oppose" (2012: 183).

Animacy modeling

Sedgwick takes up models of demons and, to a lesser extent, animals in treating Native Americans. However, that modeling is almost entirely done by the characters, and it is presented as ironically distant from the views of the author. For example, early in the novel, William Fletcher states that Magawisca "is the daughter of one of their chiefs," brought along after "this wolfish tribe were killed, or dislodged from their dens" (2012: 12). Similarly, Mrs. Fletcher states that the "wild wandering" lives of Native Americans are "little superior to those of the wolves and foxes" (14). At this point, we do not know quite what to make of these claims. Subsequently, we learn about the actual circumstances when the "wolfish tribe" was "dislodged from their dens" (12). The Pequods were attacked in their sleep, their homes set on fire, and they were prevented from fleeing the flames. It was a brutal act of cruelty, with no obvious wolfishness on the part of the Pequods but arguably demonic sadism on the part of the Europeans.

The model of demons is far more prominent. This is unsurprising, as it is partially literalized in the association of Native Americans with Satan worship and with witchcraft. While demons in Cooper are largely ethical and metaphorical, in Sedgwick's novel they are most often religious and literal. We see this in a chapter epigraph drawn from Roger Williams: "Being once in their houses and beholding what their worship was, I never durst be an eye-witness, spectator, or looker-on, lest I should have been a partaker of Satan's inventions and worships" (2012: 57). Sedgwick makes it clear that Williams was not some outlier. For example, she writes that "the notion that the Indians were the children of the devil was not confined to the vulgar; and the belief in a familiar intercourse with evil spirits, now rejected by all but the most ignorant and credulous, was then universally received" (164).

This association of the demonic model with the ignorant and credulous is taken up within the storyworld of the novel as well. For example, Jennet suggests Magawisca and Nelema, another Native American woman, may be witches, referring to theirs as "a race that are the children and heirs of the Evil One" (23; she repeats the charge of witchcraft on 40). But she is established as an unreliable and dislikable character in the course of the novel. Most readers would have little inclination to see themselves as in any way similar to Jennet; this aversion presumably extends to sharing her views on controversial topics.

A more interesting case may be found in Digby. He had been more cautious in his assessment, stating that Native Americans, or "savages," are "a kind of beast we don't comprehend—out of the range of God's creatures—neither angel, man, nor yet quite devil" (25). Clearly, Native Americans are in his view closest to demons, though that characterization does not quite fit literally. This evaluation is immediately disputed by Everell, who responds: "I think you have caught the fear, Digby, without taking its counsel ... , which does little credit to your wisdom; the only use of fear, being to provide against danger" (25). This introduces the important theme of fear blocking empathic understanding. Digby might like to think of himself as courageous. However, he is letting his understanding be determined by anxiety over the looming and unabated threat he feels regarding the Native Americans. What is more important is that Sedgwick criticizes this view by having Digby change his attitude toward Native Americans entirely. Here, Digby fears even Magawisca. But he will eventually come to see Native Americans as mistreated by Europeans, even to the extent that he is willing to violate the law to help to free Nelema and Magawisca.

The demonic model of Amerindians is developed extensively by the sinister Sir Philip. Interestingly, he does not appear to believe the racist ideology himself. Rather, he relies on "popular prejudices" regarding "the diabolical race of the Pequods" (163) in order to further his own purposes. Sedgwick's critique of Sir Philip's claims is in part a matter of this dishonesty, along with the fact that we know the specific claims are false. For example, we know that he is fabricating the claim when he testifies that he "discovered Magawisca kneeling on the bare wet earth, making those monstrous and violent contortions, which all who heard him well knew characterized the devil-worship of the powwows," including "her invocations to the Evil One" (164) and expressed through "diabolical writhings and beatings of her person." Moreover, the reader is likely to find the claims patently ludicrous, even comic, as when he explains the mechanism of communication with Satan. Specifically, "her prayers were sped" on "sulphureous gleams of lightning" (164). It hardly inspires much confidence in the legal system of the colonists when one of the magistrates, having heard these absurdities, concludes that Magawisca "is of Satan's heritage" (165). Indeed, after Sir Philip disappears, the gullible Puritans shift quickly to viewing him as a "crafty son of Belial" (197) and concluding that Satan has received Sir Philip's corpse (201).

Perhaps Sedgwick's most powerful criticism of the demonic model comes with her treatment of witchcraft accusations. Despite the terrors to which Europeans have subjected her family, the old Pequod woman, Nelema, knowledgeable in methods of traditional healing, cures Cradock of snakebite. The European response is less than grateful. The enduringly racist Jennet claims that Nelema is an "old heathen witch" who made Cradock live only "by the devil's help" (2012: 62). More generally, Nelema is an "emissary of Satan" (63). Jennet convinces Mr. Fletcher, who concludes that the "witch" Nelema used "diabolical spells" (64). Nelema is officially charged with witchcraft, and an absurd trial leads to her death sentence. Again, the whole sequence would be laughable, if its consequences were not so serious. For example, driven presumably by fear and with hints of disgust, the perfervid imaginations of the Christian community generate delusions: "Some could smell sulphur from the outer kitchen door to the door of the cell; and there were others who fancied that, at a few yards distance from the house, there were on the ground marks of a slight scorching: a plain indication of a visitation from the enemy of mankind" (67). Hope defies the law and frees Nelema, concealing the fact. In a comic revision of his earlier invocation of the animacy model, stressing his altered attitude and the falsity of the ideology associating Native Americans with the devil, Digby claims that Nelema was freed by an angel (67).

Romantic love and friendship

One emotion that tends to inhibit both disgust and fear is attachment.[4] (At least experientially, it seems to be less inhibitory of anger—hence the phenomenon of "lovers' quarrels.") In connection with this, attachment bonds serve as an apt model for the enhancement of empathy across identity groups, as I have emphasized (see Chapters 1 and 2 on interracial romance). Sedgwick does make some use of attachment bonds, both those of romantic love and those of friendship. The bond that links Faith and Oneca is profound. They "are as if one life-chord bound them together" (108). Moreover, this is just as it should be, for "both virtue and duty … bind [Faith] to Oneco" (191). But this example is perhaps less effective than it might be. Again, Faith is raised as a Pequod. In consequence, she is in effect a Pequod, not a European. It is important that Sedgwick presents cultural identity as malleable. However, given this malleability, the union of Faith and Oneca appears to be principally a bond within rather than across identity categories.

Magawisca seems to have romantic feelings for Everell. But those are not reciprocated, so the question of romantic union does not arise. More significantly, the ending of the novel raises the possibility of there being genuine friendship between Europeans and Native Americans. But, despite their obvious liking for one another, Magawisca rejects the overtures of Everell and Hope. This is at least in part because Sedgwick wishes to represent the defiance and determination of Native Americans. She does not wish to present them as anxiously seeking the favorable opinion of Europeans. (We will return to this point below.) Much as her representation of malleable cultural identity limits the consequences of joining Oneco with Faith, this stress on defiance limits the possibilities for ongoing friendships across racial lines.

Irony regarding characters' ideological blindness

Irony is one of the most frequent techniques used by Sedgwick to criticize racial outgrouping within America. This is perhaps most striking when Sedgwick reveals the (often absurd) prejudices of a character. For example, Magawisca sacrifices her arm to save Everell's life. Winthrop comments bizarrely that "it was a noble action for a heathen savage" (2012: 157). The suggestion seems to be that it would not have been "noble" but commonplace for (putatively) civilized Christians, something perhaps akin to giving up one's seat on the bus (to take an anachronistic example). This irony serves to expose the depth and virulence of the ideological biases held by the European Americans.

It is worthy of particular note that Hope Leslie too has such prejudices, suggesting that unbiased whites are indeed few and far between. For example, when Magawisca says "Hope Leslie, thy sister is married to Oneco," Hope exclaims "God forbid!" and "shudders as if a knife had been plunged in her bosom." Hope continues, expressing "scorn" for Magawisca's "race" (106), as she exclaims: "My sister married to an Indian!" (105). Sometimes a character's error is evident simply from what he or she says. Sometimes, Sedgwick puts the critique in the mouth of an interlocutor. Here, Magawisca rightly senses disgust in Hope's response and asks Hope if she thinks her "blood will be corrupted" by her sister's contact with a Native American (106). Sedgwick subsequently elaborates on this disgust. When Hope sees her sister "in her savage attire, fondly leaning on Oneco's shoulder," she has "a sickening feeling," a "revolting of nature," that prevents her from embracing her sister and instead leads her to withdraw (129) almost as if she is ready to vomit. Despite her place in the novel generally, Hope—along with her attitudes—is heavily ironized in such events and exchanges.

The point applies to spirituality as well. In contemplating her sister's Pequod culture, she invokes her mother's pain and suffering and cries out: "O, God! restore my sister to the Christian family" (106). Magawisca responds compellingly, pointing to her own mother's pain and suffering, and asking Hope: "Think ye not that the Great Spirit looks down on these sacred spots, where the good and the peaceful rest, with an equal eye? Think ye not their children are His children, whether they are gathered in yonder temple where your people worship, or bow to him beneath the green boughs of the forest?" (106). (On the other hand, there are complications in Sedgwick's treatment of Pequod spirituality, a topic to which we will return.)

Explaining stereotypes

As we saw in discussing Cooper's novel, the explanation of stereotypes can be important in criticizing identity divisions and associated ideologies. Sedgwick uses this technique with particular effectiveness. Specifically, she gives the reader a clear sense of what has driven Mononotto to the acts of cruelty he commits. She does this by having Magawisca recount the British massacre of her village. The British came at night when everyone was asleep; they surrounded the village and opened fire. As Everell quickly infers, they "rush[ed] on sleeping women and children" (2012: 29). Despite this recognition, Everell restates what he "heard" previously, that "our people had all the honour of the fight." Magawisca is incredulous. She explains that, as the two sides fought, the air was filled, not only with the blasts of the weapons, but with "the piteous cries of the little children" and "the groans of our mothers." When the English began to lose ground, they set fire to the Pequod huts. She goes on: "In vain did our warriors fight for a path by which we might escape from the consuming fire; they were beaten back," driven into the "fierce" flames. Hundreds died; "our homes had vanished. The bodies of our people were strewn about the smouldering ruin ... the strong and valiant warriors—cold—silent—powerless as the unformed clay" (29–30). Subsequently, the narrator writes about the representation of this event "in the history of the times, where, we are told, 'the number destroyed was about four hundred'; and 'it was a fearful sight to see them thus frying in the fire, and the streams of blood quenching the same, and the horrible scent thereof; but the victory seemed a sweet sacrifice, and they gave the praise thereof to God'" (32–33; Sedgwick is quoting William Bradford [1962: 184]). Subsequently, the British execute her captured brother in cold blood (30; Sedgwick provides a footnote citing references to show that her representation is historically accurate on this point).

As Roxanne Dunbar-Ortiz (2014: 57–58) explains, such "total war" against Amerindians—"war whose purpose is to destroy the will of the enemy people or their capacity to resist, employing any means necessary but mainly by attacking civilians and their support systems, such as food supply"—was standard in the history of European–Native American conflicts. In John Murrin's (1987: 336) words, "settlers ... adopted a ferocious style of waging war," engaging in "wars of subjugation and even annihilation." They were "deliberately terroristic" and "they, not the Indians, began the systematic slaughter of women and children."

It is important to note that the scene in Sedgwick's novel parallels—and presumably in part responds to—the abduction scene in Mary Rowlandson's 1682 *Narrative of the Captivity and Restoration of Mrs. Mary Rowlandson* (also known as *A Narrative of the Captivity, Sufferings, and Removes of Mrs. Mary Rowlandson*). In that influential (and powerfully written) work, European settlers are attacked by Native Americans, who set fire to homes and prevent the helpless victims from escaping. Thus, Rowlandson writes that "now might we hear mothers and children crying out for themselves and one another, 'Lord, what shall we do!' Then I took my children (and one of my sisters', hers) to go forth and leave the house: but as soon as we came to the door, and appeared, the Indians shot so thick, that the bullets rattled against the house" (Rowlandson 1791: 6). The events recounted by Rowlandson postdated those recounted in Sedgwick's novel by about four decades, so the relations between the two groups were not the same. (Unsurprisingly, and in her case more forgivably, Rowlandson engages in the usual forms of antagonistic outgrouping of Amerindians, drawing on the usual domains, including a synthesis of animal and demon models in her reference to them as "hell-hounds" [9]. On the other hand, Rowlandson ends up presenting a portrait of individual Amerindians that is much more sympathetic than one might have expected from a captive.)

Again, the problem with explaining stereotypes is that it risks enhancing the cognitive prominence of the stereotype. Magawisca speaks of how her father "plac[ed] himself at the head of one band of the young men," "shouted his war-cry, and … pursued the enemy" (Sedgwick 2012: 30). This leads to the slaughter at Bethel. Though the number killed in that encounter was miniscule in comparison with the hundreds of Pequods killed by British forces, the dead are individuated in a way that is likely to have emotional consequences for the reader. For most readers, the murder of Everell's infant brother is likely to be far more salient and emotionally consequential than the deaths of the anonymous children indicated by Magawisca's account of the British attack.

Despite this, I believe Sedgwick does a very good job of establishing that Magawisca's father "was a changed man" (30) after the terrible British attack. The stereotype came to fit him only after the massacre of his people and the execution of his son. As she explains, her father "had been the friend of the English; he had counselled peace and alliance with them; he had protected their traders; delivered the captives taken from them, and restored them to their people" (30). The suggestion here is that it is European policies of violence against Native Americans that have given rise to stereotypical Native American violence.

Defiance

It seems that many members of dominant groups—men, European Americans, straight people—assume that members of dominated groups—women, Native Americans or African Americans, gays and lesbians—cherish a fond desire to be accepted by the dominant group and will react with gratitude to anyone who does accept them. But being oppressed, exploited, and denigrated is at least as likely to anger people, to inspire antipathy, even if prudential considerations lead them to conceal these feelings. In keeping with this, many progressive writers—including Sedgwick—do not condemn intergroup anger in the way that they might be inclined to reject disgust or to question fear. (Nussbaum [2016] argues compellingly against such tolerance of anger, but I suspect her arguments—with which I wholly agree—represent very much a minority position on the topic.) Whatever one's assessment of anger, it does seem clear that dominated groups are rarely passive in the face of domination. As, for example, Edward Said (2012) emphasized, they resist. This does not simply mean that they act vengefully, wreaking terror on innocents due to personal grievances. It means that they act as principled advocates for the rights of their group. This is an aspect of Sedgwick's novel that has almost no presence in Cooper's novel.

Sedgwick states the main point explicitly at the opening of the novel: "The Indians of North America are, perhaps, the only race of men of whom it may be said, that though conquered, they were never enslaved. They could not submit, and live" (2012: 3). European Americans tend to misunderstand this because "our histories … represented" resistant Native Americans "as 'surly dogs,' who preferred to die rather than live." However, if Native Americans had "their own historians or poets," these writers would, "with more justice, have extolled their [ancestors'] high-souled courage and patriotism" (3). In some ways, Sedgwick is setting out to provide something of what Native American historians and novelists could have provided and something of what they eventually would provide.

It is also important that the resistance or defiance that Sedgwick celebrates most is not that of the men, but that of such women as Nelema and Magawisca. We find a powerful example of the former when Nelema responds to Mrs. Fletcher's warm enthusiasm for her son, Everell. Nelema explains: "I had sons too—and grandsons; but where are they? They trod the earth as lightly as that boy; but they have fallen like our forest trees, before the stroke of the English axe. Of all my race, there is not one, now, in whose veins my blood runs. Sometimes, when the spirits of the storm are howling about my wigwam, I hear the voices of my children crying for vengeance, and then I could myself deal the death-blow" (22). There is nothing timid or acquiescent about the oppressed in Sedgwick's novel. On the other hand, Sedgwick has the good sense to recognize that this is not necessarily to the good. The people who killed Nelema's family are different from the people who would be killed if she took revenge. Collective punishment is wrong whether practiced by European Americans or Native Americans. Nelema rather understates the point when she acknowledges that "when the stream of vengeance rolls over the land, the tender shoot must be broken, and the goodly tree uprooted, that gave its pleasant shade and fruits to all" (22).

Magawisca's view is more nuanced. When asked to defend herself at a trial by the colonial court, she responds as follows: "I am your prisoner, and ye may slay me, but I deny your right to judge me. My people have never passed under your yoke; not one of my race has ever acknowledged your authority" (164). She rightly denies the legitimacy of the court, which has asserted its jurisdiction not democratically, but by force. The moral complexity of situations faced by many Native Americans in these conditions is expressed well early in the novel. Magawisca is uncertain about whether she should inform the Fletchers of an impending danger. Her "first impulse had been to reveal all to Mrs. Fletcher; but by doing this, she would jeopard her father's life. Her natural sympathies, her strong affections—her pride, were all enlisted on the side of her people; but she shrunk, as if her own life were menaced, from the blow that was about to fall on her friends" (34).

This reference to "friends" returns us to the end of the novel. Magawisca seems then to act as if the members of an identity group are all one person. She rejects the friendship of even Hope and Everell, saying that "the Indian and the white man can no more mingle and become one than day and night" (191). The judgment is particularly striking because it recalls her earlier comment to the colonial court and her reference to Sir Philip: "The sunbeam and the shadow cannot mingle … . Can we grasp in friendship the hand raised to strike us? Nay" (168). But, of course, neither Hope nor Everell is assimilable to Sir Philip, except racially. In this context, Magawisca's rejection of a bond of friendship with Everell and Hope may seem little more than racist—and, indeed, it is racist (as presented), just as it is racist of Mononotto or anyone else to engage in collective punishment based on race. All this suggests some complexity and ambivalence in Sedgwick's treatment of Native American resistance.

Spirituality

There is also complexity and ambivalence in Sedgwick's treatment of spirituality. The moral excellence of many Native Americans is stressed throughout the book. Early on, William Fletcher says of Magawisca's mother: "This poor savage's life, as far as it has come to our knowledge, was marked with innocence and good deeds; and I would gladly believe that we may hope for her, on that broad foundation laid by the apostle Peter: 'In every nation, he that feareth God and worketh righteousness, is accepted of Him'" (2012: 13). Almost at the end of the novel, the narrator observes that Magawisca "seemed, to her enthusiastic young friends, one of the noblest of the works of God—a bright witness to the beauty, the independence, and the immortality of virtue" (193). Thus, Native Americans do not appear to be morally or spiritually inferior to Europeans.

But this does not mean that the novel treats Christianity and Native American religion as equal. The stance of the novel on this issue is unclear, and I suspect that Sedgwick wavered in her views on the topic. Thus, for Magawisca the great virtue of Everell was that he "admitted the natural equality of all the children of the Great Spirit" (151). This may seem to imply a natural equality of a religion of the Great Spirit and that of Christianity. Conversely, the narrator appears critical of the fact that "good people, who take upon themselves the supervisorship of their neighbours' consciences, abounded in that age" (16). Part of that supervisorship would presumably include attention to religion and work to convert the "savages."

But what are we to make of Hope's late "thought that a mind [such as Magawisca's] so disposed to religious impressions and affections might enjoy the brighter light of Christian revelation—a revelation so much higher, nobler, and fuller than that which proceeds from the voice of Nature" (192). Hope is, after all, the hero of the book and the character who most actively defies convention to do good. Then there is the saintly Esther, who is eulogized in the closing paragraphs of the novel. She strives to convert Magawisca, principally (it seems) for Magawisca's own benefit. She explains that "I set before her her temporal and her eternal interest—life and death. I prayed with her—I exhorted her; but oh! Everell, she is obdurate; she neither fears death, nor will believe that eternal misery awaits her after death!" (160). Most importantly, Sedgwick includes a footnote, evidently in her own voice, stating that "we cannot but hope that the present enlightened labours of the followers of Eliot will be rewarded with such success as shall convert the faint-hearted, the cold, and the skeptical into ardent promoters of missions to the Indian race" (203).

The elevation of Christianity over Native American beliefs is related to Sedgwick's clear imagination of the nation as European, which is suggested by her praise of the pilgrims as "our" forebears, who chide us because "we forget that the noble pilgrims lived and endured for us" (43). The pilgrims' excellence was not merely national; it was also spiritual—"an exiled and suffering people, they came forth in the dignity of the chosen servants of the Lord, to open the forests to the sun-beam, and to the light of the Sun of Righteousness" (44), as if the crimes recounted by Magawisca were an example of Righteousness. She goes on to apparently celebrate how "the consecrated church" replaced "the rock of heathen sacrifice" (44). Our forefathers from Europe, then, "braved death" due to "an enthusiasm kindled and fed by the holy flame that glows on the altar of God; an enthusiasm that never abates, but gathers life and strength as the immortal soul expands in the image of its Creator" (44). There are other, more local issues as well. For example, God seems to favor the European Americans, as "Providence" (135 and 197) or "Heaven" (137) intervenes for Hope while apparently striking Mononotto dead by lightning (135). (This is an instance of the common nationalist idea that God is on our side against the [demonic] national enemy [see Hogan 2009: 118–123].)

Of course, everyone is free to consider his or her own beliefs as correct and to try to convince others to agree. I do not mean to condemn Sedgwick for that. The point is simply that the cultural egalitarianism she appears to affirm at some points is not held consistently throughout the work.

Ideological retreat?

The preceding observations bring us to the topic of ideological regression in Sedgwick's novel. In *Sexual Identities*, I discuss how some authors present a fairly radical position on sexuality or gender at some points, only to retreat into partial orthodoxy at other points (Hogan 2018b: 68). It seems that Sedgwick's novel involves something along these lines as well.

Consider again the violence perpetrated against Native Americans and that perpetrated by Native Americans. As we have seen, Magawisca's account of British violence against her people is chilling and unequivocal. Moreover, it resulted in roughly one hundred times the number of deaths that were caused by the Amerindians at Bethel. Even so, there is something deeply distressing about the details of Native American violence. The clearest case of this comes with the image of infanticide so often associated with the demonic outgroup. We read that a "savage" took up an "infant boy" and "tossed [him] to the ground." The child survived the fall and "clasped the naked leg of the savage with one arm, and stretched the other towards him with a piteous supplication, that no words could have expressed." But "one of the Mohawks fiercely seized him, tossed him wildly around his head, and dashed him on the door-stone" (Sedgwick 2012: 39). The victims of British violence are not portrayed anywhere near so effectively.

Moreover, as to numbers of dead, Sedgwick goes on to state that "such events, as we have feebly related, were common in our early annals, and attended by horrors that it would be impossible for the imagination to exaggerate. Not only families but villages, were cut off by the most dreaded of all foes—the ruthless, vengeful savage" (43). She recurs to savage massacres later on, stating that "in the years 1642 and 1643 there was a general movement among the Indians. Terrible massacres were perpetrated in the English settlements in Virginia; the Dutch establishments in New-York were invaded, and rumours of secret and brooding hostility kept the colonies of New-England in a state of perpetual alarm" (110). Sedgwick's views on the conflicts between Europeans and Amerindians are not so straightforward or consistent as might be inferred from Magawiska's account of the British attack on her village alone.

Conclusion

On the whole, *Hope Leslie* is a remarkably progressive novel for its period and even in some ways for our own. Sedgwick expertly deploys a range of techniques to oppose colonial military policies as both un-Christian and imprudent. She tries to give white readers a sense of the condition and perspective of Native Americans. She opposes the use of demeaning cognitive models that are so pervasive in understanding and responding to outgroups. She represents not only the unjustified violence of the Europeans, but also the resistance and spirit of the Native Americans. Nonetheless, it is never clear that Native Americans are part of colonial America. There is a separation between the races—due in part to the cruelty of both sides, but also due to the apparent racism of even the best-intentioned Native Americans, such as Magawisca (though Hope too exhibits racism at points). Sedgwick also seems to retreat from her criticism of British violence and to stress Native American cruelties. Finally, I believe that *Hope Leslie* is in several respects politically and aesthetically superior to its more famous precursor, *The Last of the Mohicans*. But it lacks the sort of hybrid character found in Hawkeye, as well as the love hinted at between Uncas and Cora, and (perhaps most strikingly) the clear spiritual egalitarianism of Munro, all of which suggest the value of bringing together the different traditions of Europe and Native America to form a new, more inclusive society.[5]

Notes

1. As Edward Foster (1974: 91) puts it, it is "entirely possible that … Sedgwick's novel is in part an answer to Cooper's" *The Last of the Mohicans*. Nina Baym (1992: 68) draws the connection more vigorously, writing that "*The Last of the Mohicans* spurred Catharine Maria Sedgwick to write *Hope Leslie*." Margaret Higonnet (1998) provides an overview of some of the observations of earlier critics regarding Sedgwick's relation to Cooper.
2. Sedgwick's novel is consistent with current psychological research in this respect, as "fear, anger, and contempt/disgust" are the most widely discussed "important contributors to intergroup conflict" (Maitner et al. 2017: 115).
3. On the development of attachment bonds between real (as opposed to fictional) Amerindian families and abducted Europeans, the refusal of some Europeans to leave their Amerindian families, and the cultural assimilation of Europeans into Native American cultures (all reminiscent of Sedgwick's Faith), see Axtell (1987).

4 On attachment and trust, see Hogan (2018a: 161) (commenting on Kringelbach and Phillips 2014: 116). On the complex relation between attachment and disgust, see Hogan (2011b: 75, n.8).
5 With regard to the last point, it should be clear that I am disagreeing with a range of critics (see, for example, Foster 1974: 91–92), who criticize Cooper for not presenting an interracial marriage (though he does so, in the case of Munro) and who praise Sedgwick for presenting a marriage across identity groups (though, it seems clear, the marriage of Faith does not really cross cultural identity categories; moreover, it is an equivocal example, based as it is on abduction).

4

WILLIAM APESS

A Native American writes back

There are two key discourse differences between William Apess's writings and those of James Fenimore Cooper and Catharine Maria Sedgwick. First, he is not white. Thus, in speaking about European–Amerindian relations, he does not have an initial, spontaneous identification with the dominant group. He is broadly humane and sympathetic; therefore, he does not outgroup Europeans in prejudicial and demeaning ways. (We will return to his treatment of whites.) However, he clearly does not see himself as one of them, nor does he have to struggle with biases in favor of the dominant group. Second, he is aware that there may be some Native American readers of his work. Even if the Amerindian readership were confined to his wife, he would not automatically expect his reader to begin with assumptions that privilege Europeans. In consequence, he presumably wishes to frame and phrase his writing in such a way as to be effective for a white readership while also retaining the trust and endorsement of his Native American readers. Even so, Apess's main target readership is whites—a point explicit in one of the two writings we will consider, "An Indian's Looking-Glass for the White Man."

Apess's address to Europeans is dictated by the main purposes of his work—responding to and to some extent correcting the social denigration and oppression of Native Americans. In other words, I take it that the rectification of disabilities imposed upon Amerindians is the central thematic aim of the piece. This may seem to put it in the same category as some parts of *The Last of the Mohicans* and *Hope Leslie*, at least according to the interpretations that I have suggested. Of course, the fact that Cooper and Sedgwick in some parts and to some degree return to dominant ideology might suggest a difference even here. Indeed, Apess does appear to be able to avoid dominant ideology more consistently. But there is a more fundamental divergence. Cooper (Chapter 2) and, more obviously, Sedgwick (Chapter 3) do have a genuine interest in the welfare of Native Americans qua Native Americans. But it seems that, at least to some extent, their opposition to divisions of racial identity categories serves national purposes. In other words, part of what is wrong with such divisions is that they impede national unity.

At points, Apess might appear particularly concerned with national unity as well. For example, in his autobiography, *A Son of the Forest*, Apess refers to the U.S. military, stating that "I could not think why I should risk my life and limbs in fighting for the white man, who had cheated my forefathers out of their land" (1992: 25). More strikingly, he ends "An Indian's Looking-Glass for the White Man" with the assertion that only when "the mantle of prejudice" has been "torn from every American heart" will it be possible for "peace [to] pervade the Union" (1992: 161). But the rhetorical point of such appeals to unity seems very different here. It is a matter of addressing the self-interest of the European majority. When Apess comments on fighting with U.S. forces or on "peace" throughout "the Union," he is reminding his white readers that a situation of European–Amerindian division involves violence that is not in the interest of Europeans either. By orienting his thematic appeal in this way, Apess is not, believe, taking national unity as his goal, with diminution of prejudice serving as a means of achieving that goal. Rather, for Apess, the main goal is always advancing the interests of Native Americans. The appeal to the nation, rather, suggests that at least many of his white readers may be inclined to oppose mistreatment of Native Americans, not as an end in itself, but first of all instrumentally as a means to national unity and peace.

Indeed, there is a suggestion in the autobiography that, insofar as Apess identifies national interest as important, he is concerned with Native Americans as a nation, not with the United States. Thus, he devotes only a little over half of his autobiography to his individual life. The remainder (45 of 97 pages) concerns "the origin and character of the Indians as a nation" (52). Seeing "the Indians as a nation" is a nation-building project. In furthering this project, Apess draws on the common model of the nation as a person. We see this not only in the parallel with Apess's individual life, but also in the attribution of a "character" to the Indian nation.

This last point brings us to the way that political complexity enters Apess's works. I mentioned already that he does not seem to fall into dominant ideology in the course of the work. In writing this, I was referring to Apess as the author or narrator. Apess as a character does sometimes suffer from self-doubt related to being Native American. However, the author never endorses these self-doubts. The ambiguity in the case of Apess concerns the degree to which he does or does not succumb to the inclination to outgroup Europeans and to assume the superiority of Native Americans as an ingroup. He certainly invokes Amerindian ingroup bias, as we will see. The question is—to what degree does he endorse this bias, rather than using it only as a rhetorical technique to challenge European American self-aggrandizement?[1]

On the other hand, there is a complication of even this complication. At times, Apess does seem to make a genuine appeal for national unity. At other times, he appears to be interested only in liberating Native Americans from oppression. Moreover, it is certainly clear that he does not consider the latter a mere means to the former. Justice for Native Americans is a more important goal for him than national unity. Nonetheless, there are hints that his most encompassing desire really is for peace and unity. But this is peace and unity of humankind. Thus, it is not a national concern at all, neither for "the Indians as a nation" nor for "the Union" (thus, in the latter case, a nation of both Amerindians and Europeans). This is the peace and unity found in God, which is not nationally defined. We see this, for example, when he affirms that "Christ died for all mankind" and that "age, sect, color, country, or situation made no difference" (Apess 1992: 19). Indeed, all the terms are important here. "Color" repudiates racism; "country" repudiates nationalism; "age" repudiates the tyranny of adults over children (clear from Apess's grandparents and family of indenture both); "sect" repudiates the religious biases that poison the relations between Methodists and other Christians, and among different groups of Methodists (as Apess recounts); and "situation" repudiates class (with its brutal mistreatment of the destitute, the indentured servants, the enlisted soldiers, and others discussed by Apess).

Explaining stereotypes and critiquing ideology

Before considering this complexity, however, we should review some of the main techniques used by Apess to critique European colonialism and racism. He shares a number of these techniques with Cooper and Sedgwick. Consider, for example, the explanation of stereotypes. Right at the outset of the autobiography, he recounts how his grandmother beat him viciously. This sort of savage violence is stereotypically associated with "savages." Apess explains the violence by reference to alcoholism (much as Cooper explains Magua's initial mischief). Of course, as demeaning stereotypes go, the alcoholic Indian may be only a slight improvement on the violent Indian. But Apess goes on to explain this stereotype as well. Thus, he writes that he blames alcoholism "in a great measure [on] the whites, inasmuch as they introduced" alcohol, "seduced them to a love of it," and used the resulting disorientation to deprive Native Americans of "their lawful possessions" (1992: 7).[2]

As the preceding point indicates, Apess also simply sets out literal criticisms of European American brutality. Like Malcolm X at the start of Spike Lee's eponymous film from 1992, though not so confrontationally, he indicates that whites have been responsible for the greatest number and most extensive crimes perpetrated by any race. He asks rhetorically: "Can you charge the Indians with robbing a nation almost of their whole continent, and murdering their women and children, and then depriving the remainder of their lawful rights, that nature and God require them to have?" (157). He enhances the emotional impact of these criticisms (as does, for example, Sedgwick) by framing that brutality as a betrayal of the trusting kindness and hospitality of Native Americans. He explains that "the whites ... had been welcomed to their land in that spirit of kindness so peculiar to the red men of the woods," who "extend the hand of friendship," only to find "their daughters claimed by the conquerors" (4).

Sometimes, he establishes the presence and effects of ideological beliefs in order to critique them. For example, at one point in the autobiography he explains that he had become mortally afraid of Indians. He then goes on to explain that "the great fear I entertained of my brethren was occasioned by the many stories I had heard of their cruelty toward the whites—how they were in the habit of killing and scalping men, women, and children." However, he goes on to say that these stories leave out the fact that whites "were in a great majority of instances the aggressors" (11). This is particularly noteworthy, as he shows the effect of ideologically guided storytelling—and, indeed, its effect on a Native American, whose inclination would presumably be to favor, rather than fear, the identity group with which he was socially identified.

Like a number of other writers, Apess also uses shift in perspective to counter-ideological effect. For example, he asks whites if they "would like to be disfranchised for all [their] rights, merely because [their] skin is white" (156). Similarly, he instructs his readers to "suppose an overwhelming army should march into the United States for the purpose of subduing it and enslaving the citizens" (31). The idea may seem at first unimaginable for European Americans, who would have little motivation to envision themselves in the place of their dominated foes. On the other hand, what Apess is doing should be very familiar to Christians, as it is in part simply a matter of following out a central precept of Christianity, the "Golden Rule." This precept states that "all things whatsoever ye would that men should do to you, do ye even so to them" (Matthew 7:12, KJV). To follow this precept, one must imagine oneself in the position of the other person, and thus shift perspective in just the way Apess is asking.

Spirituality and empathy

I point to the Golden Rule here because Apess's approach to intergroup relations is fundamentally religious. Specifically, it is a matter of showing Christian Europeans that their racism and colonialism are incompatible with the religious precepts that they espouse. This is a specific version of a common rhetorical technique in which the writer takes up the ethical principles of his or her antagonist and holds the antagonist to those principles. Such a strategy is particularly forceful when one's antagonist has invoked those principles against the very group one is supporting. Christian Europeans commonly belittled Native American peoples for their "pagan" religious practices. Apess shows that the Europeans have no right to invoke Christian principles against anyone.

Thus, Apess asks his reader: "Did you ever hear or read of Christ teaching his disciples that they ought to despise one because his skin was different from theirs?" (158). He goes on to cite St. Paul rejecting differences between "Greek" and "Jew," "Barbarian" and "Scythian," "bond" (or slave) and "free," for "Christ is all and in all" (158; see Colossians 3:11, KJV). Indeed, it is particularly hypocritical for Christians to reject non-Europeans, for Jesus himself was not European, but of a "colored people" (160). Apess reasonably suggests that, were Jesus alive in then-contemporary America, his skin color would lead to his rejection by many Christians, who would "shut" their "doors" to him (160).

Apess also identifies theological inconsistencies in the colonists' racism. It is a commonplace of antiracist writing that God made all human beings. Thus, we should treat one another equally. Apess gives this a striking twist, making it a much more challenging and critical response to racism. Specifically, if someone believes that nonwhites are thoroughly inferior, objects meriting little more than disgust, that belief would seem to suggest a tacit judgment about God. As Apess puts it, "if black or red skins or any other skin of color is disgraceful to God, it appears that he has disgraced himself a great deal—for he has made fifteen colored people to one white" (157). As this case shows, his appeals to the conscience of European Americans have a sting to them. That is in part a matter of maintaining his own dignity. But, in specific cases, it also may suggest the operation of some ingroup bias on his part.

Empathy and modeling outgroups

Anyone who has read even a few pages of *A Son of the Forest* or "An Indian's Looking-Glass" knows that Apess tries to cultivate empathy for Native Americans. He begins the latter work by portraying reservations as places that reduce Native Americans to "the most ... abject, miserable race of beings in the world" (1992: 155). The confines are filled with "children half-starved" and "almost ... naked." In their desperation, women with no means of supporting themselves are "seduced by white men" who abandon them to become "prostitutes" and alcoholics (155).[3] At the start of *A Son of the Forest*, Apess particularizes Native American suffering by reference to his own life and that of his siblings. The family was "clothed with rags" and "suffering from cold and hunger" (5). He also provides an exemplar for white readers, a case of compassion that they might imitate. Specifically, he explains that "some of our white neighbors ... took pity on us and measurably administered to our wants, by bringing us frozen milk" (5). He also provides an exemplar for broader social policy. When he is beaten brutally, his arm "broken in three different places" (6), he convalesces for a year "at the expense of the town" and "receive[s] the attention of two surgeons" (6). This cultivation of empathy is central to the Golden Rule and thus to Apess's development of Christianity in opposition to racism.

Here, as in works by other authors, certain sorts of modeling serve to guide cognition about outgroups and to affect interpersonal stance. Though Apess does not treat any of these at length, his localized treatments of the topic are revealing. For example, at the start of "An Indian's Looking-Glass" Apess partially explains the current situation in the following terms: Native Americans "are made to believe they are minors and have not the abilities given them from God to take care of themselves" (1992: 155). Here, Apess is criticizing the childhood model, indicating that it is false, and even in some degree irreligious, as it goes against God's creation of Native Americans. After the other works we have considered, one thing that is striking here is that Apess has focused, not on the European's belief in the model, but on Amerindians' acceptance of the model. As with alcohol, the model is introduced by Europeans. But at this point, Apess is focused on the deleterious effects of the model on Native Americans themselves and the way in which it contributes to a sense of dependency and a feeling of helplessness. It is to a degree self-fulfilling, as it fosters a debilitating reduction in their self-efficacy (to use the technical term for a person's sense of what he or she may be capable of accomplishing [see Maddux and Gosselin 2012: 199]).

Other prominent models work their way into Apess's writing as well, this time with the focus on European prejudice and cruelty (rather than on Amerindian psychology). For example, the kindly Furmans, who had given the destitute Indian child milk, also reveal a proneness to the racist outgrouping of Native Americans. At one point, Mr. Furman accepts without question a false accusation against young William and whips him. Drawing on the animal model, he denounces the child as "you Indian dog" (1992: 12). Subsequently, when Mr. Furman beats him again, he invokes the demonic model, claiming that "the devil had taken complete possession" of the child (16). In his history of Native Americans, Apess quotes another author who neatly characterizes the nature and consequences of the former (animal) model. The Indian may be "regarded as a ferocious animal, whose death is a question of mere precaution" (60).

Apess also draws on more novel metaphors for the ingroup–outgroup relation between Amerindians and Europeans. A particularly interesting case of this may be found in his invocation of the Parable of the Good Samaritan. At the end of "An Indian's Looking-Glass," he reminds his readers of the story of the man who was waylaid by robbers and left broken and bereft on the roadside. Respectable Jewish travelers passed him by, offering no help. But a Samaritan came along and, seeing the man, came to his aid, using his own money to house the victim until he recovered (see Luke 10:30–37). Apess appeals to European Americans to aid the Native Americans, who have been similarly wounded and robbed. The obvious point here is that Apess is appealing to the spiritual authority of Christianity and the empathy of European Americans. In doing this, he brings together spirituality with a more innovative use of modeling and with a shift in point of view, thereby synthesizing several techniques in his opposition to racism. Perhaps the most significant part of this modeling is not the assimilation of Amerindians to the victim of robbery. Perhaps, it is the alternative models that Apess offers his white readers. In the past, they were the robbers. Now, they have the possibility of being the good Samaritans.

Apess seeks to advance his political project by assimilating Native Americans to Jews, the Chosen People of God. I am not referring here to a subdued implication of his writings. Apess believed that Native Americans were literally Jews, the descendants of the lost tribes of Israel (53, 82). More significantly, Apess must have been aware that one main point of the parable was antiracist. Samaritans were seen as inferior by Jews; they were a group "against whom the Jews felt a strong racial antipathy" (Brinton 1973: 36). Jesus chooses a Samaritan for his story to bring home to his audience that it is good work, not ethnic identity, that is important in the sight of God. That (antiracist) point is obviously central to Apess's purposes. But it is also important that Apess places Europeans in the position of the parable's outgroup, the Samaritans, not the parable's ingroup, the Jews. This is in part a matter of preserving his self-respect. Always associating oneself with the outgroup is dispiriting. Apess opposes that by shifting the alignments from what whites might expect.

On the other hand, this reversal of the dominant social hierarchy is probably not only strategic. It seems also to result from Apess's own spontaneous tendency to identify categorically with Native Americans and thus to have the bias associated with that identification. I do not mean to criticize Apess for this; I merely want to note that his response to Europeans may have some of the same complexities and ambivalences as the responses of Cooper and Sedgwick to Amerindians. There are other points in his writing that may suggest this as well. For example, Apess insists on the relation between Native Americans and the Jews, giving the former a special, ethnic relationship with Jesus, thereby associating God more closely with his ingroup (a common practice; see Hogan 2009: 118–123). He also insists that Native Americans have the original human skin color (1992: 10). Thus, he represents his ingroup as the norm and the (European or white) outgroup as deviating from the norm with respect to their definitive difference (skin color). He also maintains that Native Americans "will occupy seats in the kingdom of heaven" before the whites (51). All this could simply be rhetorical provocation. But it may also suggest genuine ingroup bias. (Again, I am not condemning Apess for this; it is far more forgivable in his case than in that of European settlers, given the history of the groups.)

Beyond this, Apess seems at times to suggest both the animal and even the demonic models, which are now applied to Europeans. On the other hand, these are applied in much milder forms, and are connected with pacific impulses, such as patronizing pity, rather than with violence. For example, at one point he overcomes his anger at some Europeans by telling himself that "they had not the sense and wisdom of the brute creation" (36). Elsewhere, he explains that some people pretended to be his friends and tried to seduce him into a life of crime. Those who did so "were not my brethren [i.e., they were not Native Americans] but whites" (36). Though inexplicit, this suggests a model of the Satanic seducer. Apess does not use these models to justify mistreatment or revenge, but rather to dissuade himself from sin. Moreover, he does not reduce white people to their race category. Rather, he makes it clear that they are individual people, some of whom are wicked and some of whom are good. Most importantly, no ingroup bias distorts his clear vision of my personal ingroup, residents of Connecticut, of whom he astutely writes that "in the land of steady habits, I found the people very benevolent and kind" (37).

Emotion

We have been dealing with Apess's appeals to emotion in referring to his cultivation of empathy and his concern with interpersonal stance. However, we have not touched on particular emotions as they bear on racial divisions. Such emotions are of course numerous. But one stands out in Apess's writings—attachment. We see the centrality of attachment in two ways. First, the natural development of attachment is disrupted by the violence of racist oppression. Second, the formation of new attachment bonds—prominently in romantic love—may serve to heal the wounds caused by attachment disruption and may begin to respond to the divisions between identity groups.

Initially, the second point seems familiar from other works. Like Cooper before him, Apess at times seems to suggest the value of interracial romance, though on closer inspection it may be that he simply opposes racial segregation. Specifically, he denounces antimiscegenation laws as "disgraceful" (1992; 159) and affirms people's right to select their own spouse (160) without having that choice constrained by legal exclusion of an entire class of people. Thus, he clearly does not oppose interracial marriage. However, he does not really celebrate it as a social reconciliation either. Indeed, he repeatedly indicates that, historically, interracial unions have often been a matter of white men raping or exploiting Native American women (see, for example, 4 and 155). The establishment of attachment bonds does facilitate Apess's sense of interracial reconciliation, but it does so very differently than one might expect.

Romantic union certainly has benefits in Apess's view, but it has benefits when it is founded on genuine feelings of attachment and serves to repair the attachment losses and insecurities of one or both of the partners. That repair occurs perhaps most obviously in Native American unions with other Native Americans. Moreover, it is with regard to the initial, frayed attachment relations, the relations requiring repair through romantic union, that we find Apess's deepest and most consequential worries in this area. Specifically, the colonial condition and state of constant war in which Native Americans find themselves are harmful not only for their physical well-being (e.g., when they are wounded in battle, or deprived of food and proper shelter through displacement), but also for their emotional well-being and especially for their attachment relations.

Early in the autobiography, we learn that Apess was deprived of his parents at an early age. He was given far from adequate care by his grandparents, due to poverty and alcoholism. He sometimes had to rely on food from neighbors—prominently, milk (5). As Apess makes clear, the impoverishment and cultural degradation of many Native American groups were due to European colonization, which thus resulted in a fundamental attachment insecurity. Indeed, he paints a utopian picture of Native American life before European colonialism (7). The attachment needs of the young William are made clear by his deep feelings for the Furmans. He insists that the Furmans took him in due to "attachment" (7). But they did not adopt him as a son. Rather, he entered their family as an indentured servant. As we have already seen, Mr. Furman beat him and expressed clear racism at crucial points. Moreover, when Apess became troublesome for the family, they "sold" him (15). At first, he did not understand this and ran away from his new owner to reach what he thought of as his home only to be returned to his legal proprietors.

Apess's religious devotion is closely connected with his feelings of attachment deprivation and the roots of that deprivation in European colonialism and racism. For example, he is overwhelmed with feelings of being "friendless, unpitied, and alone" (20), thus deprived of an attachment bond. One might expect him to analogize this state to being in a wilderness. In fact, he does the opposite, wishing "to become a dweller in the wilderness" (20). On the one hand, this suggests a sort of spiritual retreat, perhaps bringing to mind John the Baptist (famously "the voice of one crying in the wilderness" [John 1:23, KJV]) or even Jesus (who also went into "the wilderness" [Matthew 4:1], where he "fasted forty days and forty nights" [Matthew 4:2]). On the other hand, the wilderness recalls the forest, the place of the Native Americans, the place where—Apess's title informs us—Apess is genuinely a son. However, unable to return to the precolonial Amerindian society of the forest, he finds himself rescued from this utter isolation by Jesus (21). As a result, he "embraced the whole human family" with "love" (21). Religion allows him to feel, at least for a time, that the immediate family he had lost early in his life, and the ethnic family he had lost in the encompassing history of European colonialism, may be replaced by the more enduring, spiritual family of all humankind in Jesus. His need for religion is ultimately a need for secure and reciprocal attachment bonds. Moreover, the unity of humankind in Jesus may be the only way he can envision overcoming the racial antagonisms that have caused so much suffering to him and other Amerindians and that have so devastated his attachment bonds.

Thus, the healing effects of attachment bonding operate very differently here than in the interracial romance. This is not to say that romantic love—or adult, sexual, attachment bonding—has no place in Apess's writings. It has an important place. But that too is different. Specifically, the crippling of attachment recurs throughout the course of the autobiography. Later, he once again finds himself "friendless." His response is predictable—"the desire of my heart was to get home" (1992: 35). But he cannot definitively say just where home is. In practice, he seems to attain some sense of emotional stability only when he meets his wife and marries—thus only when he at last establishes a secure attachment bond in a particular, personal relationship (as in fact one would expect from the psychology of attachment). But this is not unrelated to the social context of colonialism and Native American identity. Apess is able to meet his future wife and is open to the possibility of forming a genuine attachment bond with her because he "returned to [his] *first love*" (46). He explains: "I went then to my native tribe" (46). It is difficult to pinpoint what he means by his "*first love*," but he appears to mean his "native tribe." He leaves European American society and returns to the group and the place of his earliest attachment bonds. Unlike the whites with whom he had been in contact, then, he meets "a woman of nearly the same color as myself" (46), thus a woman with whom there was no need to overcome racial antagonism. It is only when that debilitating colonial hierarchy is removed that Apess can begin to repair his long-standing attachment loss and insecurity.

Conclusion

In sum, Apess draws on some of the same techniques as Cooper and Sedgwick in his response to the subnational division between Native Americans and Europeans. He to some extent explains stereotypes. More often, he engages in a sort of revisionist history, maintaining that the relations between the colonists and Amerindians were very different than European Americans have commonly believed. In connection with this, he on occasion engages in more pointed and rhetorically developed forms of ideological critique—setting up the ideological belief (e.g., in the danger posed by Amerindians) only to undermine it. Unsurprisingly, he seeks to cultivate empathy in his readers and, like Cooper and Sedgwick, he draws on religion to do so. Indeed, Apess is more consistently and intensely Christian in his appeals than either Cooper or Sedgwick. Thus, his work to develop readers' empathy—and his technique of reversing perspective (also shared with Cooper and Sedgwick)—are more closely bound up with the Golden Rule. He too draws on and undermines age and animacy models used by Europeans in thinking about and responding to Native Americans.

Despite important similarities, Apess is also in some ways strikingly different from the other two authors we have considered so far. Most obviously, he is Native American himself. As such, his spontaneous categorial identifications are likely to be with Native Americans, rather than with Europeans. In addition, he is more aware that Native Americans will constitute part of his readership and that he therefore needs to address them as well as whites. This may have led, for example, to greater sensitivity to the self-esteem of Native American readers and possible slights to that self-esteem due to, say, excessive solicitousness of white people's approval. In keeping with both differences, Apess's criticisms sometimes have a sharpness, a biting irony at the expense of whites, that one does not sense in Cooper or even Sedgwick. This is connected with Apess's occasional expression of apparent ingroup biases himself (e.g., in the very limited and nonaggressive use of animacy and age models for European Americans), as well as with his complex and at best ambivalent response to interracial romantic union. On the other hand, Apess does not generalize about European Americans and, at least self-consciously, he appears to believe that there is ultimately only one true identity group: the human family as a whole, united in Jesus.

I say, "at least self-consciously," because at various points Apess seems to reveal a profound longing for Native American union, even suggesting a sort of Native American nationalism. The longing for union is inseparable from the most affecting part of Apess's work, his indication that colonialism and racism disfigure human attachment relations and lead to deep attachment insecurities. In many ways, Apess's spirituality and his antiracist and anticolonialist work (connected with that spirituality) are driven by a need to soothe and perhaps begin to heal the wounds to attachment bonds that he and so many others have sustained in traumatic life situations brought on by racism and colonialism. That healing may point toward a unified national identity, but not necessarily for the same nation as that envisioned by European American authors such as Cooper and Sedgwick. In other words, Apess's imagined nation seems likely to be fundamentally Amerindian, whereas the imagined nation of Cooper or Sedgwick appears to be fundamentally European American.

Notes

1 It is worth noting that Apess's position with respect to Native Americans is in many ways parallel with Sedgwick's position with respect to sex. This includes the issue of whether Sedgwick may unselfconsciously assume a sort of female ingroup superiority over males. One difference, however, is that Sedgwick probably expected that a much larger percentage of her readers would be ingroup members (thus women, in her case).
2 Unsurprisingly, Apess was not alone in this assessment, as Peter Mancall (1995: 174–177) discusses, and as we saw with Magua in Cooper.
3 Apess also indicates that Native American women were not only seduced, but raped (subjected to "violence of the most revolting kind upon [their] persons" [7]). The problem continues to this day. Andrew Schwartz (2018: 7) reports a 2010 survey of "American Indian and Alaska Native women living in Seattle," in which "94 percent reported they had been raped or coerced into sex."

5

UNCLE TOM'S CABIN

The childhood model and delegitimating U.S nationalism

Harriet Beecher Stowe's famous and profoundly influential novel[1] has been a sort of touchstone for me in thinking about subnational divisions in the United States and the ways in which those divisions are treated in literature. It develops many of the techniques we have been considering, now in relation to African Americans rather than Native Americans, but it does so in unique and innovative ways. Indeed, it was through work on Stowe's novel that I first came to realize the extent to which an author may hold contradictory views on complex topics and the extent to which those contradictions may be understood by reference to varying goals and contexts in the author's writing.[2] Since I have treated these points at length elsewhere (see Hogan 2013: 113–149), I will only summarize them here. On the other hand, my previous analysis did not relate Stowe's concerns to the topic of American identity; I will therefore focus particularly on that relation.

As many critics have noted, Stowe is both racist and deeply antiracist. In fact, I disagree with many criticisms of Stowe, especially regarding the magnificent character of Uncle Tom.[3] But it is undoubtedly the case that she makes overtly racist comments in the course of the novel. What is particularly striking is that often Stowe will make statements about Africans that do not cohere with her portrayal of Africans. We are used to this in cases of concealed or unconscious racism, where the author makes antiracist statements, but then falls back on racist stereotypes when creating characters. But what Stowe does is often the opposite and might remind us of Georg Lukács's ideas about Balzac. Lukács (1981: 40) argues that Balzac made reactionary statements, but he portrayed characters, situations, and events in a progressive way. That is what we often find with Stowe. Thus, we see her develop African characters in ways that are inconsistent with her racist generalizations.

For example, the narrator, presumably speaking for the author, tells us that Africans are not enterprising (Stowe 2003: 108) and that they lack industry (358). In part, this is not a criticism, since she uses the words ambiguously. On the one hand, to be enterprising means something along the lines of *taking initiative for personal, material gain* (basically, active greed). We find this quality in the villains of the novel—Haley and Legree, for example. It is largely the case that Africans in Stowe's novel are not enterprising in this pejorative sense. In our terms, that might suggest a limited degree of racial ideology, but it certainly does not indicate race hatred. Moreover, even its racial ideology does not seem to have any implications for social hierarchization—at least any that would be harmful to Africans—since active greed is presumably something we would like to discourage in society. The other meaning of *enterprising* or *industrious* is roughly *taking initiative to advance social well-being or knowledge*. Africans in Stowe's novel seem to exhibit rather more initiative than Europeans in this commendatory sense of the term. We see this in cases ranging from Eliza's flight to save her son to George's invention of new technology and his later commitment to the advancement of Africans.

In order to clarify these points terminologically, I distinguish between the "implied author" and the "implicated authors." Implicated authors are the local suggestions of authorial attitude, the particular ideas indicated by localized statements or characterizations. For example, the narratorial comment that Africans are "naturally ... unenterprising" (108) implicates a racist authorial judgment. The point is reinforced when a sympathetic character (St. Clare) comments that Africans need to be trained into having "industry" if they are going to become "men" (358). At the same time, the implicit characterization of George as enterprising implicates an authorial view that Africans can be more industrious than Europeans. Moreover, Tom is explicitly referred to as "industrious" (369). These various implicated authors are *prima facie* incompatible with one another. The implied author is, so to speak, the most global implicated author, the author suggested by the work as a whole, with its indication that the author found that work suitable and complete or at least suitable and complete enough for publication. A critical delimitation of the profile of an implied author, then, will ideally include an account of the contexts, purposes, or other factors that make sense out of the contradictions among the implicated authors.

For example, part of the contradiction regarding enterprise and industry is a simple matter of verbal ambiguity, though part of it is also a matter of thinking about broad categories (which fosters stereotyping) versus thinking about individuals (which can overrule stereotypes [see Holland et al. 1986: 219, 221]). Other factors enter into other local contradictions. For example, Stowe is appealing to a variety of audiences. In some parts of the novel, she seems to have one type of reader in mind, while in another part she appears to have a very different reader in mind. In the "Concluding Remarks," she explicitly distinguishes readerships—"men and women, of the South" (504), "Farmers" of New England (505), "mothers of America" (505), "Northern Christians" (506), and others.

Empirical research shows that minimally different contexts can significantly alter one's response to fundamentally identical situations. For example, when test subjects were told about refugees fleeing a country by train, they tended to advocate military intervention, having assimilated the situation to that of World War II. In contrast, the identical problem, except that the refugees were represented as fleeing by boat, provoked greater opposition to intervention, on the model of the Vietnam War (see Holland et al. 1986: 313–314). An author's implied reader may define contexts of this sort as well. If Stowe was speaking with a Southern slaveholder, she probably used different arguments and presupposed different shared premises than if she was speaking with a neutral Northerner or someone opposed to slavery but passively acquiescing in its practice. There would be similar effects on her literary creation when one or another such audience was more salient at a particular point in her writing.

There are also differences in the types of argument one might make. In some cases, a stereotype might simply and unequivocally support oppressive social, legal, or economic structures. In other cases, however, a stereotype might support an argument against such oppression. To take a simple example, viewing a group—say, women—as children contributes straightforwardly to their oppression when the context is political enfranchisement. But it may work against oppression when the context is one of protective legislation (e.g., having to do with sexual assault). Anyone who has had any involvement with political activism is likely to recognize that activists often shift their presuppositions in just this way, in effect contradicting themselves in different contexts, though they may be entirely unaware of this. The same points hold for contradictions between implicated authors. This does not mean that Stowe cynically employed false stereotypes when it served her purposes. That certainly happens and might be taken as an apt characterization of propaganda. However, in both fiction and policy debate, this sort of shifting can occur unselfconsciously. Indeed, as the preceding experiment suggests, it occurs all the time. This tendency is almost certainly enhanced in writing a work of fiction, where the contextually shifting ideas and attitudes are largely implicit in characterization, metaphor, and trajectories of action, as opposed to explicit arguments that articulate premises, inferences, and conclusions.

One aspect of Stowe's novel that is particularly relevant to the present study is her use of the childhood model for outgroups. It shows unusual complexity in its relations among implicated authors and implied authorship. There seems to be less complexity in her treatment—arguably, rejection—of national unity, which is also obviously of direct relevance to our concerns. Before going on to these, however, we need to consider some general points about the novel's themes and techniques, specifically its author's cultivation of empathy, as well as some thematic and technical differences entailed by its author's appeal to different classes of reader at different points during the story.

Stowe on slavery and empathy

As is well known, Stowe wrote her novel with thematic, real-world purposes in mind. Most immediately, she wished to foster opposition to the Fugitive Slave Act of 1850.[4] This act required residents of the free states, on pain of imprisonment and heavy fines, to cooperate in the capture of escaped slaves and their return to slavery. More broadly, Stowe sought to oppose the institution of slavery in general. With respect to her readers (whom she almost certainly envisioned as European

American), her goal was to encourage them to behave morally, that is, in keeping with God's will—thus, refusing to cooperate with the continuation of slavery. With respect to slaves, her goal was that they should receive just and humane treatment, which was possible only through the abolition of slavery.

These moral and humane goals regarding slavery are the primary and explicit animating forces for the work. However, they are intertwined with a secondary, more implicit concern—the nature of the United States. We saw in Sedgwick (Chapter 3) some skepticism regarding the extent to which European Americans and Native Americans might be reconciled and joined in a unified nation. The deferral of interracial friendship at the end of her novel suggests a similar deferral of national integration. There are other qualifications to the imagination of national unity in Cooper (Chapter 2), whose vision of the future United States appears to include some elements of Native American culture, but a diminishing presence of Native Americans themselves, and Apess (Chapter 4), who hints at a nation that is primarily Native American, as the nations imagined by our other authors are primarily European American. Stowe may express an even more profound skepticism about a nation that lives up to its ideals of universal, democratic egalitarianism. Indeed, as we will discuss below, her acerbic references to patriotism seem to express both anger regarding the state of the nation and despair over any genuinely egalitarian unification across races in the future.

On the other hand, whatever Stowe's views on the possible, future legitimacy of the nation, she is clearly pursuing an antislavery program. She is, therefore, addressing a key aspect of subnational identity division. In doing this, she uses many of the techniques we have considered thus far (e.g., explaining stereotypes, as when she has St. Clare explain to Ophelia that slaves are dishonest because they quickly learn that there is no other way for them to survive [2003: 242]). Like other authors we have considered, she does this to a great extent by seeking to cultivate the reader's empathic response. As she puts it in the "Preface," "the object of these sketches is to awaken sympathy and feeling for the African race, as they exist among us" (xviii). Moreover, also in keeping with tendencies we have observed before (and will observe again), she does this to a great extent by appealing to attachment bonds. Stowe draws particularly on the story genre of family separation and reunion,[5] from Tom's separation from his family and the stories of George, Eliza, and Harry at the outset, to Cassy's reunion with her daughter Eliza and George's reunion with Mme. de Thoux at the end. In keeping with this, and with Apess's attention to attachment disruption and insecurity due to colonial violence, she has one character remark that "the most dreadful part of slavery, to my mind, is its outrages on the feelings and affections—the separating of families, for example" (139).

In order to foster empathy, Stowe uses the usual technique of shifting perspective, trying to bring the reader to simulate the point of view of an outgroup member, in this case trying to shift the perspective of a European American reader into that of an African American. For instance, George and his wife, Eliza, are slaves of different masters. George's master is generally cruel and has recently said that he will separate George from his wife and child. Eliza appeals to his faith, saying: "O, George, we must have faith. Mistress says that when all things go wrong to us, we must believe that God is doing the very best" (19). The mistress in question is Mrs. Shelby, a humane woman in whom many white readers are likely to see something of themselves (perhaps giving themselves too much credit in the process). In any case, some Christian readers may be inclined to share the providential sentiment expressed in Mrs. Shelby's comment and echoed by Eliza. But Stowe is clearly aiming to foster a type of Christianity that is more engaged in the world and more egalitarian, in keeping with the sympathy she expresses for Quakerism in the course of the book. (On Quaker egalitarianism, and its theological foundation, see Brinton 1973: 27–28; Quaker activism included work to make "peace with the Indians, opposition to slavery, reform in prisons and institutions for the insane, and a multitude of educational undertakings" [Brinton 1973: 58].) In connection with this, she directly brings in George's perspective, tacitly encouraging the reader to imaginatively adopt this perspective, at least momentarily. Specifically, George criticizes Mrs. Shelby's Panglossian optimism, a form of passive providentialism that is undoubtedly shared by at least some readers even today. Specifically, George responds: "That's easy to say for people that are sitting on their sofas [not unlike the reader of Stowe's book] ... but let 'em be where I am, I guess it would come some harder" (Stowe 2003: 19).

Elsewhere, Stowe addresses the reader more directly, connecting him or her with the slave and the slave's experience. For instance, when Tom weeps over separating from his family, she in effect directs the reader to adopt a parallel interpersonal stance by reminding him or her that Tom's grief over attachment loss is just the grief anyone feels over attachment loss. Specifically, Tom wept "just such tears, sir, as you dropped into the coffin where lay your first-born son; such tears, woman, as you shed when you heard the cries of your dying babe. For, sir, he was a man—and you are but another man. And, woman, though dressed in silk and jewels, you are but a woman, and, in life's great straits and mighty griefs, ye feel but one sorrow!" (44).[6]

Though the point is clear enough, it is worth quoting two further passages. The first is one of the most famous in the novel. In this case, Stowe does not merely point to parallel emotional experiences, but calls on the reader to engage in effortful empathy, imagining herself in the place of a slave mother seeking to save her child from being sold. "If it were your Harry, mother, or your Willie, that were going to be torn from you by a brutal trader, tomorrow morning—if you had seen the man, and heard that the papers were signed and delivered, and you had only from twelve o'clock till morning to make good your escape—how fast could you walk? How many miles could you make in those few brief hours, with the darling at your bosom—the little sleepy head on your shoulder—the small, soft arms trustingly holding on to your neck?" (56). The concrete detail of the description is designed to guide our imagination in such a way as to link the reader's concrete experiences of holding a loved child with the experiences of the slave mother.

Finally, Stowe also undertakes to produce perspectival changes that bear on reasoning (and biases of reasoning) in connection with law and religion. For example, after he has escaped, George meets a sympathetic white person who suffers moral conflict over George's actions. Specifically, he sympathizes with George's condition, but he has been convinced that the Bible urges submission to authority. George responds with characteristic acumen, asking "if the Indians should come and take you a prisoner away from your wife and children, and want to keep you all your life hoeing corn for them, if you'd think it your duty to abide in the condition in which you were called. I rather think that you'd think the first stray horse you could find an indication of Providence—shouldn't you?" (135). No one claimed that white men and women abducted by Native Americans should simply accept the condition of slaves. The entire idea would have appeared ludicrous to any European settler, despite the verses quoted from the Bible supposedly in support of slavery. Yet the position of those European captives was directly parallel to the position of African slaves.

Stowe most obviously seeks to foster empathy by developing pathos, the suffering of the characters. But her antislavery work is not confined to compassion. She is consistent in developing admiration for her African American characters as well. This should serve to make the reader's compassion less superior and patronizing. Eliza is almost superhuman in her escape from Haley, leaping from one floating sheet of ice to another across the river. More significantly, George is the most intelligent and accomplished character in the novel, an industrial inventor of great ingenuity, despite his very limited opportunities; Stowe stresses that George is modeled on a real person, an African American in Kentucky (see 13n.). Tom shows great intellectual capacity reforming St. Clare's management of the plantation through "soundness of mind and good business capacity" (230). More significantly, he is the most spiritually excellent character in the novel, allowing himself to be martyred rather than betray a fellow slave, and being paralleled repeatedly with Jesus.[7] (We will consider some of these points again when we turn to Stowe's treatment of cognitive models for outgroups.)

Stowe's implied readers

As I noted briefly above, Stowe develops her goals and techniques somewhat differently for different audiences. In the "Concluding Remarks" that end the novel, she names different categories of readers—Southern men and women (504), New England farmers (505), Northern Christians (506), and so on. Probably the most crucial division is the obvious one between Northern and Southern whites. (Unlike Harriet Jacobs [Chapter 6] and Frederick Douglass [Chapter 7], Stowe does not appear to have envisioned much of a nonwhite readership—and, in any event, European Americans were the ones she needed to convince and motivate.) In each case, Stowe sought to develop characters who might serve as models for readers' emulation and characters who might promote self-criticism in readers. With respect to Northern whites, the models for emulation would include the Bird family, not excepting the flawed character of Senator Bird, who initially supports the Fugitive Slave Act (90) but subsequently aids Eliza and Harry in their flight. An even more exemplary case is the Hallidays, especially the saintly Rachel. Stowe seeks to foster self-criticism through the complex character of Ophelia, who is committed to the abolition of slavery but finds African people themselves rather disgusting. Thus, she exhibits racism at the level of individual interaction while repudiating it at the broad sociopolitical level.

Southern whites find a model for action in George Shelby, who concludes the story of the Shelby plantation by emancipating all the slaves. Mrs. Shelby is also exemplary to some degree, though circumstances limit the extent to which she is able to act on her good impulses. The characters who should lead to self-criticism on the part of white southerners prominently include Mr. Shelby and St. Clare, gentle and sympathetic men who end up causing great suffering due to their involvement in the slave system. They also serve to indicate that slavery is a destructive and inhumane institution, even in those rare cases where the slave masters are themselves individually humane. In contrast, the function of such a character as Legree does not involve identification of any kind, but helps to develop a "worst case scenario" showing what slavery can involve when the master is particularly cruel.

It is also worth mentioning that Stowe pays particular attention to women readers and, of these, especially mothers. As noted above, she appeals to mothers explicitly in portraying Eliza's escape. Indeed, motherhood is Stowe's explicit and implicit model for the loving beneficence that she wishes to foster in whites with respect to slaves. This is why her ideal is arguably Rachel Halliday. In keeping with this, Jane Tompkins stresses the novel's recurring "story of salvation through motherly love" (1985: 125).[8] On the other hand, Stowe does present the manly physical courage of George and Tom as exemplary as well.

Childhood model

Like the other authors we have considered, Stowe too responds to standard forms of cognitive modeling. On the other hand, her precise relation to these models, particularly the childhood model, is unusually complex and revealing, though also somewhat equivocal. Stowe does refer to animacy models. For example, she reverses the application of the animal model when she suggests that Loker and Haley, the slave catcher and dealer, are doglike (2003: 74–76). She effectively takes up the image again when she has George explain that he is treated worse than a dog (e.g., in terms of food and physical abuse [127]). As many critics have noted (without reference to outgroup modeling), she closely links Legree and Legree's plantation with Satan and Hell, respectively.[9] In direct contrast with this, she repeatedly assimilates Tom to Jesus. But the most complex use of modeling in the novel comes with Stowe's use of age grades, specifically the use of the childhood model.

Stowe's use of the childhood model for African Americans is striking for several reasons. For one thing, it is contradictory. At times, she clearly accepts the model, while at other times she critiques it, or at least undermines its validity through her representation of African American characters. In addition, when Stowe adopts the childhood model, she often does so for antislavery purposes.

I will not dwell on the many cases where Stowe asserts the childlike character of Africans. They are frequent in the book and range from general statements such as "There is no more use in making believe be angry with a negro than with a child" (83, *sic*), to more particular reflections such as the narrator's comment on Tom's "touching simplicity" and "child-like earnestness" (33). Sometimes, Stowe does not use the word "child" but portrays Africans in a way that tacitly assimilates them to children, as when the narrator comments that "the negro mind, impassioned and imaginative, always attaches itself to hymns and expressions of a vivid and pictorial nature" (32), or when she depicts the antics of the slaves Sam and Andy. An important part of the childhood metaphor is that it applies not only to individuals, but also to the outgroup as a whole. As such, it is commonly used to characterize their fitness for self-governance or, conversely, to assert the "white man's burden" of taking guardianship for the group. In connection with this, Stowe's narrator (who is, to all appearances, speaking for Stowe in this) comments on the idea of establishing a state for freed slaves in Liberia. She writes: "To fill up Liberia with an ignorant, inexperienced, half-barbarized race, just escaped from the chains of slavery, would be only to prolong, for ages, the period of struggle and conflict which attends the inception of new enterprises" (507). She elaborates on the point, referring to maturity, in keeping with the age model. Thus, she writes that Africans need to attain "moral and intellectual maturity" before they are sent to Liberia, "where they may put in practice the lessons they have learned in America" (507). Of course, Stowe is right that you cannot merely dump people in a place and expect them to spontaneously form themselves into a working nation. But that has nothing to do with the people's maturity; it applies to everyone.

Again, Stowe also at times contradicts this model and related stereotypes, for the most part implicitly. For example, at points Stowe puts comments about Africans as children in the mouths of unreliable characters, which directly suggests their falsity. Thus, Marie St. Clare—a self-deluded and dislikable character—comments that her slaves "are nothing but grown-up children. ... what a provoking, stupid, careless, unreasonable, childish, ungrateful set of wretches they are" (197). Almost any assertion from Marie St. Clare is likely to provoke the reader's skepticism. More significantly, Stowe often portrays African Americans as more adult than European Americans. Thus, she presents George as "manly" (not boyish), so much so that his owner experiences a "consciousness of inferiority" (13). Tom is "simple and childlike" (166), but Haley reports that he has a "'stromary [extraordinary] talent for business" and that his "calculatin' faculties" are "oncommon" (169)—not what we would ordinarily consider to be childlike talents. Indeed, Tom is far superior to both Shelby and St. Clare in running their plantations. A contradiction that I find particularly amusing concerns Tom's introduction to St. Clare's estate, which he admires. Stowe explains: "The negro, it must be remembered, is an exotic of the most gorgeous and superb countries of the world, and he has, deep in his heart, a passion for all that is splendid, rich, and fanciful; a passion which, rudely indulged by an untrained taste, draws on them the ridicule of the colder and more correct white race. St. Clare ... was in heart a poetical voluptuary" (185). In the first of these two sentences, Stowe tells us that Tom likes the ornate St. Clare estate because he is a negro, while the "white race" does not go in for that sort of thing. Then, where we might expect an example, she tells us that this ornate design is just what St. Clare liked, reminding us that the estate—which is presumably "splendid, rich, and fanciful" and thus "negro"—was designed by a member of the "white race."

For our purposes, the most important elements of the childhood metaphor come in two areas. The first is a matter of attachment relations and parenting. (The second concerns Stowe's views on childhood and spirituality.) In keeping with the metaphor, some versions of white supremacist ideology characterize Europeans as parental figures for Africans. In the case of fathers, Stowe clearly undermines this characterization. As in Jacobs and Douglass, literal white fathers of Africans are (explicitly or implicitly) slaveholders who deceive or coerce the women involved and sell their offspring like so many cattle. A striking example is the man Cassy thought of as her husband but who sold her and her children, separating them from one another as well. Though peripheral to the narrative, such characters are clearly despicable, very far from models of paternal behavior. Slaveholders may be metaphorical fathers as well as literal ones. They do not fare much better in that role. For example, St. Clare comments that "we are too lazy and unpractical, ourselves, ever to give [the slaves] much of an idea of that industry and energy which is necessary to form them into men" (358). In short, white men are not particularly suited to a paternal role with respect to Africans, whether it be literal or figurative.

It is perhaps unsurprising, given Stowe's apparent views on gender, that adoptive mothers do better. A lovely example comes when Rachel Halliday asks Eliza about her escape to Canada, saying: "And what'll thee do, when thee gets there? Thee must think about that, my daughter" (153). Stowe's narrator explains that "'my daughter' came naturally from the lips of Rachel Halliday; for hers was just the face and form that made 'mother' seem the most natural word in the world. Eliza's hands trembled, and some tears fell on her fine work" (153). Stowe sensitively represents the difference between the genuine parental concern of a character such as Rachel, a concern that is not affected by the racial difference between herself and Eliza, and the patronizing attitude that is part of white paternalism. Stowe's representation of the Quaker community does, moreover, leave open the possibility that men too could have this genuinely beneficent attitude, though she clearly thinks it is more in the character of women, perhaps mothers in particular.

Despite the childhood model, Africans too are parents, and Stowe represents them as parents in the novel. Crucially, despite the childhood model, they are excellent parents—both to Africans and to Europeans. Our first exemplar of motherhood in the novel is Eliza. As noted above, Stowe calls on her readers to consider just how fast they would walk to save their child from a slave-trader (56). This is, again, first of all a matter of cultivating readers' effortful empathy. But it is also a matter of setting up Eliza as an ideal that European readers may admire and even regard with a degree of wonder.

The parental superiority of African mothering is explicit in the St. Clare household—and this includes African mothering of white children. We see this when Evangeline St. Clare returns home after a long absence with her father. She warmly greets her mother, Marie St. Clare, who pushes the child away, complaining that her head aches (see 186–187). In contrast, Evangeline also warmly greets her black governess, "Mammy," who reciprocates the child's warm affection and enthusiasm. Indeed, African fathers are similarly admirable, even with respect to white adults. For example, Tom regards St. Clare with "fatherly solicitude" (231). More strikingly,

Mr. Shelby refers to Tom as "boy," but does not treat him with the care of an adult for a child. In contrast, Tom exhibits clear paternal affection and care for Shelby. Indeed, despite the small age difference between the two, Tom has had a paternal role in Shelby's upbringing. As Tom explains, "I was jist eight years old when ole Missis put you into my arms, and you wasn't a year old. 'Thar,' says she, 'Tom, that's to be your young Mas'r; take good care on him,' says she. And now I jist ask you, Mas'r, have I ever broke word to you, or gone contrary to you, 'specially since I was a Christian?" (62). The paradoxical position of both parent and child is exhibited particularly effectively in his relation with little Eva. As if she were the parent, Eva explains that "I read to him [Uncle Tom] in my Bible." But Tom takes the more important parental role in that "he explains what it means" (210). Thus, Eva has a technical skill of a parent, but Tom has the deeper knowledge and wisdom.

It is, of course, important that Tom's wisdom concerns religion. Indeed, a crucial part of Stowe's use of the childhood model involves the spiritual elevation of Africans by means of that model. Specifically, Stowe draws on the appeal to childhood spirituality to suggest that Africans are in fact superior to Europeans in what, to Stowe, is most important. Thus, we find St. Clare commenting to Tom that "it seems to be given to children, and poor, honest fellows, like you, to see what we can't." St. Clare goes on to wonder how that has occurred. Tom responds with reference to Luke 10:21 that God has "hid from the wise and prudent, and revealed unto babes" (343). For anyone familiar with the Gospels, this and other passages also recall Matthew 18:3 (KJV): "Except ye . . . become as little children, ye shall not enter into the kingdom of heaven."

I and, I imagine, most readers today are inclined to fault Stowe for accepting the childhood model even in a local and contradictory way. Nonetheless, she should be respected for taking up aspects of the model that served the interests of Africans. European propagandists were likely to ignore positive aspects of the model, elaborating on the political and economic disabilities it appeared to justify. However, these are directly and forcefully challenged by Stowe's different development of the model.

Again, the childhood model was applied not only to individuals, but also to the group as a whole. In consequence, it was understood to suggest something about the group's maturity and ability to govern itself, to be independent. As we have seen, Stowe at least sometimes accepted this application of the model. However, she was quite unusual in following through its implications insofar as these were positive for Africans. If "we" (Europeans) are adults and Africans are children, then some day Africans will take our place as we pass to senescence. Stowe affirmed this, linking it with a spiritual teleology. Thus, Stowe writes that "if ever Africa shall show an elevated and cultivated race—and come it must, some time, in the great drama of human improvement— ... the negro race, no longer despised and trodden down, will, perhaps, show forth some of the latest and most magnificent revelations of human life. Certainly ... they will exhibit the highest form of the peculiarly Christian life, and, perhaps, as God chasteneth whom he loveth, he hath chosen poor Africa in the furnace of affliction, to make her the highest and noblest in that kingdom which he will set up, when every other kingdom has been tried, and failed; for the first shall be last, and the last first" (204).

Race and nation

The preceding point brings us to the issue of national identity. Stowe's book is certainly important for its response to the outgrouping of Africans by Europeans and the consequences of this outgrouping, most significantly the rationalization of racial slavery. But it is relevant to the present volume only to the extent that it is in some way addressing the topic of U.S. identity. After the first century or so of U.S. independence, prominent writers appear to become less interested in national unification and perhaps less hopeful for the realization of egalitarian ideals. Stowe is, I believe, an early example of skepticism about U.S. nationalism. In some ways, this is unsurprising. Stowe's novel preceded the Civil War, but it is driven by some of the concerns that were central to the war, particularly concerns bearing on the way national unity (and thus the preservation of national identity) had become an excuse not only for individual acts of gross inhumanity, but also for a legal system that routinized atrocities. Stowe's relation to this conflict is well represented by President Abraham Lincoln's characterization of her in 1863: "The little woman who wrote the book that made this great war" (Kazin 2003: ix). In some ways, this novel involves a fundamental rejection of U.S. national identity, even while affirming its ideal of universal, democratic egalitarianism.

Indeed, Stowe arguably presents us with an in some ways radical form of skepticism about U.S. unity, reconciliation, and identity—a *national delegitimation* of the sort that we might associate with the counterculture dissidence sparked by the Vietnam War over a century later. It may well be that, as some critics have argued, Stowe's solution to the race problem in the United States is tainted by the sort of disgust at Africans exhibited by Ophelia. Indeed, this is just the sort of complexity and ambivalence we would expect from what we have already seen. But Stowe expresses a range of other attitudes as well, in some ways hinting at radical black separatism and Third Worldism as these developed in the 1960s. There are also more particular parallels with the 1960s, such as the elevation of Canada as an admirable alternative to the United States.

Specifically, Stowe does not suggest that whites and blacks can be reconciled by interracial love, like the friendship of Hawkeye and Chingachgook in Cooper. Indeed, despite the beneficence of Rachel Halliday, George Shelby, and a few others, it is not entirely clear in Stowe's novel that white people will ever change in large enough numbers—or that enough former slaves and their descendants will be able to overcome the trauma to which they or their ancestors were subjected—in order to produce a genuine, enduring reconciliation between blacks and whites. Stowe seems far more pessimistic than Sedgwick, who allows that Magawisca may someday return to friendship with Hope and Everell. For Stowe, there is only one option that will secure black people's well-being, restoring them to autonomy and allowing their development into the bearers of God's final message to humankind.

That solution is national independence for African Americans, who should be resettled in their new homeland of Liberia in West Africa.

The (justified) anger of African Americans is articulated by George at a number of points in the novel. For example, speaking to a well-meaning but somewhat confused European American, George explains: "You have a country; but what country have I, or any one like me, born of slave mothers? What laws are there for us? We don't make them—we don't consent to them—we have nothing to do with them; all they do for us is to crush us, and keep us down" (2003: 126). Stowe suggests little more than scorn for celebrations of U.S. national identity as she has George continue: "Haven't I heard your Fourth-of-July speeches? Don't you tell us all, once a year, that governments derive their just power from the consent of the governed? Can't a fellow think, that hears such things? Can't he put this and that together, and see what it comes to?" (126). Later, she has George take up the ideals of the American Revolution again, now in favor of the independence of Africans, parallel to the independence of the American colonists. George writes: "I have no wish to pass for an American, or to identify myself with them. It is with the oppressed, enslaved African race that I cast in my lot. ... The desire and yearning of my soul is for an African nationality. I want a people that shall have a tangible, separate existence of its own" (491–492). With only a few changes, such as "British" for "American," one could imagine such a sentiment being expressed by George Washington rather than George Harris. The general point is surely much the same.

Stowe articulates arguments in favor of this independence through George. Specifically, George writes in a letter that it is not possible for an individual to break the chains of slavery that bind Africans in the Southern United States. One can achieve such a large political goal only as "part of a nation, which shall have a voice in the councils of nations. ... A nation has a right to argue, remonstrate, implore, and present the cause of its race—which an individual has not" (493). This is not a scheme that George or Stowe believes Africans should be required to finance themselves. Thus, George asserts that "we have the claim of an injured race for reparation" (493). In her "Concluding Remarks," Stowe agrees with George on this topic, asking the reader: "Does not every American Christian owe to the African race some effort at reparation for the wrongs that the American nation has brought upon them?" (507).

Some critics have seen a sort of segregationist attitude in Stowe's advocacy of an independent Liberia (see, for example, Ammons 2000). There may be some element of this. Again, it is possible that Stowe shares a degree of disgust for Africans with Ophelia, an antislavery woman from New England, like herself. As St. Clare chides Ophelia: "You would not have them abused; but you don't want to have anything to do with them yourselves. You would send them to Africa, out of your sight and smell" (202). If there is any link between Stowe and Ophelia, we should first acknowledge that Stowe has engaged in an admirable self-criticism in this passage. The fact that she could engage in that self-criticism may suggest that there are other reasons for her black separatism. In addition to those articulated by George, there is the role of Africans in human salvation, which has been prophesied by Stowe. Again, Africans are to lead the way to new spiritual realization as they move from a putative racial childhood to a putative racial adulthood. This is why Stowe, in her "Preface," characterized the future state as "an enlightened and Christianized community ... on the shores of Africa" (xviii).

For our purposes, it is of course important that Stowe advocates a kind of black nationalism. It is no less important that this goes along with a systematic delegitimation of U.S. nationalism, and thus an apparent repudiation of U.S. categorial identification. This is signaled, among many things, by Stowe's references to patriotism. It seems that Stowe, at least as the implied author of this novel, might best be characterized as an internationalist "Christian patriot," to take up a phrase used by George Harris (494). This can be reconciled with black nationalism because of Africa's future role in the extension of divine self-manifestation in a teleological history. That is why George can follow his reference to Christian patriotism with an affirmation of "glorious Africa" (494). In contrast, Stowe stresses the incompatibility of Christian ideals with "the glory of the Union" (i.e., the United States [147]) and the laws of that "glorious Union" (150), which require Northern cooperation with (un-Christian) slavery.

Indeed, Stowe has withering sarcasm for the idea of U.S. (national) patriotism. Speaking of slave-catchers, she writes that "the catching business ... is rising to the dignity of a ... patriotic profession" (80). She refers to Senator Bird as "a patriotic senator," in that he had been "spurring up the legislature of his native state to pass more stringent resolutions against escaping fugitives, their harborers and abettors!" (100), since this was done to preserve the union of North and South. Once the senator sympathizes with Eliza, however, he finds that he is "in a sad case for his patriotism" (101). Similarly, when Northerners seek to protect escaped slaves fleeing the barbarous cruelties of slavery into Canada, Americans are "too well ... patriotic to see any heroism in it" (224). The mention of Canada serves to remind us that Stowe presents that country as a greatly superior alternative to the United States, a sort of promised land for the runaways. The latter nation is, indeed, almost like an evil twin of the former. In keeping with this, there are points at which Stowe seems to entertain the possibility of African Americans simply moving to Canada and becoming genuine citizens of that nation, rather than forming a new nation in Africa. Thus, before he takes up advocacy of Liberia, George states that "when I get to Canada, where the laws will own me and protect me, that shall be my country" (128).

We find much the same national delegitimation in Stowe's explanation of how Haley transports slaves on a ship that celebrates the nation and its freedom by its symbolic display of "the stripes and stars of free America waving and fluttering overhead" (138). She is similarly scathing about the U.S. legal system, which is presumably fundamental to its identity as a nation. Thus, she explains how American law "coolly classes" the "feeling, living, bleeding, yet immortal" person as a "thing" that is no different in kind from "the bundles, and bales, and boxes, among which she is lying" (148). She goes on to write that one might "think that American legislators are entirely destitute of humanity," given "the great efforts made in our national body to protect and perpetuate this species of traffic" (151).

Conclusion

Stowe's treatment of subnational, African–European divisions in the United States is complex and obtrusively inconsistent, combining racism and antiracism. This is true principally with respect to ideological beliefs, though she may exhibit some emotional ambivalence in her attitude toward Africans as well. On the other hand, her opposition to oppressive or discriminatory social and legal practices appears unwavering. The ideological ambiguity is sometimes a matter of explicit generalization ("Africans are …") versus particular characterization ("Tom is …"). This is perhaps unsurprising, as cognitive research shows that particular knowledge tends to supersede stereotypes for a given target (Holland et al. 1986: 215). Nonetheless, it is striking that Stowe will frequently characterize Tom, George, Eliza, or others in ways that are blatantly inconsistent with her generalizations.

This contradiction is particularly evident in her treatment of the childhood model. She repeatedly links Africans with children and Europeans with adults. But she shows that Tom is a better plantation overseer than either his master Shelby or his master St. Clare. Similarly, George is a brilliant inventor who makes his master feel inferior (2003: 13). Moreover, one of the primary differences between adults and children is that the former act in a caregiving, parental role for the latter. But Stowe repeatedly shows Africans to be more committed, affectionate, and effective parents than Europeans (with some limited exceptions, prominently Rachel Halliday).

In certain cases, Stowe's contradictions are connected with her purposes. Those purposes prominently include opposing the Fugitive Slave Act and, more generally, convincing her readers that it is profoundly immoral and un-Christian to be in any manner or degree complicit with slavery. To that end, she employs a range of the usual techniques. These include establishing exemplars for emulation (i.e., characters whom readers might view as more desirable versions of themselves) as well as flawed characters who may serve to foster a self-critical attitude in readers, with both calibrated for different categories of reader (principally Northern and Southern). She also shifts the reader's usual perspective on the outgroup, often explicitly appealing to the reader's parallel experiences or urging empathic effort, in both cases fostering a parallel interpersonal stance. Stowe draws on the usual set of emotions, stressing attachment particularly and developing the painful attachment insecurity and separation anxiety that are intrinsic to the system of slavery. Stowe does not focus on interracial romantic love, of which she appears to take a rather dim view (as it was commonly a matter of sexual assault by white owners against black slaves).

As to her contradictions, Stowe not only criticizes standard ideological models for outgroups, she also takes up the childhood model to oppose oppression. She does this in two ways. First, with respect to individuals, she invokes the ideal of childhood innocence and faith, indicating that an African such has Tom has a fuller, Christian spirituality and a more profound relation with God precisely because he is childlike. Second, with respect to Africans as a group, she takes seriously the implication that, if Africans are children now, they will eventually become adults at a time when Europeans will have declined. She elaborates on this implication by reference to

Christian teleology in which the last race to achieve the dominant, mature position—thus, Africans—will also be the culmination of God's earthly revelation.

The final point suggests some of the nationalist concerns broached in the book. Specifically, Stowe supports what might be thought of as a black nationalist agenda. Through the voice of George Harris, she indicates that there is only one way of securing the freedom and autonomy of African Americans, and that is the establishment of an African nation for them—Liberia. This nation will also permit Africans to develop the Christian teleology that Stowe posits. Thus, her politics in this regard may be referred to as "Christian patriotism." In connection with this, Stowe has little if anything positive to say about U.S. patriotism, and she exhibits little if any commitment to U.S. unity or identity. In this way, her novel suggests a delegitimation of U.S. nationalism and thus U.S. identity—though not of the universal, democratic egalitarian ideal.

Notes

1 On the novel's influence, see Crane (2004).
2 The complexity of Stowe's racial attitudes has been recognized and explored by critics (see, for example, Otter 2004 and Tawil 2006). Their recognition of her "romantic racialism" is particularly valuable (see Frederickson 1971: 97–129). There has also been some discussion of differences in readers' responses to the novel (including the sexualization of the work; see, for example, Noble 2000: 126–146). However, as far as I am aware, no critic has clarified the nature and patterning of Stowe's variable and apparently contradictory attitudes, in part because they lacked the conceptual and empirical resources provided by recent cognitive science and social psychology.
3 See, for example, Warhol (2002) on some of the misunderstandings of this character.
4 A copy of the act is available at http://avalon.law.yale.edu/19th_century/fugitive.asp (accessed 3 May 2019).
5 On the prototypical form of this genre, see Hogan (2011a: 185–236).
6 This sort of appeal was particularly important at a time when many European Americans apparently doubted that Africans had attachment feelings, at least any of the quality and durability of those experienced by Europeans. Stowe presents cases of this sort in her novel (6, 139), but they were hardly confined to fiction. For example, Edward Baptist (2016: 192) reminds his readers of "Thomas Jefferson's claim that separation from loved ones mattered little to African Americans." This is part of a general tendency of group identification. Specifically, research indicates that we tend to see "both ingroups and outgroups" as possessing "primary or animal emotions (e.g., 'anger'), but "only one's ingroup fully possesses secondary, human emotions (e.g., sympathy)" (McFarland 2017: 643). It is important to note that this tendency is reduced among people who strongly identify with all humanity (Mc Farland 2017: 644).
7 On Tom's connection with Jesus, see, for example, Gilmore (2004: 72) and Karcher (2004: 207).
8 Tompkins stresses the feminist or women-centered aspects of the novel, rather than its concern with slavery. In consequence, her account of the emphasis on motherhood develops different concerns than those considered here.
9 See, for example, Josephine Donovan's (1991) chapter entitled "Inferno."

6

HARRIET JACOBS, WOMEN'S FRIENDSHIP, AND ANTINATIONALISM

Like all the other writers we have considered, Harriet Jacobs seeks to cultivate empathy or compassion on the part of the reader. But there are differences from other writers as well. The first task Jacobs has to accomplish is to establish a firm sense that African Americans have an emotional life and thus that it is possible for readers to have a parallel interpersonal stance toward them. One does not have an interpersonal stance toward emotionless objects. Of course, it is not necessarily the case that her readers self-consciously believe that African Americans are emotionless. But they may all too readily act on an unselfconscious presumption that Africans may have impulses (such as hunger) without human emotions—rather what we would expect from the animal model. Jacobs addresses this attitude explicitly at several points in the memoir. For example, she comments of her mistress that "it had never occurred to Mrs. Flint that slaves could have any feelings" (2016: 126). More concretely, she tells her master that there is a man whom she wishes to marry, a free African American. Dr. Flint (the master) replies: "If you must have a husband, you may take up with one of my slaves." Linda (Jacobs's fictional name for herself) responds: "Don't you suppose, sir, that a slave can have some preference about marrying? Do you suppose that all men are alike to her?" (34). Initially, Dr. Flint is willing to grant that Linda has a sex drive, but not that she has romantic feelings. The irony here is of course that Dr. Flint is the one who apparently lacks tender, affectionate feelings, experiencing principally an imperious lust.

On the other hand, Jacobs does not wish simply to make the reader feel badly for slaves. If feeling badly is bound up with a reader's sense of superiority, then it can become a demeaning sort of pity. Being the object of such pity may be hurtful to one's pride or self-esteem. More importantly, it may make the reader's benevolence dependent on the inferiority and self-deprecation of those whom he or she pities. Unsurprisingly, Jacobs does not affirm her self-respect by, say, engaging in the manly art of fisticuffs (as to some extent occurs with Frederick Douglass [Chapter 7]). But, when faced with discrimination in the North, she anticipates Mahatma Gandhi by engaging in nonviolent noncooperation, with success that is (if we judge by Jacobs's report) apparently greater than that commonly achieved by violent means. Thus, she explains of one group that had treated her as inferior due to her skin color: "Finding I was resolved to stand up for my rights, they concluded to treat me well" (150). She then generalizes the point, writing: "Let every colored man and woman do this"—roughly, refuse to cooperate with discrimination—"and eventually we shall cease to be trampled under foot by our oppressors" (150). Of course, as in the case of Douglass (or, indeed, that of Gandhi), the specific circumstances matter. One thinks, for example, of the slave, Demby, who refused to cooperate with an order given by an overseer in Douglass's (2017: 1181) *Narrative of the Life of Frederick Douglass*; he was simply shot. As Bertrand Russell (1968: 288) pointed out, nonviolent noncooperation has a chance of succeeding only if there is some degree of moral or empathic constraint on the part of the oppressor.

Like Stowe, Jacobs seeks to foster admiration for her characters by stressing their more autonomous and positive accomplishments as well. The clearest example of this is her grandmother's business (2016: 9). Despite her condition and background, Jacobs's grandmother initiated and developed a baking business that earned her considerable profits. Indeed, the grandmother's owners have to borrow money from her, as she is more enterprising, harder working, more financially disciplined, and more skilled than they are.

I hardly need to remark that Jacobs differs from Stowe (Chapter 5) in being black—and from Douglass (to whom we turn in the next chapter) in being a woman. Thus, she has a set of experiences as a black woman that make the condition of black women salient for her in a way that they are not salient for these other authors. Specifically, she is more keenly aware of the sexual dangers that slavery poses for black women in the South.[1] Moreover, one has the sense that Stowe was perhaps somewhat prudish about sexual matters. That does not seem to have been the case with Jacobs. Jacobs felt, quite rightly, that the sexual vulnerability of female slaves should be exposed and criticized. On the other hand, it faced her with the dilemma of how this could be done without reinforcing white prejudices—for example, without further identifying Africans with animality and bestial drives. (Again, the irony is that it was in fact the slave-owners who could most reasonably be characterized as animalistic.[2])

These various concerns—the fostering of compassion, cultivation of respect, and exposure of sexual violence—might seem to pull in somewhat different directions. But, in fact, they all contribute to the particular sort of empathy that Jacobs seeks to elicit and the particular feelings that she wishes to depict and convey to readers. Specifically, Jacobs spends a great deal of time developing a representation of Linda's moral sensibility. To a considerable degree, her suffering is not bodily misery. Dr. Flint does physically harm her, but those incidents are infrequent and serve more to underscore his bad character than to cultivate empathy with Jacobs's physical pain. The primary anguish experienced by Jacobs with regard to Flint is guilt about her loss of chastity. Thus, a key part of the compassion developed by Jacobs involves not animalistic urges but rather the putatively highest moral and religious feelings. Indeed, when Jacobs does foster empathy with her (Linda's) physical suffering, it is largely a matter of the terrible ordeals that she experiences when in hiding. Thus, the physical pain is not a sign of weakness against the greater power of the slaveholder. It is, rather, a sort of self-mortification undertaken in the service of moral principle; Jacobs suffers terrible pain and deprivation in order to evade the immoral pursuit of Dr. Flint. In this way, she implicitly undertakes to foster and integrate the reader's compassion and respect.

Moral aspiration or a sensitivity to moral guilt is not the only emotion that Jacobs emphasizes in this context. The other is attachment—which, in Jacobs as in Stowe, is closely related to moral feeling. Specifically, Jacobs seeks to cultivate the reader's compassion by detailing her attachment deprivation and by stressing the degree to which her moral feelings are inseparable from her attachment bonds with both her grandmother and her children. As to the former, her guilt over her own fallibility is intensified by her fond wish to please and to emulate her grandmother, who is a paradigm of ethical virtue but who is also ready to accept others' moral weaknesses, and who is thus someone who truly follows the model of Jesus. As to her children, Jacobs shows herself to be devoted to their well-being and industrious in the pursuit of their liberation from slavery. Moreover, this devotion and industry sometimes lead to her own deprivation, her separation from her children, despite her painful longing for them. Indeed, in this way she to some degree surpasses her grandmother, whose one fault is (arguably) that she is too unwilling to be deprived of her beloved children and grandchildren, even if an attempt to escape from slavery would be best for them.

Some standard techniques

Unsurprisingly, in pursuing her goals Jacobs draws on many of the same techniques that we have come upon in other authors. These include shifts in perspective and stereotype reversals. A stereotype reversal occurs when a negative trait or behavior commonly associated with one identity group is attributed to members of the opposed identity group, as when Catharine Maria Sedgwick (Chapter 3) links scalping with European Americans, rather than with Native Americans. For example, at least today it is a commonplace that rebellious servants—including slaves—would adulterate the food of their masters with, for example, spittle as an act of (concealed) aggression motivated in part by the disgust exhibited by the masters for the servants. But Jacobs refers to such adulteration by the masters, the main difference being that the masters had no need to conceal their acts. Thus, she reports that "if dinner was not served at the exact time on that particular Sunday, [Mrs. Flint] would station herself in the kitchen, and wait till it was dished, and then spit in all the kettles and pans that had been used for cooking. She did this to prevent the cook and her children from eking out their meagre fare with the remains of the gravy and other scrapings" (2016: 15).

She also reverses standard models. For example, she draws on the angel and demon models to characterize not Africans but European Americans—or, rather, many European American slaveholders. She recounts the barbarous murders committed by one slaveholder, including the torture of one slave, who was confined in a cotton gin for days until he was eaten by rats. "The master who did these things," she explains, "boasted the name and standing of a Christian, though Satan never had a truer follower" (43). On the other hand, like William Apess (Chapter 4), Jacobs does not condemn white people generally or employ outgroup models in racist ways. Indeed, her invocation of Satan typically involves a condemnation of social institutions, rather than individual people or even groups of people. This is why she refers repeatedly to "demon slavery" (47, 71, 134). The Hell of her existence and that of other slaves is not so much a matter of individual white people's choice or character. It results principally from the larger situation. Ultimately, it is the institution of slavery that is demonic. The people become devils because of the social practice, not the reverse.

As the example of the self-proclaimed "Christian" suggests, Jacobs also appeals to the principles asserted by European Americans. For example, she refers to the rationalization of slavery by the selective appeal to biblical passages. Specifically, she explains that slaveholders and others who enable demon slavery "seem to satisfy their consciences with the doctrine that God created the Africans to be slaves" (40). She writes "seem" here because she does not believe that the argument is valid, but also, perhaps more importantly, because she does not accept that slaveholders genuinely believe their biblical rationalizations. In any case, she goes on to give a brief argument against putatively Christian support of slavery. That support is "a libel upon the heavenly Father, who 'made of one blood all nations of men!'" (40; Jacobs's contention here is particularly reminiscent of some of Apess's arguments).

On romantic love and racism

As I have discussed above, romantic love provides a narrative structure that recurs in treatments of subnational division. Different authors express greater or lesser faith in the possibilities of interracial union as a literal means toward and a metaphorical representation of interracial reconciliation. Authors also take up romantic love more generally in considering the ways in which intergroup conflict impedes or destroys the happiness of lovers—though this is a common way of developing stories of romantic love generally, not solely in relation to pressing issues of subnational division. Jacobs takes up both ways of treating romantic love. She is, however, deeply skeptical about the value of interracial union—literally or metaphorically—in conditions of slavery. More precisely, Jacobs indicates that, as one would expect, the development, expression, and outcomes of love are deeply affected by the social structures in which the lovers are embedded. As she puts it, referring to the specific situation in which she found herself, "slavery perverted all the natural feelings of the human heart" (120). To a great extent, slavery did this by making relations between people into property relations. Insofar as it is possible for people to be owned like things, one's tendency to see other people as mere "means" to one's own egocentric gratifications is likely to be enhanced, and thus one's inclination to view or treat them as "ends in themselves" (to take up Immanuel Kant's [1956: 96–104] terminology) is likely to be diminished.

Treating others as mere means is incompatible with attachment feelings. But it is all too common a feature of sexual desire. The propensity to use others as instruments for sexual gratification may be modulated by attachment feelings, as well as by spontaneous empathy and the effortful empathy that is often a part of moral thought. In the context of slavery, interracial relations are likely to involve a widespread inhibition of empathy, due to the predominance of a complementary (i.e., antipathetic) interpersonal stance. Conversely, the principles of slavery are likely to enhance the tendency to view others purely instrumentally. It is especially likely to have this effect on masters with respect to their slaves. This suggests that, in a slaveholding society, genuinely romantic interracial relations—relations where attachment feelings are central—are unlikely to develop or to be sustained. Rather, the most exploitative aspects of sexual relations are likely to be exacerbated.

Dr. Flint's treatment of Jacobs, in addition to being at times physically violent, is never more elevated than harassment. It continually reminds the reader of the possibility—and, in other cases, actuality—of rape. Had this culminated in union between Flint and Jacobs, it would have been an extension of intergroup exploitation and subordination, a dystopian, thoroughly unromantic union, not an image of possible interracial reconciliation.

What about Jacobs's relation with Sands, the father of her children? It is certainly much better than her relations with other white men. But its problematic character is arguably even more damning for the celebration of interracial romance, since—unlike the relation with Flint—it might in principle have been romantic.[3] Indeed, the story of Jacobs and Sands is reminiscent of the first story in Lydia Maria Child's "The Quadroons." However, in that case, one feels that there was a genuine bond between Rosalie and Edward. The tragic outcome of Child's story was the result of social circumstances harming what should have been an enduring and mutually fulfilling relationship. Even in "The Quadroons," the interracial romance is not in the end a literal or metaphorical solution to racial opposition. However, it is a sign that people can overcome identity-group conflict—if the social conditions are altered to allow that.

In any case, Jacobs's relation with Sands is much more problematic than that between Rosalie and Edward. Sands is kind to Linda at the start, and he never treats her solely as a means to his own pleasure. Rather, he has at least some consideration for her needs and interests. Moreover, he helps Jacobs protect her children. He behaves far more humanely than the great majority of men in the slave states are likely to have behaved. But he never really reaches the level of what we—or antislavery activists at the time—would consider basic decency. It may be that Sands was about as moral and beneficent a white lover as was possible at that time and place. But, if so, it only shows all the more forcefully that, in Jacobs's view, interracial union is not a solution or even a valuable model.

Moreover, on the black slave's side this relation is perhaps even less a matter of attachment than it is on the white free man's side. Jacobs explains her response to Sands as in part narcissistic. Being "an object of interest to a man who is not married, and who is not her master, is agreeable to the pride and feelings of a slave, if her miserable situation has left her any pride or sentiment" (2016: 48). Even more significantly, when entering into a relationship with Sands she does not find herself swept off her feet with unspeakable delight at his presence. Rather, "revenge, and calculations of interest, were added to flattered vanity and sincere gratitude for kindness" (48). For Jacobs, Sands was principally a means. Their affair served to protect her to some degree against Flint and to wound Flint's pride. One can readily sympathize with such motives, given the haughty superiority that characterized Flint's and other white people's responses to African Americans. But such motives are hardly ideal or genuinely liberating. In short, it was a union of convenience. Its utilitarian nature is brought out nicely when Flint asks Jacobs "Do you love him?" and she explains that "I am thankful that I do not despise him" (51–52); she is basically satisfied with the bond only because it would have been difficult to enter into such a potentially useful sort of intimacy had she felt disgusted by Sands.

In contrast with interracial romance, Jacobs does allow some place for intraracial romantic love. It is, for her, the genuine and appropriate sort of love. Thus, she refers to her one true beloved—a free African American—explaining that "we are both of the negro race. It is right and honorable for us to love each other" (34). I do not know whether or not Jacobs intended this, but the phrasing certainly seems to imply that love between the "negro race" and the white or Caucasian race would not be "right and honorable." In any case, when asked by Flint if she loves this man (34)—who is, again, "colored"—she answers, simply "Yes, sir," a response quite different from the one she gives to his question about Sands.

While Jacobs's business-like relation with Sands is disappointing, this romance with the "colored carpenter" is tragic. Jacobs "loved him with all the ardor of a young girl's first love." But she "was a slave" and, as such, "the laws gave no sanction to the marriage" (33). Moreover, Flint refuses to sell Jacobs to this man, so that he could emancipate and marry her. Here, it is not the feelings of the lovers that are perverted by slavery, but the natural course of the relationship that is made tragic. Treating her beloved as an end in himself—as one would expect from their deep attachment bond—she urges him to leave the South, "to go to the Free States, where his tongue would not be tied, and where his intelligence would be of more avail to him." After he leaves, she feels "lonely and desolate" (36).

I have no doubt that this was an entirely sincere expression of her and her lover's pain. But, as such, it is also a fine example of Jacobs's ability to cultivate a reader's compassion by reference to suffering that is both a matter of attachment and of ethical feeling. Jacobs has made an ethical choice to sacrifice her happiness for the increased well-being of her beloved. Thus, the reader should not only recognize the depth of her attachment bond and therefore sympathize with her pain, but he or she should also admire the selflessness of the decision that has so intensified that pain.

The centrality of attachment

None of this is to say that all hope is lost for Jacobs or other slaves. Hope, however, does not come from romantic love. It comes from less passionate but more consistently ethical feelings that are part of romantic love—feelings of attachment. Moreover, for Jacobs these feelings of attachment—particularly maternal feelings between women—define a prototype for the reconciliation of racial antagonisms. It is not, then, interracial heterosexuality but interracial homosociality that is both the literal means and symbolic image of interracial union.

Trust is closely related to attachment (e.g., both involve oxytocin; see Oatley et al. 2007: 161–162). It is perhaps unsurprising, then, that the failures of interracial attachment bonding in Jacobs's narrative are paralleled by a loss of trust. Jacobs shows herself to have been deeply distrustful of European Americans. After her flight to the North, she finds herself alone and deeply insecure. In consequence, "I longed for some one to confide in; but I had been so deceived by white people, that I had lost all confidence in them" (2016: 143). She explains that the feeling of distrust is not idiosyncratic to her, but that it is the usual experience; anyone who "had ever been a slave" knew "how difficult it was to trust a white man" (134).

What not only gives her trust in some European Americans, but makes it possible to survive, is the warm affection of maternal women—or, sometimes, her own maternal feelings for children. In either case, Jacobs stresses women's attachment bonds as the exemplars of interracial unity and indeed a prominent means to social integration. Such interracial bonding is not confined to the free states. Early in the memoir, Jacobs recounts how her grandmother is to be sold after all her dutiful service. But when she is on the auction block, "a feeble voice said, 'Fifty dollars.' It came from a maiden lady, seventy years old, the sister of my grandmother's deceased mistress." Acting from friendly attachment and associated ethical and empathic feeling, "she gave the old servant her freedom" (15). This woman shared with Jacobs's grandmother a deep bond of friendship and "love" (76), which was expressed in their affectionate meetings in which they would sometimes grow teary in reminiscing together. This "good old lady ... paid fifty dollars for my grandmother, for the purpose of making her free, when she stood on the auction block. My grandmother loved this old lady, whom we all called Miss Fanny" (76). This case makes clear that such bonds not only represent interracial reconciliation, they also contribute literally and directly to that reconciliation, as Miss Fanny manages the emancipation of her friend.

Jacobs too finds an attachment bond and a great helper in a white woman, Mrs. Bruce, whose kindness contributed to "thawing my chilled heart" (143). Significantly, it was not just the friendship with Mrs. Bruce that had this emotionally reviving effect. It was also Jacobs's own maternal feelings, which were inspired by "the smiles of her lovely babe" (143) or, as she puts it later, "Mary, the darling little babe ... thawed my heart, when it was freezing into a cheerless distrust of all my fellow-beings" (161). Mrs. Bruce was "an excellent friend" whose "sympathizing voice" cheered and comforted Jacobs, a friend whose capacity to help and encourage Jacobs was presumably related to her being "a tender mother" (155).

Jacobs is fortunate that, when Mrs. Bruce dies and Mr. Bruce remarries, his second wife takes up the role of Jacobs's close friend and in effect repeats the benevolent act of Miss Fanny with respect to Jacobs's grandmother. Specifically, the second Mrs. Bruce determines to purchase Jacobs's freedom, showing again how liberatory social action may derive from an attachment bond. Jacobs resists, in part for reasons of moral principle. As she explains, "the more my mind had become enlightened, the more difficult it was for me to consider myself an article of property; and to pay money to those who had so grievously oppressed me seemed like taking from my sufferings the glory of triumph" (168). Mrs. Bruce goes ahead and buys Jacobs's emancipation anyway, then contacts Jacobs, informing her that she no longer needs to hide, but can "come home" (168). Of course, "home," here, does not mean the South. It means the place where she is loved, especially by Mrs. Bruce. Finally, "when I reached home, the arms of my benefactress were thrown round me, and our tears mingled" (168). Jacobs and Mrs. Bruce weep in each other's arms like lovers reunited after a long separation, or like Miss Fanny and Jacobs's grandmother, whose "spectacles would get dim with tears" (76).

This homosocial attachment bond between women takes up the role played by romantic love in the works of other writers seeking to overcome racial division. Jacobs writes: "Reader, my story ends with freedom; not in the usual way, with marriage" (170). But the freedom is the result of something that is akin to marriage in being an enduring attachment, if one unaffected by the potentially selfish interests of sexual desire, with their possibilities for using others as mere means, rather than treating them as ends in themselves.[4]

A note on emplotment

In connection with the preceding points, it is worth noting that the invocation of interracial love—whether romance or friendship—is commonly connected with emplotment patterns, recurring structures in the organization of stories (see Hogan 2003 and 2011a). In other work, I have argued that a few narrative structures have unusual prominence across cultures. These include romantic stories (in which two people fall in love and struggle against social obstacles to be united), heroic stories (of conflict between national enemies, and of conflict regarding the authority structure within the home society), family separation stories (in which parents and children are separated and seek to be reunited), and so on. Long, complex narratives such as novels commonly have a number of plotlines of different sorts, though many such works maintain a dominant emplotment structure, which may repeat across different storylines. Often, works with a prominent, romantic story trajectory, such as *The Last of the Mohicans* and "The Quadroons," take up interracial romantic love as the prime exemplar of interracial reconciliation. Indeed, I would even say that this is the case for the first part of *Moby Dick*, though the romantic structure is not as straightforward in that work and it is displaced after Ishmael and Queequeg board the ship. In contrast, works such as *Uncle Tom's Cabin* and *Incidents in the Life of a Slave Girl* draw more on family separation and reunion structures. This is consistent with their stress on attachment bonding and the connection between women's friendship and maternal feeling.

These correlations suggest that, in thinking about the reconciliation of antagonistic identity groups, we draw on different types of emotional relations—romantic love, nonsexual attachment bonds, admirable physical courage (roughly what we find in part of Douglass), and so on. In addition, when writing stories about such reconciliation and national unity, we are likely to draw on the cross-culturally prominent narrative structures. Finally, these narrative structures tend to be coordinated with particular, related types of emotion. The result is the development of genre-like patterns in treatments of racial and other subnational divisions in the United States, with some treatments following a romantic storyline, others a familial separation narrative, and still others a heroic structure.

Where is nationalism here?

But the present study is not a broad treatment of interracial reconciliation or the pursuit of justice for oppressed groups. It is particularly concerned with a more specific topic—the ways in which authors address a few key types of subnational division in relation to an encompassing, national identity, whether it is a matter of establishing that identity as a goal, invoking it as a means to other ends, or repudiating it. This leads us to the question of whether there is any such national concern in Jacobs's book.

In fact, there are strong suggestions of opposition to U.S. nationalism in the memoir, to the extent that it seems to take us back to the loyalism of the Revolutionary War period. Indeed, there are some hints of a connection with that period in the book. Most significantly, Jacobs's maternal grandmother "was the daughter of a planter in South Carolina, who, at his death, left her mother and his three children free, with money to go to St. Augustine, where they had relatives. It was during the Revolutionary War; and they were captured on their passage, carried back, and sold to different purchasers" (Jacobs 2016: 9). Jacobs does not make it entirely clear who did the capturing and selling. However, the British forces did at times appeal to slaves, as when Lord Dunmore "promised freedom to Virginia slaves who joined his forces," while George Washington rejected parallel requests from slaves (Zinn 2015: 82). This general point would encourage us to understand that the re-enslavement of Jacobs's grandmother was the fault of the colonists, rather than the English. Jean Yellin (2004: 4) confirms this, explaining that Jacobs's grandmother's family was in fact freed "under British protection," but "captured by Americans, separated, and sold."

We find other suggestions of distaste for national identification elsewhere, for example in Jacobs's comments on an obituary for her Uncle Phillip at the end of the novel. The obituary is celebratory in a way that is cruelly ironic, given the conditions of his life and the lives of his family members. Jacobs writes: "Now that death has laid him low, they call him a good man and a useful citizen." She comments particularly on the last word—"so they called a colored man a citizen!"—and concludes that these are "strange words" (2016: 170).

A more striking case comes with Mr. Thorne, a white man who happens to come upon Jacobs after she has escaped to the North. He says that he will not betray her (151). Despite this, he contacts Dr. Flint, informing him of Jacobs's whereabouts, telling him that "she can be taken very easily" and avowing that "there are enough of us here to swear to her identity as your property." Thorne is undoubtedly interested in pecuniary compensation for this intelligence. But he justifies his behavior in nationalist terms. He helps to arrange the abduction of a young woman, he writes, because "I am a patriot, a lover of my country, and I do this as an act of justice to the laws" (152). From Jacobs's point of view, and that of many of her readers, there could be few criticisms of American nationalism that would be more withering than this association of legally sanctioned inhumanity with patriotism.

It is presumably not merely a biographical accident that Jacobs turns from this (admittedly local) criticism of American identity to a celebration of English identity. Jacobs had found herself disappointed in the racism of the North. Now, she travels to

England with the Bruce family. In London, she explains: "For the first time in my life I was in a place where I was treated according to my deportment, without reference to my complexion. I felt as if a great millstone had been lifted from my breast" (155). That millstone was American racism, including that of the North. Despite the American myth that it is "the land of the free" (in the words of our national anthem), it is only upon leaving the United States that Jacobs can experience "for the first time … the delightful consciousness of pure, unadulterated freedom" (155). This celebration of the former colonial nation—reminiscent of that of Rip van Winkle (Chapter 1)—does not dissipate, but continues for her entire stay. "I remained abroad ten months," she explains, and "during all that time, I never saw the slightest symptom of prejudice against color."[5] In fact, her experience was so different in England, so natural, so much like what home should be, that she "entirely forgot" such prejudice against color "till the time came for us to return to America" (156). In contrast with patriotic love of one's country, she feels dread. As she poignantly writes, "it is a sad feeling to be afraid of one's native country" (157).

For Jacobs, it is as if the family separation and reunion narrative can never be fully resolved in the United States. Home, thus the place where she could in principle have a genuine family, could be in England, but not its pervasively racist former colony. This is connected with the fact that the first Mrs. Bruce, the friend who made it possible for her to feel trust again, the one whose infant daughter thawed her heart, was English; indeed, the trip to England is to visit Mrs. Bruce's family (155).

Conclusion

Like the other authors we have considered, Harriet Jacobs seeks to cultivate compassion for the condition of disenfranchised people, in this case African Americans, particularly slave women. Sensitive to the possibly demeaning quality of pity, she qualifies her representation of slavery in order to foster respect (and self-respect) for African Americans. In keeping with this, she stresses two sorts of suffering, both of which emphasize the humanity of African Americans and challenge white supremacism. Like Stowe, she emphasizes suffering due to attachment bonds. In keeping with this, her dominant emplotment structure is that of family separation and reunion. In addition to the pain of attachment loss, Jacobs develops the moral suffering of slaves, who are put in situations where their ability to act according to ethical principles is severely compromised; in the case of women slaves, their chastity is particularly threatened.

Jacobs uses a number of standard techniques to forward her political goals. These include stereotype reversal (shifting a demeaning stereotype from the dominated group to the dominant group), the reversal of outgroup models (e.g., assimilation to devils), and appeal to the religious and moral principles of the dominant group. However, her use of romantic love is skeptical. Interracial union is often a matter of coercion and exploitation. Even in the best cases, it is tenuous and half-hearted. A white may be a "lover," rather than a rapist, but even then he does not live up to the most minimal standards of humane, ethical behavior. This is principally because, as in the case of the slave, the legal, political, and economic situation so deeply and pervasively biases and distorts the relations between whites and blacks. That situation also harms intraracial romantic love, which Jacobs seems to see as more "right and honorable" (34) than interracial union. In this case, however, the harm occurs in dooming genuine love to tragedy, not in substituting exploitation for love (as seems to happen with even the best interracial unions).

Instead of romantic love (and the associated romantic emplotment), Jacobs foregrounds nonsexual attachment bonds, in keeping with her dominant emplotment structure of family separation and reunion. The quality of feeling here is maternal, but it manifests itself in close friendship. In consequence, Jacobs's autobiography presents interracial attachment bonding between women as both the paradigmatic model for interracial reconciliation and an important literal means for achieving liberation and unity.

A final difference between Jacobs and many other writers is that the racial unity she gestures toward does not serve U.S. national interests. American nationalism is too profoundly compromised by the institution of slavery in the South, the complicity with slavery in the North, and the pervasive racism that rationalizes both the institution and the complicity. Indeed, Jacobs suggests that U.S. patriotism may be too intertwined with racism to separate the two. She even appears to hearken back to the sort of sympathy with British loyalism with which we began in our consideration of Washington Irving. It is as if, for Jacobs, the independent United States can never really be home to African Americans and their subnational alienation might only be overcome in a transnational context.

Notes

1 Quite rightly, this has been a prominent concern in critical discussions of the book. It is sometimes combined with the other main critical concern, the veracity of the autobiography (see, for example, Foreman 1996 for such a combination). Veracity, and the related issue of historical representativeness, are of course significant issues in the treatment of slave narratives (see, for example, the selections treating "The Slave Narratives as History" in Davis and Gates 1985: 35–146). I entirely agree that this is an important topic. However, my focus is on the ways in which these works seek to treat American identity and subnational divisions. Thus, I am concerned with their thematic development, whether or not it is based on literally true autobiographical facts. (This is, of course, why I am considering fiction as well as nonfiction.)
2 Indeed, the situation was even worse than this implies. As Greg Grandin (2019: 74) notes, some slave-owners acknowledged "the regime of sexual terror enslaved women lived under" but claimed that raping black women helped to prevent men from threatening the chastity of white women; thus, the sexual assault of slaves was good in "helping to redirect the lust of white men away from white women" (2019: 73).
3 Lauren Berlant (1995: 466) points out that Sands has "isolated" moments of "real empathy for Jacobs"; however, these moments are not sustained, in part because Sands appears impervious to self-criticism, which is particularly consequential in a context where socially pervasive racism inhibits and distorts attachment bonds.
4 I obviously take a more positive view of these friendships than some critics. Advocates of a more negative construal sometimes draw on Jacobs's real-life relationships (rather than the friendships as presented in the memoir). When such critics do focus on the memoir, their negative interpretation is not, in my view, plausible. For example, Deborah Garfield refers to a passage in which Jacobs explains that "God so orders circumstances as to keep me with my friend Mrs. Bruce. Love, duty, gratitude, also bind me to her side" (Jacobs

2016: 170). Garfield (1996: 282) comments that the words "orders," "keep," and "bind" suggest "unwanted bondage." But "orders" here means "arranges" (not "commands"); "keep" means merely "sustain a particular condition" (not "prevent"); and "bind" points toward emotional bonding (not bondage).

5 Here, as elsewhere, however, repudiation of ingroup versus outgroup divisions is fragile, and divisive identity categories can easily be revived. In Yellin's account, Jacobs discovered this on her last trip to England, years after the publication of *Incidents in the Life of a Slave Girl* (see Yellin 2004: 213–214). Such political and social attitudes are much more changeable than we often believe, much more contextual and much less a matter of anything like cultural fixity—a point that is distressing when applied to antiracist attitudes (which may too easily change for the worse), but hopeful when applied to racist attitudes (which then appear less recalcitrant to amelioration).

7

FREDERICK DOUGLASS, MANHOOD, AND THE LOST HOME

Needless to say, Frederick Douglass, an escaped slave, was deeply committed to the abolition of slavery. Moreover, this was clearly an end in itself, independent of any considerations of national identity or identification. However, though it may not be obvious initially—and is certainly not obvious in the first of Douglass's three autobiographies—Douglass's opposition to slavery does connect with a deep patriotism, a genuine emotional commitment to a national identity. This becomes particularly clear in his final autobiography, *Life and Times of Frederick Douglass* (1855; hereafter LTFD).

In making his case against slavery, Douglass adopts the usual techniques that we have explored in other authors. For example, he seeks to foster a shift in perspective on the part of readers, particularly white readers. In some cases, he does this explicitly, as when (in *Narrative of the Life of Frederick Douglass* [1845; hereafter NLFD]), he calls on the reader to "imagine himself … a fugitive slave in a strange land—a land given up to be the hunting-ground for slaveholders—whose inhabitants are legalized kidnappers," and so on. In the remainder of this passage, Douglass carefully guides the imagination of the reader so that he or she may "know how to sympathize with" a "whip-scarred fugitive slave" (Douglass 2017: 1220).

I say "particularly white readers" because the implied reader of Douglass's books is not necessarily European. One difference between Douglass and most of the authors we have been considering is that Douglass is much more keenly aware of his non-white readership. Though he presumably imagined African Americans as a minority—probably even a small minority—of his readers, he clearly viewed them as important readers. He cared about his African American audience. This is particularly clear in LTFD. Toward the end of that volume, he addresses his white audience on just this topic, writing: "If I have pushed my example too prominently for the good taste of my Caucasian readers I beg them to remember that I have written in part for the encouragement of a class whose aspirations need the stimulus of success"

(Douglass 2012b). Here, Douglass is saying that white readers may find his story boastful, focusing too much on what he has achieved and what honors he has received. Personally, I do not find Douglass's self-presentation any more self-congratulatory than any other autobiography, perhaps even less so. But the key point is that he did not humbly downplay his successes, precisely because it was crucial for him to present African American readers with an example that would stand against the despair that is otherwise all too likely to affect them when faced with the enormous social obstacles in their path. At least in this respect, Douglass is saying that his African American readership is more important to him than his European American readership. The latter may have liked Douglass better if he had been more self-critical, thus more in line with the usual (prudent) self-presentation of a slave. But such a self-presentation would only have disheartened his African American readers.

This difference in simulated readership may partially account for another somewhat distinctive aspect of Douglass's autobiographies. In reading Douglass's account of his life, it is clear that—unlike Harriet Beecher Stowe (Chapter 5) or even Harriet Jacobs (Chapter 6)—he does not dwell on pathos. He does at times appeal to the reader's empathy (as in the passage just cited). But his primary focus is on cultivating respect (from non-Africans) and thus self-respect (from Africans). Even when appealing to empathy, his treatment of the slaves' condition is regularly tempered by a concern to keep them from being viewed as helpless victims.

I say that this is in part a matter of readership because it seems to me that it does not convey the whole of Douglass's own attitude. Indeed, I do not believe it conveys what is most fundamental to Douglass himself. I am not saying that Douglass is dishonest here. In fact, I suspect that Douglass's "impression management" or "self-presentation" (see Schlenker 2012) is aimed as much at himself as it is at others. In other words, I suspect that Douglass does not want to see himself as lacking agency any more than he wants others to see him as such. Indeed, he himself is one of the readers who could fall victim to despair, thus one of the readers whom he is seeking to encourage and sustain.

In discussing Douglass, I will not follow the usual format of the preceding chapters (though of course I will take up many of the same topics). Rather, I will focus on the duality in his feelings, aims, techniques, and so on. Specifically, I will begin with the obvious Frederick Douglass, the Frederick Douglass that we sense directly on reading NLFD or LTFD. From there, I will turn to what I take to be the more fundamental but more concealed Frederick Douglass, a Frederick Douglass who, despite his truly astonishing physical and moral courage—which is real and evident—is yet arguably more deeply vulnerable than any of the authors we have considered thus far. If we were to put the idea in a pop-psych idiom, we might say that the tough, independent Frederick Douglass conceals a wounded child.[1] This certainly oversimplifies the point, but it is not entirely inaccurate. What is important here is that both the tough, independent adult and the wounded child bear an important relation to Douglass's conception of himself as an American.

In the rest of the chapter, I will make reference to NLFD and Douglass's second autobiography, *My Bondage, My Freedom* (1855; hereafter MBMF). However, I will focus mainly on the final autobiography, LTFD. This is due principally to the fact that LTFD is the most encompassing work, covering more of Douglass's life than the others.[2] As such, it also includes more explicit and elaborated treatments of Douglass's relation to U.S. national identity. This choice does have the slight disadvantage that it takes up a post–Civil War text, though I have otherwise limited the analyses to pre–Civil War works. However, Douglass is an author who grew to maturity and achieved literary fame prior to that war. Moreover, his patriotism is consistent with the more general optimism that directly followed the Union victory, but that dissipated in later decades.

The public face of Frederick Douglass

This section outlines some of the main features of Frederick Douglass's self-presentation, the way he portrayed himself, not only to others, but I imagine to himself as well. Again, I am in no way suggesting that this self-presentation is false. My contention is merely that it is incomplete, specifically in making his emotional life much more homogenous than it actually was. This sort of incompleteness is not by any means unique to Douglass; in some degree, it probably characterizes all of us. Indeed, Douglass may be unusual in the extent to which his self-presentation remains true even when we recognize the more covert aspects of his mental life. For example, Douglass presents himself as physically courageous, determined, and strong in the face of oppression, cruelty, and disdain. This is true and our sense of its truth is, if anything, enhanced when we see a largely unacknowledged, but deep vulnerability in Douglass's emotional life.

Anyone's self-presentation may be understood to include a range of parameters that have predominant values. For example, self-presentation commonly involves a particular emphasis on a limited number of emotions. We all experience all emotions. But we may think of ourselves as being particularly prone to one or another (e.g., "I'm a lover, not a fighter," suggests a predominant propensity toward attachment feelings rather than anger). In his autobiographies, Douglass stresses pride—not in the sense of arrogant superiority, but in the sense of appropriate self-respect. Many antislavery writers stress the suffering of slaves in order to foster compassion. Douglass certainly has moments when he depicts the pain of slavery. But he is particularly distrustful of pity. Moreover, he was not writing for a uniformly white readership. There was little reason to promote pity among blacks, especially self-pity. What is more important, Douglass presumably did not wish to see himself as a pathetic victim—and he was not a pathetic victim. Again, he showed remarkable physical and moral courage. In keeping with this, he wished to see himself as standing up against adversity, therefore as courageous. Thus, the predominant emotions that he develops as driving his own life are pride or self-respect with courage entering when his dignity was threatened (e.g., in his physical battle with the slave-"breaker," Covey). Correlatively, he sought to cultivate respect in white readers and self-respect in black readers. As to the former, for example, he pointed in LTFD to "the low estimate everywhere in that country placed upon the negro as a man: that because of his assumed natural inferiority, people reconciled themselves to his enslavement and oppression, as being inevitable if not desirable" (Douglass 2012b). He went on to explain that "the grand thing to be done, therefore, was to change this estimation, by disproving his inferiority and demonstrating his capacity for a more exalted civilization than slavery and prejudice had assigned him."

Predominant emotions tend to go along with a broad range of other tendencies. Put differently, once the "parameter" for predominant emotion is set, a number of other parameters tend to assume default values. For example, Douglass's primary attitude toward authority was not one of, say, deference, awe, or fear. His attitude toward authority did of course vary with the nature of the authority itself. But a recurring pattern in his works reveals a skepticism about hierarchies and a defiant affirmation of independence or autonomy. He does not grant any superiority or justification to hierarchies of authority as such. The point is perhaps most obvious in his confrontation in NLFD with the slave-"breaker," Covey, with whom he engaged in a physical fight (see Douglass 2017: 1203–1204). But his advocacy of defiance was much more general. Thus, in LTFD he maintains that "the way to break down an unreasonable custom, is to contradict it in practice." A good example is his argument about the Fugitive Slave Act. He does not view the relative failure of the act as the result of compassion or empathy. Rather, "the thing which more than all else destroyed the fugitive slave law was the resistance made to it by the fugitives themselves" (2012b).

As to independence, Douglass maintained in LTFD that "no man can be truly free whose liberty is dependent upon the thought, feeling, and action of others; and who has himself no means in his own hands for guarding, protecting, defending, and maintaining that liberty" (2012b). This is, of course, bound up with the defiance of authority. Indeed, as Douglass's disagreements with President Abraham Lincoln and others attest, he was insistent on asserting his independence even when he admired an authority figure and generally accepted that authority. This is also what one might expect from his stress on self-respect. Consistent with both, it is unsurprising that "Douglass's most frequently delivered lecture was titled 'Self-Made Men'" (Foner 2018: 26).

Just as we often have some dominant attitude or concern with regard to "vertical" relationships (i.e., relationships in a social hierarchy), we often have some dominant attitude or concern characterizing our "horizontal" relationships (i.e., relationships with equals). While some writers stress romantic relations, Douglass stresses male bonding. Indeed, romantic relationships are conspicuous by their absence in Douglass's autobiographies, where his wife barely gets mentioned. In contrast, he emphasizes the importance of his close connection with the white boys in Baltimore (see Douglass 2017: 1187–1188) and with the fellow slaves with whom he planned to escape. Indeed, Douglass rarely shows any emotional dependency—except in relation to his male friends. For example, in NLFD he explains that, when their plan to escape was revealed, the main worry that haunted him and his comrades was not, say, the physical suffering of torture, but the emotional suffering of separation from one another (2017: 1212).

Unsurprisingly, the preceding points are linked with a strong gender identification as male or masculine. Douglass is deeply concerned with the ways in which slavery is a system that deprives African American men of their manhood.[3] In NLFD, he explains that he urged fellow slaves to make an effort at escape on the grounds that not to do so would show a "want of manhood" (2017: 1209). Similarly, in LTFD he treats the "manly endeavor to secure my freedom" (2012b) and celebrates one result of a "terrible battle" in the Civil War—that it showed "the quality of negro manhood." Denial of manhood to African American men is certainly one issue in slavery. But perhaps a more obvious and certainly more fundamental issue is the denial of humanity to both African American men and women. This seems to be the crucial problem, not the loss of specific prerogatives associated with gender norms. Douglass was undoubtedly sensitive to the plight of African American women—and, indeed, all women. He was, in fact, one of the earliest male supporters of women's rights and was an articulate and committed speaker on that topic (see Levine 2017: 1163). Moreover, he did not fail to recognize and criticize the more general dehumanization of Africans—male and female—through the ideology and practice of slavery. However, he emphasized the loss of manhood and the importance of African American men reaffirming their manhood.[4]

Finally, in keeping with these points, the dominant narrative structure in Douglass's writing tends to be heroic.[5] The (cross-culturally recurring) heroic genre has two components—a usurpation sequence and an invasion sequence.[6] In the usurpation sequence, the legitimate organization of society is overturned by the establishment of an unjust hierarchy, which the hero opposes, usually with martial force. In the invasion sequence, an enemy occupies the land of the ingroup and must be dislodged by the hero and the people. Douglass tends to see individual slaveholding in terms of usurpation of authority, the heroic struggle against such usurpation, and (ideally) the restoration of legitimate authority, in keeping with the usurpation sequence of the heroic genre. Once he escapes to the North, he comes to view the conflict over the extension of slavery implicitly in terms of a heroic struggle against invasion.

Here, it may seem as if Douglass is simply describing things the way they are. But, in fact, there are many different ways of emploting individual slaveholding or the territorial extension of slavery. For example, Lydia Maria Child ("The Quadroons") emplots individual slaveholding principally in relation to the romantic story structure (at least before Rosalie's death), while Stowe (*Uncle Tom's Cabin*) does so principally in relation to the family separation-and-reunion genre; Jacobs too (*Life of a Slave Girl*) stresses the family narrative, as we have seen. There is a small exception to this tendency in Stowe's treatment of George Harris, who may have been in part modeled on Douglass (see Foster 1954: 33–34). The point is consistent with the way that characters in these works tend not to confront the cruelty of slavery, but to flee or hide from it (as when Jacobs or Cassy and Emmeline conceal themselves from their owners); the way that they tend to have a more traditionally "feminine" gender identification (presumably related to the authors being women); the way that they often stress female friendship rather than male bonding; and their tendency to emphasize the cultivation of empathy and compassion rather than respect and self-respect, except specifically in relation to moral excellence, especially moral excellence bearing on putatively feminine virtues.

Douglass's inclination toward heroic emplotment is clearest in his affinity for literal military action. This is most obvious in his support and recruitment work for the Union in the Civil War, as shown for example in his article "*Men of Color, to*

Arms" (1863). It is also evident in his sympathy for the militant abolitionist John Brown. As Douglass explains in LTFD, Brown "was not averse to the shedding of blood, and thought the practice of carrying arms would be a good one for the colored people to adopt, as it would give them a sense of their manhood" (2012b), the last point being obviously consistent with Douglass's gender identification. Douglass further explains Brown's views in such a way as to link them with his own emphasis on defiance and independence, writing that "no people he said could have self-respect, or be respected, who would not fight for their freedom." Douglass himself publicly expressed the view "that slavery could only be destroyed by blood-shed." One important aspect of Douglass's affinity for Brown concerns the slavery policies for new states. Douglass (quite reasonably) construed this in a sort of invasion scenario (LTFD): "The border ruffians from Missouri had openly declared their purpose not only to make Kansas a slave state, but that they would make it impossible for free-state men to live there. They burned their towns, burned their farm-houses, and by assassination spread terror among them until many of the free-state settlers were compelled to escape for their lives" (2012b). Though he opposed the Harper's Ferry scheme on tactical grounds, he worked with Brown "to set ... in operation" some plans for which "money and men, arms and ammunition ... were needed."

Another Frederick Douglass

Again, Douglass's self-presentation is not a misrepresentation. But it is also incomplete. Indeed, it seems likely that a great deal of the explicit, visible Frederick Douglass results from his response to the experiences and inclinations that were earlier and deeper parts of his personal identity. The most important of these is the dominant complex of emotions. Again, overtly, Douglass most strongly repudiates social disrespect and the associated racial shame, seeking to foster pride or self-respect. But, covertly, there is at least some reason to believe that the most emotionally hurtful experience he had was that of attachment deprivation and that the most important or cherished emotion for him was secure attachment. In connection with this, I see the most fundamental relationship for Douglass being the relationship with mother, father, and home—not so much his biological mother and father or the place where he grew up, but the people and places that he sought out in later life as substitutes for the early loss of a mother, a father, and a home place. It follows that his most important relation with authority was a longing for parental love that would allow a sense of dependency in secure attachment. The problem was that secure attachment, and thereby a sense of dependency, presuppose trust. As Douglass is at pains to explain, everything about a slave's life drives him or her to distrust everyone, undermining almost every human relation (see 2017: 1220). The main exceptions to this, in Douglass's life, are the cases of bonding—the white boys in Baltimore or the fellow slaves with whom he plans his ill-fated escape; this enables the substitution of male bonding for the more profound desire for parental care. As all these points suggest, the most important underlying story prototype for Douglass was not heroic but familial—the prototype of family separation and reunion.[7]

I take it that this set of emotional inclinations, with its roots in early childhood, is largely pregender, thus not particularly male or masculine, and that this is part of the reason that Douglass was able to identify with women's struggles despite his explicit affirmations of manhood. After all, those affirmations, taken in isolation, might seem to represent emancipation from slavery as a goal that concerned only men, since presumably the denial of their own manhood is not what slave women found most galling about slavery.

Regarding his relations with his mother, Douglass explains in NLFD, with no evident emotion, that "I never saw my mother, to know her as such, more than four or five times in my life" (2017: 1171). Moreover, he treats his distress over not knowing his birthdate as if it were solely a matter of slave-owners not recording that date. The interests of slave-owners—and the ways in which they work to de-individuate slaves, through for example ignoring their particular birthdates—are clearly important both for slavery in general and for Douglass in particular. However, one learns one's birthday from one's parents, most obviously the mother, who was as involved in that birthday as the child. In this way, his "unhappiness" (1171) over having no knowledge of his birthday may suggest unhappiness over having no relation to a mother who might convey that knowledge.

In LTFD, Douglass is more willing to acknowledge his attachment loss. For example, he records an incident from his childhood when, by good fortune, his mother was able to rescue him from ill treatment. He explains that he was a "friendless and hungry boy" and in "extremest need" (2012b). In other words, he was defenseless child, lacking attachment bonds and (maternal) nurturance. But, in this one instance of good fortune he "found himself in the strong protecting arms his mother." This incident shows him what life should be like with a reliable and protective attachment relation. When he wakes up later, his strong, protecting mother is gone. He concludes: "To me it has ever been a grief that I knew my mother so little" (2012b). I take it that this enduring grief—a mourning of attachment loss—was one key source of his insistent striving for manly independence in later life.

Douglass predictably sought substitutes for his mother. Probably the most important substitute was Sophia Auld. When he first meets her in NLFD, he sees "what I had never seen before … a white face beaming with the most kindly emotions" (2017: 1184). It is, of course, significant that Sophia is white. Indeed, it is important that his primary mother substitute in the novel is European American, as it suggests one way in which racial oppositions may at times be resolved. But this is significant only because Sophia Auld is a mother who greets Douglass with a "beaming" face— the face with which a mother greets her child. Moreover, she soon takes on the parental role of teaching Douglass, in this case teaching him how to read and write.

Sophia Auld's maternal role in Douglass's imagination and memory is more explicit in the later autobiographies. In MBMF, he writes that, on the plantation, he had been treated as an animal. But with "'Miss Sopha,' as I used to call Mrs. Hugh Auld," he "was treated as a child now" (2012c). Indeed, he "soon learned to regard her as something more akin to a mother, than a slaveholding mistress." The bond was not ideal. But it was a bond of parent–child attachment, nurturance, and dependence.

Thus, Douglass writes that "if little Thomas was her son, and her most dearly beloved child, she, for a time, at least, made me something like his half-brother in her affections. If dear Tommy was exalted to a place on his mother's knee, 'Feddy' was honored by a place at his mother's side" (2012c). Even much later, when Douglass is attacked and injured by (white) fellow workers, Sophia Auld bandages his wounds herself, and Douglass explains that "no mother's hand could have been more tender than hers" (2012b).

But this maternal bond too, according to NLFD, is wrecked by slavery. Sophia Auld was initially "preserved from the blighting and dehumanizing effects of slavery" (2017: 1185). But as she accustomed herself to being a slaveholder and as her practical identity became increasingly integrated with the institution of slavery, "the fatal poison of irresponsible power … commenced its infernal work" (1185). Eventually, she too began to treat Douglass "as though I were a brute" (1187). Thus, slavery began his life by separating him from his biological mother, and then so corrupted his foster mother as to alienate her entirely, thereby intensifying his attachment insecurity and associated distrust.

The situation with Douglass's father is similar, though even less overt. In NLFD, he does not express much of any feeling about his father, even curiosity. As he puts it: "The opinion was … whispered that my master was my father." But, regarding this, he explains with seeming indifference, that "I know nothing" (2017: 1171). He does treat the topic of white masters fathering children with their slaves (1172), but shows little personal relation to the topic. Rather, he expresses the sort of condemnation that any of us might feel for the behavior of such fathers. When he goes on to treat his owner, he comments that he "was a cruel man" (1173). But, again, this does not appear to bear on feelings of attachment loss.

It is unsurprising that Douglass would have less emotional response to a father that he never experienced as a father than to a mother with whom he had at least moments of bonding security, however brief and infrequent. Even so, his relation to this father is not entirely absent. I take it to appear significantly in Douglass's relation to his last name, the name that, in America, typically comes from the father. Douglass begins with his mother's last name, Bailey. He discards this, opting first for "Stanley," then "Johnson," and finally "Douglass" (2017: 1221–1222). What I find striking about these names is that "Stanley" and "Douglass" are first names, while "Johnson" is a first name with the suffix "-son" added. He does not choose "Doe" or "Smith" or "Green" or any of the other countless possible names that are not (or do not include) given names. Why might this be? I take it to suggest that Douglass is in effect modeling his choice of a surname on the name of his probable father, the name he should have received had he been conceived and born in normal social conditions, which is to say, in conditions without slavery. That father's family name, according to NLFD, was "Anthony" (2017: 1173). In choosing first names—in one case, a first name to which "son" was added—Douglass is in effect choosing possibilities that are like his biological father's name, the name that should have marked him as his father's son.

Douglass did seek substitute fathers as well. But this search was more difficult. In part, the difficulty resulted from the social organization of society and the ways in which men could relate to other men. These relations were particularly inhibited across racial lines, an important factor, since Douglass's father was white while Douglass was socially classed as black (or "colored"). In addition, however, Douglass's search for a father substitute was inhibited by his own emotional background and experience. He had a real (if severely limited) emotional relation with his mother, but nothing of the sort with his father. For this reason, he seems to have tacitly imagined a father as a sort of mother with masculine characteristics.

Just as Sophia Auld is the most obvious mother substitute for Douglass, there is one apparent father substitute, which is developed in LTFD. And that is Abraham Lincoln, a "man," Douglass explains, "whom I could love, honor, and trust without reserve or doubt" (2012b). Of course, Douglass could be speaking hyperbolically here. But if we take him at his word, we find an expression of secure child–parent attachment. The attachment feeling is stated in the profession of "love," the security of that bond is found in the "trust," and the elevated—hence, parental—position of the target of his feeling appears through the word "honor." (The word may have seemed particularly appropriate to Douglass due to its use in the biblical commandment to "Honour thy father and thy mother" [Exodus 20:12, KJV].) In keeping with Douglass's own experience of attachment, he expresses his response to Lincoln in part by reference to mother–child relations. Thus, he characterizes Lincoln as having "the tenderness of motherhood," but also "the highest perfection of a genuine manhood" (2012b). As if Lincoln were literally a dear family member, Douglass explains that he keeps "his picture … before me in my study." When Lincoln is assassinated, Douglass says that the relation of Americans to Lincoln has made Africans and Europeans, not merely fellow countrymen, but "kin."

On the other hand, even then the kinship is imperfect. Just as "Feddy" was only a foster child to "Miss Sopha," so too Douglass does not feel that he has fully found his white father in Lincoln. Douglass addresses "my white fellow citizens," telling them that they "were the objects of [Lincoln's] deepest affection and his most earnest solicitude" and explaining that European Americans "are the children of Abraham Lincoln" (2012b). In contrast, African Americans, including Douglass himself, "are at best only his step-children; children by adoption." Given his life experiences, and given the nature of ingroup and outgroup definition in the United States at the time (and even now), it is hardly surprising that Douglass continued to feel attachment insecurity and associated distrust.

Frederick Douglass and attachment to the national home

For the purposes of the present study, the complex nature of Douglass's personal identity—the difference between his self-presentation and the vulnerabilities that this self-presentation passes over—is important for at least two reasons. First, as we have already seen, both bear on the interracial relations that defined Douglass's social attitudes and actions. He was, on the one hand, fiercely independent, defiant of (unmerited) authority, and deeply concerned with dignity, respect, and self-respect. But, at the same time, he appears to have no less deeply desired a relationship of trust and attachment in which he could be dependent and nurtured.

The other reason is that both his surface and underlying attitudes and propensities bear directly on his sense of himself as an American. In part, this connection operates through the close interrelation between person attachment and place attachment.[8] In NLFD, as I have noted, Douglass writes as if the deprivation of person attachments to mother and father had few emotional consequences for him. Similarly, he comments with apparent indifference that "the ties that ordinarily bind children to their homes were all suspended in my case" (2017: 1183). But in LTFD, he maintains that a relation to a home place—both individual and national—is important. "No people," he writes, "ever did much for themselves or for the world without the sense and inspiration of native land, of a fixed home, of familiar neighborhood and common associations" (2012b). Thus, we might infer that Douglass was no more indifferent to his lack of secure and enabling place attachment (home) than he was to his lack of secure and supportive person attachment (parents).

Unsurprisingly, in his pre–Civil War writing he maintains that he has just as little a bond to a national home as to a familial home. In LTFD, Douglass quotes a letter he wrote in 1846, in which he asserted that "as to nation, I belong to none" (2012b). In the letter, he goes on to explain that "I have no protection at home … . The land of my birth welcomes me to her shores only as a slave." With his references to "home" and to his "birth," Douglass suggests that he might have had an attachment relation with the United States, but slavery foreclosed that bond, just as it foreclosed bonds with his parents. Moreover, Douglass goes on to say that his antipathy to the United States is so absolute that he now finds it impossible to imagine ever feeling attachment to that nation. Specifically, he explains that "if ever I had any patriotism, or any capacity for the feeling, it was whipped out of me long since by the lash of the American soul-drivers" (2012b).

And yet, right after saying that he can no longer experience patriotic feeling, he engages in a brief panegyric on the aesthetic qualities of the national place. Such praise for the natural beauty of the nation is an almost invariable characteristic of nationalist poetry and may be seen in many national anthems. Thus, also in 1846, he writes: "In thinking of America, I sometimes find myself admiring her bright blue sky, her grand old woods, her fertile fields, her beautiful rivers, her mighty lakes, and star-crowned mountains." He, then, does experience attachment to the nation as a geographical place. But that is soon contradicted by other feelings—especially pride and self-esteem. He explains: "But my rapture is soon checked—my joy is soon turned to mourning. When I remember that all is cursed with the infernal spirit of slaveholding" (2012b).

What I find most striking in Douglass's pre–Civil War discussions of national identification is that, far from being content with a repudiation of America, due to slavery, Douglass gives us hints that he has a deep longing for an attachment bond with the United States and that his anger is directed not only at slavery but at the, so to speak, broad range of bad parenting by the United States, bad parenting that includes not only slaveholders, but also apparently the large majority of non-slaveholding whites as well.

Perhaps the most striking case of Douglass's longing for this attachment bond with the United States is to be found in a brief but deeply revealing statement in which he takes up the role of a child to the United States. Specifically, again in 1846 (qtd. in LTFD),

Douglass bitterly complains that "America will not allow her children to love her" (2012b). The point could not be clearer: Douglass desires to form a bond of patriotic love with the United States. But slavery prevents that. In keeping with this, Douglass opposes the Liberia scheme, affirming that African Americans have a genuine "love of country" and suggesting the usual sort of attachment to one's home when he notes (of course, rightly) that "we have grown up with this republic" (2012b). Moreover, he himself feels an incommunicable depth of pain—technically separation anxiety—when "compelled to leave his home and country and go into … banishment."

As I have noted above, Douglass found himself partial substitutes for his parents. But the substitutes were imperfect. Even at the best of times, Douglass was only a foster child to Sophia Auld. Similarly, he and his fellow African Americans are only "stepchildren" to Abraham Lincoln. Douglass takes up the same sort of family model again during the transition period after the Civil War but before former slaves have been enfranchised by the thirteenth, fourteenth, and fifteenth amendments. Now, he applies the model to the nation as a whole, writing in LTFD that "I was the ugly and deformed child of the family, and to be kept out of sight as much as possible while there was company in the house" (2012b).[9]

The preceding quotations already indicate a partial acceptance of national identification on Douglass's part. That acceptance develops from an ambivalent longing in the 1840s to a full affirmation of patriotic devotion after the passage of the key constitutional amendments. This becomes clear in the course of LTFD. For example, Douglass moves from considering the U.S. Constitution a "pro-slavery" document to celebrating it as "in its letter and spirit an anti-slavery instrument, demanding the abolition of slavery as a condition of its own existence" (2012b). This is important because it means that Douglass is taking up a central part of American national identity—the view that we are uniquely democratic and egalitarian. The emancipation and enfranchisement of the slaves are not, in his view, deviations from an objectionable U.S. identity. They are, rather, a long overdue expression of the national character. Indeed, he comes to see the slave states as opposed to the fundamental principles of American identity. Many in the South, he tells us, "had come to hate everything which had the prefix 'Free'—free soil, free states, free territories, free schools, free speech, and freedom generally, and they would have no more such prefixes." Thus, the Confederacy was a sort of antithesis to the U.S. with regard to national identity.

In keeping with these points, Douglass writes that "it was a great thing to achieve American independence when we numbered three millions, but it was a greater thing to save this country from dismemberment and ruin when it numbered thirty millions" and "to destroy slavery" (2012b). Here, again, the suggestion is that the destruction of slavery was in part the fulfillment of the initial assertion of national independence. In addition, what is perhaps most striking about this quotation is that Douglass first affirms the greatness of "sav[ing] this country." Thus, he is not affirming the nation as a mere means to the freedom of African Americans. To the contrary, he is celebrating the liberation of African Americans in the context of celebrating the nation, making their liberation precisely their freedom to be Americans, rather than "standing outside the pale of American humanity, denied citizenship."

Indeed, many of us who admire Douglass are likely to be somewhat uneasy with his thoroughgoing identification with "our country," his affirmation of "the national heart," his calls to "rally around the flag," his assertion of the Union's "advanced civilization," his statement that dying for one's country is the "highest point of nobleness beyond which human power cannot go," his celebration of "the star spangled banner," his conviction that the United States is bound to have "a long and glorious career of justice, liberty, and civilization," his expression of gratitude to "the noble army," his identification of patriotism as a "noble sentiment," and his assertion that "this great country" will continue "leading the world in the race of social science, civilization, and renown" (2012b).

Conclusion

Frederick Douglass too took up the usual techniques for responding to the subnational division between white and black. Like other nonwhite writers, he sought to shift the white reader's perspective, while at the same time being sensitive to the fact that not all his readers would be white. That awareness of a black readership is presumably part of the reason that Douglass particularly sought to cultivate respect in his readers—including self-respect in his black readers—rather than pity and self-pity.

But, like all the authors we have considered, there is greater complexity here as well. In Douglass's case, the various autobiographies suggest that there are two different Douglasses. First, there is the public Douglass, who stressed his self-confident perseverance in the face of disrespect and physical cruelty, affirming his independence and autonomy, drawing on heroic story structures to emplot his response to an oppressive and racist nation. But, underlying this, there was another Douglass, suffering from attachment insecurity, and tacitly emplotting his life in a story of family separation and (ideally) reunion, loss of home and (ideally) return to home. This private Douglass was not confined to his private life. It also defined his relation to the nation—the national family and national home (to take up standard metaphors that have particular resonance in Douglass's case).

One way of putting all this is to say that Frederick Douglass is very different from Harriet Beecher Stowe. On the surface, Stowe is all about love and empathy. But, when one considers her novel a little more deeply, one sees that there is a considerable strain of defiance in her main characters. Indeed, one of these characters, George Harris, actually takes up weapons in his struggle against slavery. Moreover, I suspect that many people intuitively expect Stowe to have a generally positive view of the nation. She does not seem to be much of a revolutionary, and certainly seems to be an unlikely ancestress for black nationalism. But, considered closely, her novel expresses a damning and pessimistic assessment of the United States, and does end up affirming a position rather close to black nationalism or separatism. In contrast, on the surface, Douglass is all about defiance and respect—and, indeed, he does support the use of violence against slavery. But, when one considers Douglass's writings a bit more deeply, one sees that his life is pervaded by a feeling of attachment vulnerability and a mourning for attachment loss. Moreover, I suspect that many people intuitively expect Douglass to have a generally negative view of the nation, perhaps even approximating some form of separatism. But even minimal attention to Douglass's texts shows that he longed for acceptance by the nation that he wished to love. Moreover, after slavery was abolished and slaves were constitutionally enfranchised, he developed into an enthusiastic patriot—a man with a profound sense of identity as an American and with deep attachment feelings for the United States as the land of democracy, equality, and freedom.

Notes

1 The basic idea here is not unfamiliar. For example, David Blight (2018: 12) writes that parts of Douglass's writings express "a child's screams transported by memory into the anguished heart of a lifelong orphan." In keeping with this, Blight (2018: 517) refers to Douglass's "lifelong quest for an idealized mother's care, and a home that might provide it."
2 I hope that, by the end of the chapter, readers will agree that LTFD is a rich and revealing work that has been unfairly derogated by some critics (see, for example, Houston Baker [1985: 254], who, in an otherwise sensitive and illuminating discussion of Douglass's work, rather dismisses LTFD as "verbose and somewhat hackneyed").
3 For a critical discussion of Douglass's concern with masculinity, see Newtown 2005.
4 Darryl Dickson-Carr (2001: 128) contends that, despite his support of women's rights, Douglass "regarded any sign of femininity in himself … as anathema" (cf. Maurice Wallace's [1995: 253] assertion that Douglass had a "fear of the feminine"). This does not necessarily compromise his commitment to women's rights. If one strongly identifies with a category, one may wish to embrace aspects of that identity—as socially understood—even when one does not see those characteristics as somehow objectively superior. In any event, the key point here is that Douglass expressed (both implicitly and explicitly) a very strongly male gender identification, and he responded no less strongly to any apparent threat to that identification.
5 In saying this, I am referring to the story prototype that implicitly contributes to Douglass's emplotment of his life events. There are many sorts of genres that contribute to any work. I am in no way claiming that this is the sole literary structure that contributed to Douglass's writings. (See, for example, Olney [1985] on the genre conventions guiding slave narratives.) Indeed, I will myself propose a second important genre prototype in the next section of this chapter.
6 On this genre and its cross-culturally recurring structure, see my *The Mind and Its Stories* (Hogan 2003: 109–118) and the third chapter of my *Affective Narratology* (Hogan 2011a).
7 Other critics have been concerned with the ways in which Douglass's writings take up literary structures. However, they are concerned with very different, more obvious and straightforward structures, such as those involved in autobiography (see Tawil 2016b).
8 On the connection between person attachment and place attachment, see Panksepp (1998: 265).
9 The idea of being deformed recalls the interweaving of ideologies of race and disability in rationalizations of slavery (on this connection, see Nielsen 2013: 56–65).

8

THE SCARLET LETTER

Sexuality, sin, and spiritual realization

A note on sex and national identity

It seems fairly obvious that racial outgrouping involves subnational divisions that threaten the sense of national identity. It may be less obvious that sex and gender often pose difficulties for national identity as well. On reflection, however, it should be clear that, in a patriarchal society, one half of the adult population is at least in some degree excluded from full participation in the group. In the case of nations, this is most obvious when women do not have the vote, though the point is not limited to disenfranchisement. Thus, Abigail Adams wrote to her husband—the American revolutionary leader John Adams—that women should have more rights. Modeling the status of women on that of the American colonists, she suggested the possibility of "rebellion" if women are "bound to obey the laws in which we have no voice of representation" and are thereby subjected to "tyrants" of husbands (qtd. in Zinn 2015: 110). The phrasing shows clearly that Abigail Adams saw sex as a crucial subnational division.

Of course, the issue is not confined to patriarchy, in the sense of structures of inequality in access to goods and services, and rights of participation in a group. Sexism underwrites and rationalizes that division with its view of women as intellectually underequipped to play a full role in society and with its other stereotypes about and normative regulations regarding gender. Misogyny—or, more properly, sex-based affective bias or sex-based antipathy—is a factor too, just as racial antipathy is in the case of European–Amerindian and European–African divisions. Like racial antipathy, sex-based affective bias may involve anger at the independence or "willfulness" of members of the dominated group. It may also involve fear of the harm that members of that group can cause. This is usually physical harm in the case of racial outgroups, though it may also be status injury—humiliation, for example. In the case of women, men are likely to fear status injury (hence the occurrence of "honor killings") and personal harms related to attachment dependency (thus, rejection or abandonment), but not (commonly) physical harm. Finally, disgust is often a prominent factor in misogyny (see, for example, Nussbaum 2010: 17–18; and Nussbaum 2001: 348–349). Misogynistic disgust is commonly connected with sexuality—an unsurprising development, since categorizing someone by sex is to at least some extent emphasizing sexuality. (Contrast categorizing someone by profession, nationality, or native language.)

As with race, outgrouping by sex regularly involves cognitive models. The putative incompetence, emotionality, and deficiency of women are related to a model of women as children who need the protective guidance of a parent (e.g., a husband). As to affect, sexist ideology may be linked with disdain and a sense of superiority or, stressing the childhood model, may be connected with a sort of patronizing affection. Women's sexuality and some men's associated misogyny, however, tend to draw on models from animacy. As Martha Nussbaum notes, women are sometimes seen as more animal than men are. In keeping with this idea, "derogatory portrayals of women as disgusting (smelly, oozy, full of questionable fluids) are used by men to distance themselves from their own animality" (Nussbaum 2004: 18). Nussbaum plausibly relates this disgust to the bodily evidence of reproduction marking women in salient ways. She points toward menstruation, pregnancy, and birth (see Nussbaum 2004: 16). But even women's breasts may serve to remind people (male or female) of their function. Thus, the bodily role of women in reproduction—a sort of "animal" process—may be more difficult to occlude or ignore than the bodily role of men.

Perhaps more importantly, women are also subjected to the superhuman model. They may be akin to Satan in their seductive power, or they may be literally associated with Satanic seduction, as in the case of Eve or witchcraft. Witches are prototypically older, postmenopausal women. Like the Weird Sisters in *Macbeth*, they may seduce one into crimes of greed or ambition. When women are young, their Satanic seductions are most often seen as sexual. It is probably not uncommon for people to regret sexual indulgence and to blame their partners' putative seductiveness for their lapse. Moreover, a sense of having been seduced (rather than freely choosing sexual relations) may be intensified by a rebound effect.[1] Sexual desire leads one to ignore or suppress feelings of disgust, which the smells and fluids of other people's bodies commonly provoke. After sexual relations, however, that disgust may return with greater force. (I imagine that this happens with comparable frequency to men and to women. It is simply more consequential for the more socially and personally powerful of the people involved.) On the other hand, young, nubile women may forego seduction, renouncing sexuality. In that case, they are associated with angels, rather than demons. Indeed, the widely cited virgin–whore opposition is a variant of the angel–demon division. I should note that the incompetence attributed to women in standard sexism does not carry over into the stereotyping in the most extreme forms of misogyny. The incompetence idea draws on a childhood model that is not compatible with the demonic seducer model or the aged witch model (which combines old age with Satanic connections).

To a great extent, the sorts of techniques that writers employ to criticize racial outgrouping—cultivating empathy, challenging the use of cognitive models based on animacy hierarchies or age grades, etc.—should apply to sex-based outgrouping as well. Moreover, here, as with racism, fostering feelings of attachment, including romantic love, should inhibit fear and disgust. However, sexism and misogyny arise in a context where attachment bonding and romantic love are actually normative. In other words, while blacks and whites are not supposed to intermarry in a racist society, men and women are supposed to intermarry; indeed, marriage is a key structural feature of patriarchal society. Thus, it seems clear that romantic love cannot play precisely the same role with regard to sex-based antipathy as it does with regard to race-based antipathy. Indeed, thinking about romantic love in connection with sex-based social divisions reminds us that pair bonding in marriage has divisive as well as conciliatory elements. These bear on each of the main emotions linked with antipathy. For example, for reasons just mentioned the arousal of sexual feelings might subsequently enhance disgust. In addition, the salience of romantic love might make the possibility of rejection, thus shame—with its consequent rage—more salient as well. It is not entirely clear how one might reasonably respond to these issues. As to sexuality, it is probably the case that destigmatizing sexuality will to some degree reduce sex-based disgust and probably certain sorts of sex-based shame as well. Thus, the destigmatizing or normalization of sexuality is an important addition to the techniques by which an author might challenge sex-based antipathy and subnational divisions. Unsurprisingly, however, this is not a simple matter.

New England: Puritan and Victorian

The status of women was far from enviable in colonial New England. For example, husbands had the right to chastise their wives (Zinn 2015: 106), and they exercised ownership over their wives' goods (Zinn 2015: 107). Things had not improved greatly by Nathaniel Hawthorne's time.[2] For example, following independence—despite the sensitivity to disenfranchisement that partially inspired the American Revolution—only New Jersey granted women the right to vote, and it withdrew the right in 1807 (Zinn 2015: 110). In these and other respects, women were widely assimilated to children and men to adults. It is a commonly accepted that parents have the right to chastise their children (within certain limits), that parents have disposition of the children's goods (e.g., a parent can punish a child by taking away some toy), and that children do not have a vote in social or familial decisions. Similarly, a "best-selling" instruction book from the 1700s stresses that men have "the larger share of Reason" and thus are "the Law-givers." Men also have greater "Strength," while women have more "Gentleness" and are more suited to "Compliance" (qtd. in Zinn 2015: 108). Here, too, we see the childhood model at work, with children assumed to have more fantastical thought patterns and less moral as well as physical strength.

In the colonial period, paranoid misogyny appeared in a particularly stark form in ideas about witchcraft and in trials of particular women for witchcraft. Moreover, these ideas were inseparable from the patriarchy's sense of communal identity, which was at least protonational. Consider, for example, the enormously influential work of the Puritan minister Cotton Mather (1663–1728). In *The Wonders of the Invisible World*

(1693), in keeping with common views that ingroups have a special relation with God and divine will, he wrote that "the *New-Englanders* are a People of God settled in those, which were once the *Devil's* Territories" (Mather 1862: 13, emphasis in the original; the association of Native Americans with demons was, again, commonplace and part of what James Fenimore Cooper, Catharine Maria Sedgwick, and William Apess had to respond to). Mather develops the point, drawing on the PEOPLE ARE PLANTS metaphor,[3] which is altered to accommodate immigrants, as when he writes of "the *Vine* which God has here *Planted, Casting out the Heathen, and … causing it to take deep Root*" (1862: 13, emphasis in the original).

But what does this have to do with the outgrouping of women? As it turns out, witchcraft is the means by which the national enemy hopes to reverse the advancement of the Godly nation. Roxanne Dunbar-Ortiz (2014: 36) explains that "Salem authorities …justif[ied] witch trials by claiming that the English settlers were inhabiting land controlled by the devil." More importantly, Mather (1862: 14, emphasis in the original) recounts that "we have now with Horror seen the *Discovery* of such a *Witchcraft*! An Army of *Devils* is horribly broke in upon the place." As a result, "the Houses of the Good People there are fill'd with the doleful Shrieks of their Children and Servants, Tormented by Invisible Hands, with Tortures altogether preternatural" (14). He explains that "more than One [and] *Twenty* have *Confessed*" and in their confession they have admitted being compacted with the Prince of Darkness "in his Hellish Design of *Bewitching*, and *Ruining* our Land" (15, emphasis in the original). Thus, "the Devil has made a dreadful Knot of *Witches* in the Country" and their antinational task is one of "Rooting out the Christian Religion from this Country [note the variation on the PEOPLE ARE PLANTS metaphor], and setting up instead of it, perhaps a more gross *Diabolesm* [sic], than ever the World saw before" (16, emphasis in the original).

Though there were some male practitioners of the black arts, the great majority of those judged to be witches were women (see Dunbar-Ortiz 2014: 35). Thus, it was some women who posed the greatest danger to the polity in its function as exemplar for the world. We see the anger, fear, and disgust at work when Mather (1862: 159, emphasis in the original) refers to one accused witch as "this Rampant Hag, *Martha Carrier*," who forced her own children into the soul-destroying sin of witchcraft, betraying even that fundamental attachment trust, because "the Devil had promised her, she should be *Queen of Heb*." One can almost feel Mather's stomach-churning revulsion when he denounces "this Rampant Hag."

The Puritans had a special concern with controlling sexuality, especially women's sexuality. Their general rigidity in sexual matters was related to biblical legalism. For example, several Puritans in *The Scarlet Letter* refer to Leviticus 20:10 (KJV): "And the man that committeth adultery with another man's wife, even he that committeth adultery with his neighbour's wife, the adulterer and the adulteress shall surely be put to death." On the other hand, the actual punishments enacted by the Puritans, as well as those in Hawthorne's novel, are more limited. They often included physical punishment (Edmund Morgan [1942: 602] notes that the "usual punishment" for adultery was "a whipping or a fine"). However, the punishments stressed by Hawthorne are focused on producing shame in the sinners—and general sexual shame in the community at large.[4] Here, too, in the decades after then American Revolution, the situation improved in some ways, but not in others. Howard Zinn argues that, in certain respects, this censorious attitude toward sexuality in general and female sexuality in particular intensified after 1820. Specifically, "sexual purity was to be the special virtue of a woman. It was assumed that men, as a matter of biological nature, would sin, but woman must not surrender" (Zinn 2015: 112). Such purity became part of the "cult of true womanhood" (2015: 112, quoting Barbara Welter).

Of course, the attitudes toward sex, gender, and sexuality were not uniform at the time (or ever). For example, the revolutionary writer Thomas Paine supported the rights of women (Zinn 2015: 111). Quakerism, which was much reviled by the Puritans, was a feminist "covenant," as well as antiwar and progressive in other ways. (On the Quaker view that "men and women [are] equal" and its theological sources, see Brinton 1973: 34; on Quaker pacifism, see Brinton 1973: 28.)

It is also worth mentioning Thomas Morton (1579–1647) in connection with these points. Morton was a "potent enemy of the Puritans" and the source of one of Hawthorne's short stories ("The May-Pole of Merry Mount"). Part of his antagonistic relation with the Puritans involved the fact that he "celebrated … sensuality, worldliness, and embrace of the region's indigenous peoples" (Gustafson 2017: 167). Michael Bronski (2011: 14) explains that "Morton befriended the local Algonquian tribe, whose culture he admired, and urged intermarriage between native women and male colonists. He also released the indentured servants and made them equal 'consociates.'" Thus, Morton combined sexual liberation with opposition to outgrouping Native Americans (as well as socioeconomic egalitarianism).

Of course, the most important way in which attitudes toward sex and gender were not uniform is a matter of the attitudes and actions of women themselves. Like other oppressed or underprivileged groups, women resisted patriarchy. I have noted above Abigail Adams's appeal to revolutionary ideals on behalf of women.[5] However, advocacy of changes in sex relations were not confined to private letters. In 1779, Judith Murray published her important essay, "On the Equality of the Sexes." At the time, when Hawthorne was writing *The Scarlet Letter,* plans were developed for the first women's rights convention, which took place two years before the publication of the novel. As this indicates, there were many active feminists at the time, including Margaret Fuller, a friend of the Hawthornes'.[6] It would have been difficult for Hawthorne to be unaware of or unaffected by these consequential social developments.

Hawthorne's themes

Like any author, Hawthorne has a number of real-world concerns and he returns to these, exploring, specifying, and varying them just as he explores, specifies, and varies story sequences and narrative techniques. Unlike some early U.S. writers, Hawthorne's primary concern does not seem to be the nation as such. Perhaps more in keeping with some prerevolutionary authors, his principal focus seems to be on spirituality and morality. Spirituality and morality bear most obviously on individuals.

They concern whether, for example, I pursue eternal or temporal goals, or behave in selfless or selfish ways. But my devotion or goodness is inseparable from how spiritual and ethical principles organize the society in which I live, thus defining many of the options for my daily life, including my religious and moral possibilities. The relation of spiritual or moral principles to the social and political organization of the community is emphasized by the historical vocation of New England communities to be morally and spiritually exemplary, a "city upon a hill," in John Winthrop's famous phrase ("For wee must consider that wee shall be as a citty upon a hill. The eies of all people are uppon us"). This vocation—to serve as an ideal model for other communities— was part of an enduring "conviction that America was a sacred nation with a divine purpose" populated by a "Chosen People" (Leonard and Parmet 1971: 3).[7] In Winthrop's words, "Wee shall finde that the God of Israell is among us, when ten of us shall be able to resist a thousand of our enemies."

Again, to be such a city upon a hill is to be an exemplar of spiritual and moral—as well as social and political—development for the world. The model here is the Chosen People of the Old Testament, the national group selected by God as the special carriers of His revelation. In keeping with this notion, Hawthorne's novel culminates in a sermon that is framed as spiritual, moral, and national. The Reverend Dimmesdale is going to preach the "Election Sermon," a sermon marking a political event—"the start of a governor's term of office" (Hawthorne 2017: 542, n.9). Thus, the occasion of the sermon defines it as political and communal. Hawthorne develops this relation by paralleling Dimmesdale with the Old Testament prophets. There is, however, a signal difference: "Whereas the Jewish seers had denounced judgments and ruin on their country, it was [Dimmesdale's] mission to foretell a high and glorious destiny for the newly gathered people of the Lord" (560). Dimmesdale addresses the crowd politically as "People of New England!" (563), but goes on to speak about his own individual sin. The conjunction suggests again a deep interconnection between the principles of individual spiritual and moral life, on the one hand, and the principles of social and political life, on the other. In this way, Hawthorne's initially non-national concerns end up being inseparable from what are in effect issues of national identification, even if the context of these concerns is different from that of many other authors. The convergence of devotional, ethical, and political interests is consistent with the biblical conception of Israel and the Puritan conception of their New World societies as religious, moral, and political—in effect, national—communities.

This leads us to the question of just what principles might be at stake here. In the rest of this chapter, I will argue that, at least in much of *The Scarlet Letter*, Hawthorne's views of morality, spirituality, and society crucially involve the following principles. First, he accepts the Puritan and Calvinist view that we are all deeply sinful (see, for example, Simpson 1955: 103). Or perhaps he only takes the view that it is salutary for us to think of ourselves as deeply sinful. Either way, he takes self-criticism—profound, searching acknowledgment of one's sinfulness—as essential to morality and spirituality. This self-criticism is most directly incompatible with censorious judgment directed at others. Hawthorne almost certainly does not expect his readers to simply accept as true the interpretation of Dimmesdale's final sermon as a "parable," an interpretation reported by the narrator as representing the view of "highly respectable witnesses" (566). Nonetheless, Hawthorne does seem to have agreed with one part of this interpretation, the part that asserts that "we are sinners all alike" (566). Those engaged in affirming the inferiority of others, rather than critically examining their own moral and spiritual frailty, may or may not commit particular sins in the sense of violating specific moral precepts. However, they are likely to have succumbed to the graver, overarching sin, the sin of Satan—spiritual pride, the elevation of oneself as morally and religiously superior, thus the denial of one's sinfulness.[8] Note that this practical denial of one's sinfulness may be concealed by statements of one's own sinfulness. The latter may function as a sort of self-aggrandizement, a way of managing the impression one makes on others, creating the sense that one is anything but prideful, when in fact one is proudly proclaiming one's spiritual superiority. In this view of things, self-righteousness is, ultimately, a far worse sin than, say, fornication.[9]

For our purposes, this emphasis on self-criticism and eschewal of scrutinizing others may apply to both individuals and groups. I should be concerned with my own sinfulness, not with that of my neighbor—a fundamental principle of Jesus's teaching as manifest in the often-quoted critical question, "why beholdest thou the mote that is in thy brother's eye, but perceivest not the beam that is in thine own eye?" (Luke 6:41, KJV). But the same point holds with respect to one's ingroups and outgroups. European Americans are focused on the faults of Native Americans. But they should be focused on the crimes of their own community. Men are attentive to the imperfections of women. But they should rather be attentive to their own imperfections. Though it is not Hawthorne's main purpose to say this, it seems clear that such ingroup self-criticism would almost certainly have unifying consequences if practiced by all subnationally divided identity groups.

One key result of outgrouping in hierarchical societies is that nonmeritocratic divisions of economic class come to be rationalized by dominant groups through an appeal to outgroup inferiority. From, say, a Marxist perspective, this is a key social function of the idea, derived from Calvin, that material well-being is a sign of divine election. Dunbar-Ortiz (2014: 48) writes of Calvinism (including its American version) that "although individuals could not know for certain if they were among the elect, outward good fortune, especially material wealth, was taken to be a manifestation of election." This is sometimes referred to as "prosperity theology." As Harvard Divinity professor Harvey Cox (qtd. in Massari 2014) explains, "prosperity theology is an effort to reconcile the Gospel with the American dream ... The sources for this type of theology are a certain kind of distorted Calvinism. Calvinism had an enormous influence on American institutions. One reading of it says that if you're doing well materially, God must favor you. It's a sign that you are one of the elect. If you're not doing so well, you must not be one of the elect." In terms of current psychological research, this is an instance of what is called "just-world thinking." Just-world thinking is the tendency of many people to assume that hierarchies must be broadly merited because the world is fundamentally just (see Duckitt 1992: 153). Prosperity theology is simply one historically and culturally specific version of this general psychological tendency. Prosperity theology applies less obviously to relations between men and women than it does to relations of socio-economic class. But the broader tendency of just-world thinking is clearly relevant. If women suffer social degradation, then the degradation may readily be judged as deserved (by just-world reasoning).

In *The Scarlet Letter*, Hawthorne develops his ideas about human sinfulness, pride, and self-criticism out of a single sin—adultery. Though the law punished both men and women for the sin, it was clear that the sin was more harshly condemned in women than in men. Again, in Hawthorne's own time, men were rather expected to stray; women were not (as Zinn [2015: 112] explains). But what exactly was Hawthorne's point in treating adultery, its punishment in a woman and its concealment in a man? The simplest and most obvious interpretation of a work by a Christian writer treating adultery and punishment is that the author is reflecting the view expressed by Jesus. In fact, I believe that Jesus's teaching on adultery is central to Hawthorne's story, though it appears to have had little impact on the views of many Christians during the colonial period, in Hawthorne's own time, or later.

Jesus's well-known views on this topic may be found in John 8:3–11 (KJV):

> And the scribes and Pharisees brought unto him a woman taken in adultery; and when they had set her in the midst,
> They say unto him, Master, this woman was taken in adultery, in the very act. Now Moses in the law commanded us, that such should be stoned: but what sayest thou?
> This they said, tempting him, that they might have to accuse him. But Jesus stooped down, and with his finger wrote on the ground, as though he heard them not.
> So when they continued asking him, he lifted up himself, and said unto them, He that is without sin among you, let him first cast a stone at her.
> And again he stooped down, and wrote on the ground.
> And they which heard it, being convicted by their own conscience, went out one by one, beginning at the eldest, even unto the last: and Jesus was left alone, and the woman standing in the midst.
> When Jesus had lifted up himself, and saw none but the woman, he said unto her, Woman, where are those thine accusers? hath no man condemned thee?
> She said, No man, Lord. And Jesus said unto her, Neither do I condemn thee: go, and sin no more.

Jesus's teaching does not exonerate the woman (as many of us might be inclined to do). Rather, it adjures everyone to be aware of his or her own sinfulness, rather than condemning the sinfulness of others. Hawthorne, I believe, extends the idea a bit further. First, he indicates that, in order to be good to others and helpful to others spiritually (thus good *for* them), one needs sympathy. To have sympathy, one needs to have empathic sensitivity to the other person's condition. Such empathy presupposes two things. First, it presupposes that one has suffered in such a way as to enable empathic understanding. Thus, Hawthorne writes that some people lack "throughout life" a "grief" that would "deeply touch ... and thus humanize" them, making them "capable of sympathy" (2017: 526). Second, one must have a parallel emotional stance that allows one to draw on one's own similar experiences in order to approximate the other person's feelings. In consequence, it requires that one not have one's empathy blocked by any inhibitory emotion, prominently including disdain born of pride. In a spiritual context, such pride is commonly a matter of self-righteousness, which one is able to avoid principally, perhaps only, by an awareness of one's own moral and spiritual deficiencies and sinfulness. All this suggests two points. First, as noted above, the general attitude of spiritual pride, the sin of Satan, is worse than the sins of specific acts, such as fornication. Second, rather than being a sign of God's special favor, a life without suffering may, in the end, be a spiritual catastrophe, as it limits the possibilities for one's spiritual and ethical aid to others and even one's self-criticism.

On the other hand, Hawthorne also suggests that self-criticism can be excessive. Dimmesdale is a sympathetic character. However, he struggles with a sin comparable to and often paired (and contrasted) with spiritual pride—spiritual despair, the feeling that one is so sinful that one can never achieve salvation.[10] This is the sin of Judas—not in his betrayal of Jesus, but in his subsequent suicide. Jesus does not tell the woman: "Go, meditate on the vile filth of your sinfulness, lacerating yourself physically and emotionally!" He simply tells her not to sin again. In order to avoid sin, she presumably must recognize her proneness to sin and remember—with a feeling of aversion—that she sinned previously. But that is all. Spiritual pride involves disgust at others (over whom one judges oneself to be superior). Spiritual despair involves disgust at oneself. Neither attitude is spiritually beneficial.

But how does one avoid spiritual despair? It seems that, in Hawthorne's view, one way of doing this appears rather Catholic—confession.[11] But this is not private confession; it is public admission that frees one from the need to hide one's sinfulness. One recurring idea of *The Scarlet Letter* is that Hester is in a way better off than Dimmesdale, that he suffers more because he must conceal his sinfulness. Of course, Hester suffers social ostracism, the gross mistreatment of her child, and considerable material and emotional insecurity. But she is not tormented internally as Dimmesdale is. Thus, despite her outward difficulties, she does not wither away and die at a young age. Because she has been forced to wear the "A" outwardly, the searing remorse is not burned into her heart like a spiritual brand.

This all suggests that a utopian society, for Hawthorne, would be a society in which people were openly self-critical, acknowledging their sinfulness publicly and focusing on their own moral and spiritual weaknesses, not those of others. In consequence, they would be just the sort of citizens who could serve as exemplars in a city upon a hill. Like Hester, they would be more inclined to work diligently and to help others in the community. The point is not merely personal. It bears on ingroups and outgroups. Hawthorne focuses particularly on the outgrouping of women. Indeed, his work would seem to indicate that the patriarchal denigration of women may serve to make them more moral and spiritual. The suggestion of this risks modeling women on angels and, while such modeling expresses a benevolent attitude, it remains disabling for real women. However, it seems clear that the ordinary women of Hawthorne's novel are not more angelic than the ordinary men.

Indeed, there is a rather different sort of emotional and thematic complication in *The Scarlet Letter*—for Hawthorne, like Cooper (Chapter 2), Sedgwick (Chapter 3), Harriet Beecher Stowe (Chapter 5), and others, does not present a wholly uniform treatment of his chosen out-group. Specifically, Hawthorne appears to equivocate somewhat on the topic of witchcraft, giving the reader reason to suspect its reality in the case of Mistress Hibbens. This equivocation may even to some extent appear to exonerate the Puritan community for her later execution. In addition, he seems to draw on demeaning stereotypes when he portrays the heartless "gossips" judging Hester. One might even question his representation of Pearl as "demon offspring" (567).

Here, as with other authors, the apparent contradictions in Hawthorne's attitudes are, I believe, explicable. Moreover, they are explicable largely in terms of the sorts of modeling we have examined above in relation to identity categorization. Specifically, the differences in Hawthorne's attitudes appear to be governed by age sets. The difference in this case is that the sets are literal and applied within an identity category, rather than across such categories. (This may be seen as a version of what is sometimes referred to as "intersectionality," the integration of distinct identity categories, since the age model also specifies identity categories—child, adult, and aged.) Given his focus on sexuality, it is unsurprising that Hawthorne's thematic concerns bear on destigmatizing adult women of child-bearing age, not prepubescent girls or postmenopausal women.

The case of children seems to be simply a matter of seeing them as not yet fully formed in their dispositions and as often imitative of their seniors. However, two things are somewhat disappointing about Hawthorne's treatment of the elderly. First, it appears to be ageist. Thus, we see in the novel a degree of antipathy toward older women and men. Moreover, Hawthorne sometimes emphasizes age in such a way as to suggest that the objectionable traits of these characters have resulted from aging itself. Second, in the case of postmenopausal women, this antipathy may be enhanced by some degree of disgust. In this way, misogyny is not eliminated from the novel, but rather confined to a subgroup. Such narrowing of outgroup antipathy is a recurring pattern in the criticism of identity divisions, as we saw in the case of Cooper's demonization of the Hurons.

Hawthorne in national and familial tradition

If the preceding points are correct, then Hawthorne should himself have faced these issues of spiritual and moral aspiration and self-criticism in relation to the society and tradition that formed the enabling conditions for his thought and action. In Hawthorne's case, this relation included his connection with prominent forebears, not only those of the society at large, but those of his own family as well. Thus, in the introduction to his novel Hawthorne sets out to distance himself from his ancestors, whose self-righteousness had divisive and destructive results for the society in which they lived. He begins with a "grave" and "steeple-crowned progenitor," who arrived "with his Bible and his sword" to become "a bitter persecutor" (2017: 430). He instances the progenitor's mistreatment of the Quakers, which was recalled by members of that community. It is particularly important that Hawthorne specifies the act as "hard severity towards a woman" (430; Levine [2017: 430, n.5] identifies the severity as "whipping"). He goes on to a second, more recent forebear who "inherited the persecuting spirit" by serving as a judge in "the martyrdom of the witches" (430). These are heinous examples of the evil acts allowed by the self-righteous pride of the actors, who saw themselves as enforcing the good, which their spiritually and morally inferior (female) compatriots were otherwise unable to follow. In contrast with his treatment of Mistress Hibbens in the subsequent narrative, here Hawthorne characterizes the murdered women (and men) as martyrs, thus as the spiritual superiors of his self-righteous and persecutory ancestors.

As is often remarked, Hawthorne's differentiation of himself from these ancestors is expressed not only in this introduction, but in his alteration of his surname. The objectionable precursors were named "Hathorne." Nathaniel added the "w." This is sometimes interpreted as suggesting an identification with the witches. It is certainly suggestive of a type of marking with a letter, of the sort we find in both Hester Prynne and Arthur Dimmesdale—though it is a public mark, like that of the former, not a concealed one, like that of the latter. Indeed, in this introduction, Hawthorne suggests a connection between the Puritan prosecution of adultery and the prosecution of witches. Specifically, his attention to an incriminating letter turns up later in the introduction when he uncovers the scarlet "A," the mark of adultery. Hawthorne places the "A" on his own chest, suggesting his identification with the adulteress. When he does this, he feels a "burning heat" (443). In context, that burning serves to associate the adulteress with the witches.[12] Though witches in Salem were not burned, burning is widely known as a common punishment for witchcraft and almost certainly takes on that resonance here. The connection helps to orient the entire following narrative toward a critique of communal violence against women deriving from self-righteous pride. In connection with this, it is worth noting that Plymouth Colony adopted the less ambiguous "AD" to mark those guilty of adultery.[13] Hawthorne uses the more equivocal "A." This is no doubt principally because that is mentioned in *The Annals of Salem* of 1827 (see Murfin 1991: 12). However, it is no accident that the A is (as we will see) readily open to positive construal as well, making the adulteress a saintly or angelic figure like the martyred witches—or like the elevated figure of Jesus's follower Mary Magdalene, who had also been tainted with sexual sin.[14] (Or perhaps like Hawthorne's own mother, as Nina Baym [1982] has noted.)

Hester, sexuality, and the moral goodness of sin

Again, the key point about Hester's adultery and her public recognition of her sinfulness is that it enables her moral and spiritual development. Most importantly, "the scarlet letter ... gave her a sympathetic knowledge of the hidden sin in other hearts" (Hawthorne 2017: 473). It allowed her to recognize, understand, and respond in a helpful way to the moral and spiritual dilemmas of others. That is why she can point to the scarlet letter and invoke "what I have learned from this!" (486) as the source of her ability to teach Pearl ethics and religion.

Hester's situation is representative of the situation of many women punished for sexual sin. There is a social double standard. But that social inequality is supported by a natural asymmetry. Women bear the signs of sexual relations in two obvious ways that men do not—first, in the rupture of the hymen; second, in pregnancy. There is something inherently unfair in the fact that Hester must suffer for her violation of sexual norms, whereas Dimmesdale—who was, obviously, no less involved—can conceal his act. Just-world thinking might rationalize this by presenting the woman as a (Satan-like) seductress. But Hawthorne clearly does not portray Hester in this way.

Indeed, rather than drawing on the demonic model, Hawthorne turns to the superhuman alternative in the animacy model. He introduces Hester, even before the start of the story proper, as a sort of "angel" in some people's view, due to her good works (444). The idea returns, in a more general way, when the letter "A" appears "in the sky" (512), suggesting divine intervention. People interpret it to abbreviate "Angel" (512). Though these interpreters fail to draw a connection with Hester, the reader surely does so (as Hawthorne no doubt intended). This is possible because Hester's mark is the letter "A" alone and not, for example, "AD."

In context, this particular sign refers to Dimmesdale as well, since both are spiritually elevated by the recognition of and remorse for their sin.[15] Dimmesdale's spiritual excellence is manifest in the power of his sermons. In keeping with the preceding points, his utterances were felt by his congregation to be "like the speech of an angel" (462). As with Hester, a sense of sinfulness gives Dimmesdale "sympathies so intimate with the sinful brotherhood of mankind ... that his heart vibrated in unison with theirs, and received their pain into itself," leading him to touch them with "persuasive eloquence" (504).

Even so, the principal angel in the novel, the main character whose sin is not seductive and Satanic, but spiritually elevating, is Hester. As to the letter, the people find themselves so deeply affected by Hester's "helpfulness" due to her "power to sympathize," that they take the letter to stand for "Able" and to be a "symbol" for her vocation as "Sister of Mercy" (514). This connection with the religious order founded less than two decades before Hawthorne wrote his novel would appear to suggest some sympathy with Catholicism (though this is usually identified only later in Hawthorne's life).[16] The connection is even more obvious when Hawthorne first introduces Hester at the start of the narrative. There, he explains that her "misfortune and ignominy" formed "a halo" (455). This may seem ironic, and might well be taken as ironic on first reading. However, the subsequent development of the story indicates the spiritually and morally salutary effects of this public acknowledgment of her sin and thereby makes sense of the conceit. The same point holds for the linking of Hester and Pearl with the Madonna and Child. Hawthorne writes that a Catholic might be reminded of "the image of Divine Maternity" (456). The narrator continues that one "should" be reminded "only by contrast" (457). But this normative judgment seems at least in some degree ironic. Surely, there is only contrast in the eyes of the church elders and the "gossips" in the audience. But even mentioning that this is how spectators "should" respond suggests the possibility that it is not in fact how they do respond. After all, later in the novel there is just such divergence between the ordinary people and the censorious church elders. We see this when the ordinary people reinterpret the "A" for this "Sister of Mercy." Hawthorne writes that the "learned men of the community" were "longer in acknowledging ... Hester's good qualities than the people" as the "prejudices" of the former were more "fortified" by "reasoning" (514). Moreover, beyond the connections with the Blessed Virgin, there are hints of a link with Jesus, as when Hester explains that she wishes she could "endure [her lover's] agony" (463). There is an obvious way in which this is parallel to the role of Jesus, for it involves taking on and suffering for someone else's sins—what she is already doing, if in a more limited way than she wishes.

Finally, it is worth stressing that the issue of Hester's sin is Pearl, who is named for the pearl "of great price" (474) that stands for the Kingdom of Heaven (see Matthew 13:45–46). Allegorically, it is indeed through her sin that Hester gains Pearl, that is, the pearl of great price, that is, the Kingdom of Heaven. In keeping with this, Hawthorne links Pearl with "Eden," the lost paradise that is achieved again only through entering the Kingdom of Heaven. Moreover, even considered non-allegorically, the birth of Pearl is hardly an execrable event. As Benjamin Franklin (2017) famously indicated in "Speech of Miss Polly Baker" (1747), providing the occasion for the birth of another soul of God's creation can hardly be damnable.

Of course, to say that many people eventually saw spiritual elevation in Hester is not to say that everyone did so or that people did so from the beginning. The public condemnation of Hester is an act of shaming that serves principally to allow those surrounding the mother and child to feel proud of their own superiority and to express disgust over Hester and sexuality (perhaps female sexuality in particular). The narrator strongly condemns this shaming, saying that there is "no outrage ... against our common nature" that is "more flagrant" (456). Some recent writers would agree. For example, Martha Nussbaum argues forcefully against both the decency and the efficacy of shaming.[17] In any case, the narrator's judgment suggests that there is significant irony in characterizing the magistracy as acting with "mercy" (456). The perverse nature of mercy in the novel's colonial society is brought out particularly when Hester suggests that what Chillingworth presents as "mercy" is in fact more like "terror" (467). In this, Chillingworth appears only to be a more extreme case of what we see with the Puritan community.

In each case, shaming is closely connected with the response of disgust. Expressions of this dehumanizing emotion occur repeatedly in the novel. Consider, for example, John Wilson, the nemesis of Anne Hutchinson, with whom Hester is associated. (As Ross Murfin [1991: 13] puts it, the opening of the novel indicates that the reader should "regard Anne Hutchinson and Hester Prynne in the same light.") Wilson refers to "touching the vileness and blackness of [Hester's] sin" (462). His visceral revulsion at Hester is almost palpable. In ironic contrast, Hawthorne has him literally touching Dimmesdale as he says this. To make matters worse, the narrator explains that Wilson felt "shame," thus a degree of self-disgust, not over his spiritual pride, but over being "kind" (461).

As the preceding point illustrates, disgust is not invariably directed toward others. The self-laceration that almost sinks Dimmesdale under despair is a matter of profound self-disgust. We see this, for example, when he refers to himself as "utterly a pollution" (504). Though less objectionable than its prideful alternative, it poses a genuine spiritual danger. This danger appears not only in the risk that Dimmesdale will commit suicide, but in his temptation to give up any attempt at (unachievable) salvation and simply commit gratuitous sins (as presented in a series of "temptations" [544–546]).

Women and spiritual independence

It is commonplace to observe that one sure way for a woman to provoke the ire of many men in a patriarchal society is to assert her independence. The point is no less true when the independence is moral and spiritual than when it is financial. In Hawthorne's ethically and spiritually oriented view of society, that moral and spiritual independence is particularly important, both to the women themselves and to the larger society. Thus, the stifling of such independence is a crucial feature of patriarchy that needs to be altered in creating a morally and spiritually viable national community.

Of course, Hawthorne does not come out and say any of this. Indeed, this may not adequately represent the general view developed in the book. But it almost certainly represents part of that view as developed in parts of the book—beginning in the introduction with the reference to the victims of the witchcraft trials as undergoing "martyrdom" (2017: 430). The first reference of this sort in the narrative proper, found in the very first chapter, is to "the sainted Ann Hutchinson" (452). As Zinn (2015: 108–109) explains, Hutchinson interpreted the Bible and criticized ministers, principally to women followers. Most significantly for our purposes, she rejected the idea that worldly success was a sign that one was "predestined for salvation" (Murfin 1991: 13). As Michael Colacurcio (1972: 471) summarizes, "'the chosen of man' are not necessarily 'the sealed of heaven.'" Hutchinson was subjected to two trials and to banishment, which ultimately led to her death. As Zinn (2015: 109) explains, there was a well-known incident at one of her trials where the officials "did not allow her to sit down until she was close to collapse." It seems likely that Hawthorne (2017: 464) expected his readers to remember this scene when Hester is made to stand on the scaffold, unable to escape her "too intense suffering by a swoon." This is only one of the cases where Hester is implicitly or explicitly connected with the rebellious spiritual teacher.

Hawthorne's attitude toward Hutchinson is further suggested by the connection between Hutchinson and nature, specifically one particular rose bush beside the prison door. The narrator recounts how that rose bush may offer solace to those entering the prison or to those leaving to be executed. As such, it expresses the "pity" of "Nature"—a pity shared by the compassionate Hester and Dimmesdale, but not by the stern Puritan fathers or the "gossips." There is "fair authority for believing" that the rose bush "had sprung up under the footsteps of the sainted Ann

Hutchinson, as she entered the prison-door" (452). The anecdote suggests the spiritual grace of Hutchinson, grace so great that it causes nature to blossom in the way we associate with divine creation. It also associates her with the solace given by the rose bush—and given, too, by both Hester and Dimmesdale.

A further link is introduced subsequently when Pearl is asked who made her. She responds that she "had been plucked by her mother off the bush of wild roses that grew by the prison-door" (487). Initially, this appears to be simply a frivolous bit of childish nonsense. Whatever meaning we attribute to Pearl herself, however, it seems clear that Hawthorne wished to convey something here. The most obvious suggestion is that Pearl's independence of thought and action (like that of her mother) has grown out of the thoughtful, questioning spirituality of Anne Hutchinson. For Governor Bellingham and other patriarchs, the right answer would be that she was made by "the Heavenly Father" (486), a patriarch in their image. Pearl is instead offering a maternal lineage (in keeping with Hutchinson's "gender deviance" [Bronski 2011: 13]), one linked with nature and compassion rather than with rigorous legalism and hierarchical authority. The point is connected with Hester's provision of help to others—"women, more especially" (568). She was, again, "a Sister of Mercy" (514); for example, "none" was "so ready as she to give of her little substance to every demand of poverty" (513). In keeping with this, one of the Puritan accusations against Anne Hutchinson was "substituting a covenant of works for a covenant of grace" (Simpson 1955: 35).

I do not mean to say that Hawthorne self-consciously saw these passages in such terms. Rather, he developed a given scene until it seemed right to him and we are in a position to make some sense out of why he felt that it was right. On the other hand, Hawthorne was far from unconscious regarding something along the lines of a female spiritual lineage. In a lengthy passage, the narrator speculates that, had she not had the task of raising Pearl, Hester might have "come down to us in history, hand in hand with Ann Hutchinson," as a religious leader—indeed, "a prophetess" (516), only to be condemned to death by the Puritans. These conjectures by the narrator lead to a remarkable passage suggesting that Hester too struggled with a certain sort of despair. However, her despair was not precisely spiritual. Unlike that of her partner, the Reverend Dimmesdale, she did not fear that she could not be forgiven by God. She feared, rather, that it was impossible to make life worth living for women. The only solution to the depressed condition of women would require that "the whole system of society ... be torn down, and built up anew" (516). For women to take up "a fair ... position" (516) in society, there would need to be a change even more profound than that from monarchy to democracy or colony to independent country. Indeed, one might infer that an independent, democratic nation has not successfully achieved either independence or democracy if it persecutes its female prophets and prevents women from assuming a "fair" place in the community, a place where their spiritual and moral insights and compassion can have the full scope that would benefit not only women but men as well.[18]

At the end of the novel, Hester returns to her former home. The "people brought all their sorrows and perplexities and besought her counsel." Hester "comforted and counselled them." She particularly consoles the women with the view that eventually, with God's providential guidance, "a new truth would be revealed, in order to establish the whole relation between man and woman on a surer ground of mutual happiness." Moreover, "the angel and apostle of the coming revelation must be a woman" (568). She feels that she cannot be this "prophetess," due to her sinfulness. But, again, it is precisely her recognition of this sinfulness that makes her a prophetess for the distressed women who come to her.[19]

Malleable children, wrinkled witches, and demonic old men

But, again, Hawthorne is not consistent in his recognition and critique of patriarchy. Indeed, at times, his celebration of Hester risks the sort of shift within a problematic that we saw with Cooper (see my discussion of problematics and ideology in Chapter 2), in this case a shift from whore to virgin and from demon (or demonic accomplice) to angel. In keeping with this, he seems to equivocate on Mistress Hibbins, who explicitly claims a link with the Evil One and who seems to provide evidence of that link by her apparent access to knowledge that should not have been available to her. She is introduced as "a witch" (Hawthorne 2017: 453) and not, for example, "a woman later accused of witchcraft." Subsequently, she calls out to Hester, inviting her to go into the forest at night and meet "the Black Man" (489). She appears to make an attempt at drawing Pearl into a compact with this Black Man as well (see 526–527). She is perhaps capable of reading people's thoughts (546). She "affirmed a personal connection" with "the Evil One" (557). She knows about the forest meeting between Hester and Dimmesdale; she appears to know about the "A" on Dimmesdale's chest, and she (correctly) prophesies that Hester will see that letter (557). The "gossips" who feel that Hester has been treated too kindly receive only slightly less derogatory treatment from Hawthorne.

These points indicate that, like the other authors we have considered, Hawthorne is not entirely consistent in his critical response to dominant ideology and to antipathy directed at the outgroup. As noted above, the pattern here appears to involve a common division of females into different age grades—children, adults, and the aged. Men who find it possible to support the rights of nubile women and to recognize their talents and achievements may find themselves repulsed by women whom they do not consider to be desirable sexual partners, prominently including postmenopausal women. In this case, the "essence" of a given person is not seen as simply a matter of sex, but of the intersection of sex with age. We see examples of this in the identification of Mistress Hibbins as "the old dame" (527) and the "ancient lady" (556). The age grading is even clearer in the case of the "gossips." They are "the old dames" (453). One is "a hard-featured dame of fifty." One is "the ugliest" of the group (454), suggesting that they are generally unattractive. Three are characterized as "autumnal matron[s]" (454). Only the "youngest" of the group has compassion for Hester and is presented to the reader as sympathetic.

On the other hand, it is only in part a matter of restricted misogyny (like Cooper's restricted race antagonism). Though there are differences in Hawthorne's attitude toward men and women, some of this animus toward the "witch" and the "gossips" is the result of generalized ageism. Of course, that does not make the attitude blameless, but it does make it different from misogyny, and thus of limited relevance to the issue of overcoming sex opposition and unfair sex-based hierarchization within the national community. To see this as generalized ageism, we need only look at the representation of men in the novel, particularly the great villain of the novel, the "devil" (518), Chillingworth. Even more than any of the women, he is insistently defined by his age. He is not merely an "old physician" (496) and an "unfortunate old man" (502). He is also the "dark and terrible old man" (565), a phrase that suggests a connection between his (demonic) darkness and his age. He is "the wrinkled scholar" (467) and the disgust-provoking "deformed old figure" (521).

Conclusion

For Hawthorne, as for many of his American forebears (both kin and not), a spiritual and moral community is the necessary foundation for an ideal national community. In Hawthorne's case, rather more than that of his forebears, such an ideal spiritual and moral community would be made up of compassionate and genuinely helpful individuals with parallel emotional stances toward others. Compassion and helpfulness require awareness and public acknowledgment of one's own sinfulness (and that of one's ingroups) as well as personal suffering to attune one's empathic sensitivity to other people's pain. This is consistent with Puritanism in affirming the deep sinfulness of all people. However, it rejects the prosperity theology that is often a part of Puritanism, since it views suffering as a necessary condition for spiritual elevation, rather than seeing success as a sign of divine preference. In this context, in addition to particular sins that violate moral precepts, there are two overarching, spiritual sins, sins of disposition rather than sins of particular actions. The worse of the two is pride, the self-righteousness that focuses one's ethical and religious scrutiny on others rather than on oneself. The other is despair, the sense that one is just too sinful to be forgiven. Though spiritual and ethical self-criticism are crucial to spiritual and ethical development, they should not lead to despair, but should be modulated in part by attention to compassion and associated aid to others.

A crucial subcommunal—including subnational—identity division is that between men and women. In a patriarchal society, this division makes it virtually impossible for women to be treated fairly. They are subjected to a biased standard, especially with respect to sexual sins. They are also restricted in the scope given to their spiritual and moral reflection and action, which deprives the whole society of what it could gain from the guidance of women. Given the depth and ubiquity of this division, it is particularly destructive of a democratic project. To rectify this situation, society may require women prophets inspiring fundamental changes in social organization.[20]

Despite these implications, Hawthorne's novel—like the other works we have considered—is marked by thematic ambiguity and emotional ambivalence. Specifically, the novel does not entirely jettison antipathy toward women, but restricts it to a subclass of the outgroup, here the aged. On the other hand, this may be less a case of restricted misogyny than a case of unrestricted ageism, since it applies to both men and women.

Notes

1 Such an effect is documented empirically in the case of suppressed racism (see Kunda 1999: 344–345 and Dovidio et al. 2017: 277); it seems likely to operate similarly in misogyny. We will return to this topic in the next chapter.
2 As Alison Easton (2004) explains, Hawthorne drew on both colonial and nineteenth-century ideas and practices surrounding gender and sexuality. This is unsurprising. The former were obviously important for the setting of the story, but the latter made the story bear more directly on Hawthorne's own world and that of his readers. In addition, there are of course aspects of the work that are not confined to either period, allowing readers in subsequent centuries to connect with the novel as well.
3 It is conventional in conceptual metaphor theory to use all capital letters to signal a basic metaphor structure (such as, PEOPLE ARE PLANTS), as opposed to a particular instance of that structure (such as, "Jane's grandparents put down roots in Kansas farm country").
4 For historical precedents of Hawthorne's depiction, see, for example, the 1658 Plymouth Colony law on adultery, which is available online in The Plymouth Colony Archive Project, http://www.histarch.illinois.edu/plymouth/Lauria2.html (accessed 18 May 2019).
5 See her letter of 31 March 1776 to John Adams (in Gustafson 2017: 672–673).
6 On Hawthorne's complicated relationship with Fuller, as well as some resonances of Fuller and her writings in *The Scarlet Letter*, see Mitchell (1998).
7 There is some controversy over precisely what Winthrop intended by this now-famous phrase. A particularly influential account was articulated by Bercovitch (1970). For a recent alternative account, see Rodgers (2018).
8 For an influential account of spiritual pride, see Edwards (1995).
9 Critics have, in different ways, noted the criticism of self-righteousness in the novel. For example, Larry Reynolds (2008: 168) argues that "ultimately, Hawthorne wishes us to discover that the most dangerous persons in the novel are not those characters" whose "unruly passions" lead to sexual transgressions; it is, rather, "those who perpetuate a society masking cruelty as righteousness, despotism as justice."
10 As Stephen Chester (2006: 518) puts it, spiritual despair is "the fate of those who know themselves sinners but who do not experience grace."
11 Some years after writing *The Scarlet Letter*, Hawthorne developed an interest in Catholic confession, unsurprisingly, given his more general concern with the topic of confession. See the articles by Henry Fairbanks (1957) and Olivia Taylor (2005) for thoughtful accounts of the similarities and differences in Hawthorne's ideas about confession over the course of his career.
12 Other critics have of course noted this link. See, for example, Murfin (1991: 16) on the association of Hester with the "accused witches prosecuted by [Hawthorne's ancestor] John" and Reynolds (2008: 162) on how Hawthorne "imagines himself as a persecuted witch."
13 See The Plymouth Colony Archive Project, http://www.histarch.illinois.edu/plymouth/Lauria2.html (accessed 18 May 2019). Leslie Fiedler (1992: 230), referring to this practice, states that "historically, a woman found guilty of adultery would have been condemned to wear the two letters 'AD.'"
14 Erroneously, it seems. On the (scripturally baseless) sexualization of Mary Magdalene, see Oshiek (2000: 122).
15 Because the recognition of one's sinfulness is the crucial issue for Hawthorne in this novel, he does not follow the standard romantic or antiromantic plot sequences that we might otherwise expect. That is why "the novel cannot be read in approving sympathy for doomed lovers (nor, for that matter, disapproval)" (Easton 2004: 90).
16 David Leverenz (1991: 267) suggests, more guardedly, that the narrator (not necessarily the author) exhibits "anti-Puritan, even Papist bias" at the start of the novel.

17 See Nussbaum (2016: 197–200). Robert Sapolsky (2017: 546–548) may appear to isolate exceptions, such as the shaming of corporations; however, it does not seem correct to characterize the exposure of corporate malfeasance as "shaming" the corporation, which after all cannot feel shame.
18 T. Walter Herbert (2004) makes it clear that Hawthorne personally felt constrained by the system of sex and gender relations and thus felt that he would benefit from such a social transformation. However, he finds Hawthorne ambiguous on the issue of whether that system can be changed or is natural. This sense of ambivalence results in large part from his awareness of Hawthorne's statements about sex and gender outside the novel. It is probably the case that Hawthorne was changeable in his views on this topic, perhaps like most people. What seems clear, however, is that there is a gender-egalitarian view that Hawthorne puts forward in the course of the novel, a view that responds to the state of American society and its painfully imperfect realization of its ideal identity. This seems clear even if Hawthorne contradicted that view, as he did, outside the novel or elsewhere in the novel itself.
19 Sacvan Bercovitch (1991: 345) considers it something of a conundrum that Hester freely "takes up the letter" at the end. But, given the key importance of recognizing one's own sin, and the intimate relation between this and counseling others, such a free acceptance of the letter is precisely what one would expect, precisely what shows Hester's spiritual—and social—achievement. As John Erskine (1918: 26) recognized a century ago, Hester's "sin leads her straightway to a larger life"; that and her "ostracism" permit her "to enter upon a life of mercy and good works which would have been closed to a conventional woman." Indeed, Erskine goes on to note that "she becomes more loving, more sympathetic, more tender; and intellectually … emancipated from the narrowness of her age." That emancipation, in turn, enables her to see "how completely the social scheme must be altered before woman can enjoy true equality with man" (27). Some of the earliest commentators on the novel recognized the general point, as when George Loring noted in 1850 that, without sin, "virtue cannot rise above innocency" (qtd. in Tompkins 1985: 21; as Tompkins discusses, Loring's intent is often misconstrued by modern critics).
20 Earlier critics have, of course, noted some elements of feminist critique in the novel. I take it that this critique is principally a matter of religious ethics and national ideals. Readers interested in a very different sort of feminist approach to the novel might consider, for example, Shari Benstock's (1991) discussion of an alternative "logic" that "confus[es]" the "representational codes" of the novel's society.

9

POE'S "THE BLACK CAT"

An allegory of misogyny

It probably seems odd to take a story by Edgar Allan Poe as a second literary response to the subnational division created by sex identity.[1] It seems odd, first of all, because the story in question does not appear, on the surface, to be about women and men at all. It seems to be about cats. Bear with me. I believe a good case can be made that it really is about women—or maybe about gay men—but not, mostly, about cats.[2] A less obvious reason for it being an odd choice—and this one is valid—concerns Poe's aims in treating the identity division. He has no obvious interest in national identity. Rather than nation-building, one could see his work as engaging in something more like demystification. He largely secularizes issues that earlier writers may have seen as religions. A crucial part of this involves psychologizing concerns of the spirit or soul, and developing the psychology in a material way. Misogyny and associated violence against women are topics for Poe, I imagine, less because he objects to them morally or as limitations on national unity and more as complex cases of extreme psychological states. On the other hand, this is all part of Poe's national importance. He is an admired and loved American writer in part because he addresses the themes of significance for American nation-building, even if he treats them as objects of fascination and psychological study.

But, why do I think the story is about women? One reason is that, very near the beginning of the story, just after he introduces the topic of cats, Poe takes up a key topic from American history, a central element in American self-understanding in relation to women—witchcraft. Specifically, the narrator invokes "the ancient popular notion, which regarded all black cats as witches in disguise" (Poe 2017a: 671). Though Poe does not develop this point, he establishes it at the outset, thereby orienting the reader's subsequent interpretation and response. But this is not all. The cats in the story are repeatedly associated with the narrator's wife. Most obviously, when he sets out to kill the second cat, he ends up killing his

American Literature and American Identity   143

wife.³ Moreover, he inadvertently buries the cat with his wife, and it is the voice of the cat that reveals her murder. Other connections are less direct. For example, he wakes at night "to find the hot breath of *the thing* upon [his] face" and to feel its "weight" (674, italics in the original). Though this can happen with a pet, the more obvious reference for the breath and weight of a bedmate is one's spouse.

Personally, I am particularly struck by the fact that the narrator goes to "a den of more than infamy" (673), a phrase that, to my ears, suggests that the place was selling more than alcohol. In this den, he picks up … a cat. One imagines that contemporaries of Poe went to dens of more than infamy not to get a cat, but due to an interest in something that is vulgarly referred to by another name for "cat." (I should note that the sexual use of "pussy" was already to be found a century before Poe, as attested in the *Oxford English Dictionary*.) As if the connection were not already clear, the narrator offers money for it to the owner of the establishment, as one might pay in a brothel, and he "caresses" the cat (673). This sexual association with the cat may be further suggested by the imagery of fire, for after he kills the cat, the result is a fire; specifically, he wakes to find that "the curtains of my bed were in flames" (672).

Finally, it is a commonplace in literature (and, sadly, in life) that, on returning home, a belligerent drunk will beat his wife (not his cat). And, indeed, that is just what the narrator does. When he begins to drink, he first verbally abuses his wife, then engages in "personal violence" against her (671). Later, too, the narrator confesses that his "frequent, and ungovernable outbursts of fury" had his "wife" as their "usual" target (674)

In short, the story insistently links the two cats with women. Moreover, from witches to wife-beating, it does so in a way that links the actions of the story with misogyny. But that still does not explain why I might wish to consider this story in particular. As it happens, I believe that the story provides a valuable framework for thinking about misogyny.

Before turning back to the story, however, I need to say something more about the nature of misogyny. As, for example, Martha Nussbaum (2018) has noted, misogyny may involve "bodily disgust" at women, but this disgust is "not incompatible with sexual desire." Straight men feel sexual desire for women. But at the same time, many of them feel disgust at women's bodies. How can one possibly feel both misogynistic disgust and desire? My suggestion would be that the sexual desire system, when activated, inhibits disgust. This is ordinary and part of what emotion or motivation systems do (e.g., disgust inhibits hunger). The sexual desire and disgust systems may partially share elicitors, though presumably different aspects of those elicitors. For example, the touch of a partner's genitalia may arouse desire, while their odor may arouse disgust. When the desire has dissipated, the inhibition of disgust ends. Sometimes, inhibition leads to a rebound where ordinary levels of the inhibited idea or attitude rise after the inhibition is lifted. We see this in some cases of racism and other forms of bias. For example, Ziva Kunda (1999: 344) explains that "the initial suppression" of a stereotype "led to an increase in its activation and use in other settings encountered shortly thereafter" (if this seems too "cognitive," rather than "affective," it is worth noting that the rebound effect leads to behavior suggesting aversion or disgust—such as sitting "further away" [1999: 345]—and not simply to abstract judgments). This would appear to be particularly likely in cases where the desire focused one's attention on some of the same objects that are elicitors of disgust. In any case, it makes sense of the possibility of desire and disgust coexisting in one person for the same target. (See Figure 9.1.)

In addition to rebound effects, it seems likely that sexual disgust would vary with one's own sexual shame. In other words, one would expect that increased shame would be linked with increased arousal of the disgust system. That enhanced arousal of disgust may be more directed at oneself than at one's partner. But the two are likely to be closely interconnected, given the difficulties we often have with identifying emotion elicitors. Specifically, we often attribute the cause of an emotion to the wrong object or event (see Clore and Ortony 2000: 27; Gilbert and Wilson 2000: 183; and Zajonc 2000: 48). Such misattribution is frequently a matter of taking some salient object in our environment as the cause of our feelings. In the case of disgust, even if one feels disgust at one's own actions, there would seem to be a reasonable likelihood of explaining that disgust by reference to

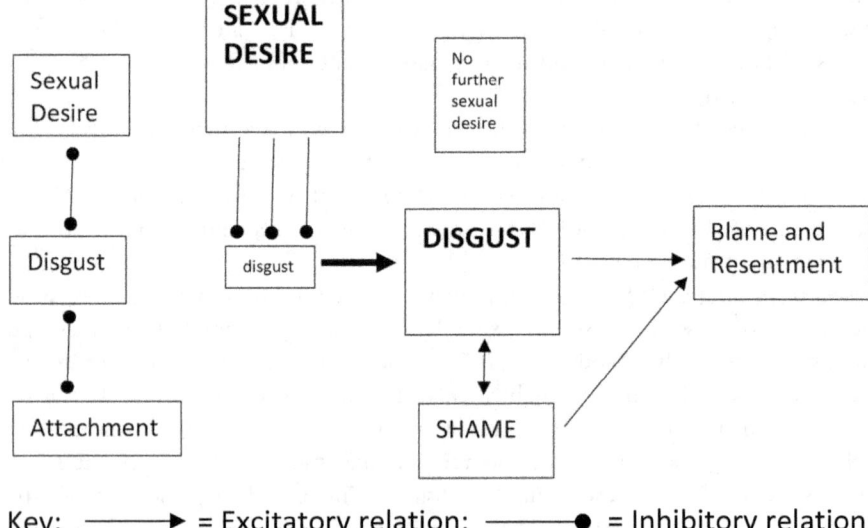

Key: ⟶ = Excitatory relation; ⟶• = Inhibitory relation

FIGURE 9.1 *Desire and Misogyny*. The motivation systems of sexual desire and attachment may be understood as having mutually inhibitory connections with disgust. Strong sexual desire may greatly inhibit disgust. However, when the sexual desire wanes, disgust may increase due to a rebound effect. This rebound effect may be enhanced in cases of self-disgust or shame, which itself may be intensified by more general disgust arousal. The aversive feelings of disgust and shame may, in turn, foster blame of and resentment against the target of (earlier) sexual desire and (current) disgust.

one's partner, since she or he is presumably the most salient element of one's environment or one's recollection (given the sexual context of the shame). Moreover, shame makes one acutely sensitive to observation. As Robert Sapolsky (2017: 547) puts it, "feeling shame is about wanting to hide" (see also Scheff 2011: 455 on shame and "withdrawal"). A partner's observation—even if it is unrelated to disgust—may make us more aware of our shame and thus more ashamed.

In this context, we begin to get a sense of some of the factors that lead to misogynistic disgust and to their association with witchcraft. Witches are old and ugly, thus manifesting the repulsive bodily features that trigger disgust. But their function is also to seduce us. Thus, they lure us into the very acts that make us feel disgust for ourselves as well as for them. Understanding the operation of disgust and shame in misogyny also helps to explain other aspects of Poe's story. Why, for example, does he first harm the cat by cutting its eye? It is presumably the same reason that the narrator of Poe's (2017b: 667) "The Tell-Tale Heart" kills an old man because of his "Evil Eye." The eye is the means and symbol of someone else's observation, and thus a deep source of one's own shame. The narrator of "The Tell-Tale Heart" explains: "He had the eye of a vulture. ... Whenever it fell upon me, my blood ran cold" (2017b: 666). Cutting the cat's eye is a way of, in some degree, avoiding being seen.

After he "caresses" the cat in the "den of more than infamy" (2017a: 673), the narrator expects to feel some degree of fondness. However, instead, he feels "disgust" and "a certain sense of shame" (673). This seems to me to rather strongly suggest an act of greater significance and intimacy that petting a stray cat. Indeed, it seems most clearly consistent with a postcoital rebound effect. Moreover, it is presumably no accident that disgust and shame are two of the most prominent emotions here, along with "hatred of the beast" (673), just as disgust and shame appear to be particularly important in misogyny or hatred of women.[4]

Finally, the concluding lines of the story stress the cat's "solitary eye of fire" (676). The emphasis on the eye again recalls that shame is intensified by observation and that the narrator here (like the narrator of "The Tell-Tale Heart") is driven into rage by that observing eye—a fitting point because shame tends to manifest itself either in hiding or in rage (see Scheff 2011 and Walker and Knauer 2011). The fire is, first of all, the fire that punishes the narrator for his initial crime. But we may also begin to guess its source in the "burning" that we idiomatically associate with shame (as well as sexual desire).[5] Finally, it is important to note that the narrator blames the cat for having "seduced me into murder" (676). Of course, a man who feels shame and disgust would be likely to accuse his partner of seducing him into sexual sin, not murder. But the key point here is that he blames his shame, disgust, and rage on a seduction, thus the sort of harmful deception associated with witches and prostitutes (recall the "den of more than infamy" [673]), and thus with women more generally, in sexist ideology.

I will conclude these brief observations on Poe's story by noting a possible problem. These are tomcats. Does that make a difference? In fact, I do not think it is crucial. However, it may serve to suggest something about anti-gay violence as well as misogyny. The narrator's trip to "a den of more than infamy" (673) could equally be read as a trip to a gay bar. The secretive character and the indirect and convoluted hints of sexuality would fit same-sex sexual desire in a homophobic society. So too would the main character's shame, disgust, and violence. In this way, the story could be understood as a precursor not only to some American feminist literature, but to such gay American narratives as James Baldwin's *Giovanni's Room* (1956).

Conclusion

Due to the brevity of this chapter, there is no need for me to summarize it. However, it is important to underscore a point that I made in the introduction. The suggestion of misogyny and sexual violence in the story are not obvious on first reading. But, even if one is skeptical about the details of my interpretation, it seems clear that the story draws on the model of male antipathy toward women and the brutality associated with that. Indeed, one could argue that homophobia and homophobic violence draw in part on misogynistic attitudes. The importance of such connections suggests the centrality and pervasiveness of misogyny and sexism in many people's understanding of and response to a range of social groups. (This is in keeping with Ashis Nandy's [1983] observation that the colonial modeling of Africans and Indians on children and the aged was often mediated by modeling colonizer–colonized differences on gender.) Moreover, analyzing the story has allowed me to suggest a partial account of the operation of misogyny in relation to sexuality. Though Poe does not address national identity in the story, misogyny and our comprehension of its relation to sexuality are clearly of central importance to our understanding of patriarchy, perhaps the most pervasive and enduring violation of universal, democratic egalitarianism.

Notes

1 A feminist approach to Poe may be less counterintuitive to viewers of Jean-Luc Godard's *Vivre Sa Vie* (1962), which treats the status of women in France at the time the film was made. Godard reads long passages from another Poe story ("The Oval Portrait") in one scene of the film. These passages bear in a straightforward way on the film's political engagement and its feminist concerns.
2 The story may also touch on racial issues, given the (somewhat occluded) importance of race for Poe, as argued by Joan Dayan (1995).
3 The woman who dies prematurely is an extremely important recurring motif in Poe's work. Interpreters of Poe have connected this motif with Poe's loss of "nurturing females" in real life (Weekes 2002: 149) and stressed its significance for his narrator's "angst and guilt" (Weekes 2002: 150). Though I have not seen any critical analyses of "The Black Cat" (Poe 2017a) that explore it as a story about misogyny, these general concerns are consistent with widely recognized patterns in Poe's work.
4 Poe does offer an explanation for the narrator's behavior. It is a manifestation of "the spirit of Perverseness" (671), the impulse to reject moral and social norms and affirm oneself simply by doing what one "knows [one] should *not*" do (672, italics in the original). "Perverseness" might seem to suggest sexuality, but that usage appears to postdate Poe's story. Nonetheless, Poe's account may not be wholly incompatible with what I am

suggesting. The characterization of the perverse act as "vile" (672) appears to hint at an element of disgust underlying the perverse act, as well as a sense of disgust at oneself, thus shame. Perhaps that self-disgust is what leads to the "unfathomable longing" to do "violence to [one's] own nature" (672).

5 This association may in part be related to blushing (see Shah 2016: 69, n.13), but it is also a matter of the common mapping of emotions onto temperature (cf. Kövecses 2000: 38).

10

JUDITH SARGENT MURRAY

Women's virtue and the equality of the sexes

Judith Sargent Murray is best known as the author of a pathbreaking 1790 work, "On the Equality of the Sexes." That essay places her in the forefront of writers treating the relations between men and women in the new nation.[1] Though she is less known today for her creative or imaginative writing, Murray was also a playwright. In this chapter, we will consider two of her plays, *Virtue Triumphant* of 1795 and *The Traveller Returned* of 1796. Despite her clear feminist credentials, Murray's relation to feminist concerns is complex and, at least to twenty-first century readers, ambiguous. She certainly gestures toward issues of the "equality of the sexes," as well as national identity. But it is sometimes difficult to determine just what ideas the plays endorse regarding these topics.

Here, we might return to our division among patriarchy, sexism, and misogyny. In her "Equality" essay, Murray touches on all three. But her main concern is with the possibilities for women's practical identity development, particularly their intellectual development. In other words, her focus is on what has constrained women in their activity and self-cultivation. Such constraint is a particular aspect of patriarchy, with implications for women's active, worldly equality as part of the nation. There are some small hints of that in her plays. But, in contrast with the "Equality" essay, the plays seem principally concerned to defend women against one sort of misogyny. This issue is not absent from the essay, and is particularly connected with the "supplement" added to the original essay. In that supplement, Murray defends Eve against the (misogyny-supporting) accusation of having caused the fall of all humanity. On the other hand, even in that case, Murray's main concern is women's quest for self-cultivation, which is represented by Eve's desire for "knowledge" (see also Genesis 1–11). Moreover, in the plays the opposition to misogyny is not exactly a defense of women. It is, rather, a defense of some women along with an appeal to other women that they should be virtuous. Put differently, it is not really a critique of sexism. To advert to the techniques we introduced in previous chapters, we might say that Murray is less interested in debunking stereotypes about women than explaining why women might behave in objectionable ways. Murray's plays are less moralistic than, for example, Hannah Webster Foster's widely read 1797 novel, *The Coquette*. Foster shows the (female) reader the dire consequences of frivolity and sexual freedom, which lead to social disgrace, psychological anguish, and premature death. This is not what we find in Murray. But Murray's plays are still moralistic in a way that raises problems for any straightforward feminist interpretation of the works—at least as we would understand feminism today.

In this way, Murray presents us with another case of the sort of ambivalence that we have found so often in the preceding analyses, though the precise operation of that ambivalence does not seem to be quite the same as what we have discussed in other writers. To some extent, what we seem to see in Murray is a difference between the formulation of abstract principles (equality of development) and the simulation of concrete particulars. When Murray states general ideas, she has one set of primary concerns and related beliefs and aims. When she imagines particular conditions and actions, however, those primary concerns and (tacit) beliefs shift to some degree, leading to stories that are only partially compatible with the general ideas. One might initially expect that general principles and concrete simulations would be consistent with one another, as the concrete particulars would conform to the general principles. But, in actual cognitive processing abstract ideas are likely to rely on categories related to one another by forms of entailment. In contrast, the simulation (or imagination) of particular causal sequences (as in the creation of a story in fiction) is likely to draw on particular experiences and conditions, especially those that are salient. (For example, Smith's bad experiences with an unreliable Volvo are likely to guide his simulation of the performance of another Volvo, even if he is familiar with the statistics about Volvo reliability and these show his experience to have been very unusual [see Nisbett and Ross 1980: 15].) Murray's particular experiences occurred within a context where patriarchal structures and sexism were in all likelihood pervasive. This would tend to make both the patriarchal structures and the sexism fade into the background, thus becoming part of what is presupposed in simulation, rather than what is varied in simulation and—through that variation—open to criticism. (This seems to me less true of misogyny. Expressions of hatred of or disgust at women appear to be more localized and episodic, thus more salient.) In this context, the political complications of Murray's plays become more comprehensible.

"On the Equality of the Sexes"

Before examining the plays, we should briefly consider some main points from Murray's "Equality" essay. She begins with psychology, taking up a critique of sexism. Specifically, she explains that "intellectual powers [may] be ranged under these four heads—imagination, reason, memory and judgment" (2017: 773). She goes on to argue that women are clearly not deficient in imagination or memory. Regarding memory, she appeals to everyone's experience of seniors reminiscing about their youth, an activity in which (she says) old men do not outdo old women.

Murray's argument about imagination is more elaborate, but also more problematic. She begins by referring to women's shifting tastes in fashion, thereby invoking a trivializing stereotype to support a feminist egalitarian conclusion. She goes on to cite a more obviously destructive stereotype, stating that "another instance of our creative powers is our talent for slander" (2017: 773). Here, someone might reasonably defend Murray's claim by pointing to psychological research on male and female aggression. As Greg Lukianoff and Jonathan Haidt (2018: 155) explain, empirical studies do indicate that "girls … are more 'relationally' aggressive; they try to hurt their rivals' relationships, reputations, and social status." This is broadly consistent with Murray's claim about slander. However, it is important that slander or related activities be put in the larger context of aggression, with the recognition that "there's no overall sex difference in total aggression," even though there are differences in "the preferred ways of harming others" (2018: 155). In any case, Murray goes on to comment that, the "great activity of mind" evidenced by fashion sense and slander shows that, if women found their creative "activity properly directed," surely "beneficial effects would follow" (2017: 773).

This comment leads to the main focus of Murray's essay—the cultivation of women's intellectual talents. She seems to accept the stereotype that women are inferior to men in reason and judgment. Research on cognitive biases may suggest she did not so much underestimate the rationality and wisdom of women as overestimate the rationality and wisdom of men. In any case, like other authors we have considered, Murray presents us with an explanation of the stereotype. Specifically, she accounts for putative female inferiority by reference to women's exclusion from self-cultivation, particularly intellectual pursuits. She subsequently extends the point to the stereotype of female frivolity (which is not only a misguided stereotype, but one that is bound to a particular socioeconomic class). Thus, she claims that, for example, an unmarried woman, without the option of becoming learned, "seeks to fill up time from sexual employments or amusements" (774). More generally, she claims that there is "too much justice" in accusations that women "amus[e] themselves" with "trifles" (774). However, this lack of serious commitment to worthwhile pursuits results from an absence of intellectual opportunities. She goes on to affirm the especial benefit of intellectual pursuits for women in that greater depth and breadth of learning would lead women to a more thorough appreciation of and devotion to God. This was a rhetorically appropriate form of appeal to her readers at the time. However, it too is less likely to strike readers today as the most feminist approach to the topic, since it does not appear to justify women's self-cultivation as an intrinsic right, comparable to that of men, but only as an instrumental value serving religion.

A note on American identity and American literature

Neither of the plays we will be considering is focused on U.S. national identity. But both bring in national concerns clearly and even obtrusively, despite their seeming marginality to the main story events. In part, this is a matter of Murray's concern—common to U.S. writers at the time—of developing an American literature and, perhaps even more importantly, an appreciative readership for American literature. In one of her essays, Murray laments "the paucity of national attachment in our country" (Murray 2018: 160). She goes on to maintain that "perhaps our deficiency in national partiality is in nothing more apparent than in the little taste we discover for American Literature" (161). She particularly stresses "supply[ing] the American stage with American scenes" (162). In this way, both her plays may be viewed as, in part, attempts at establishing a specifically American theater and thus as involved with national identity.

The point becomes clearer when we note that Murray adopted the pseudonym "Philo Americanus"—roughly, "Lover of America"—to pen the introductions to both plays (see 14 and 116). In the case of *Virtue Triumphant*, this Americaphile frames his introduction by establishing his purpose as national. He is "attached to my country" (13) and therefore wishes to advance its "eminence" (14). Part of achieving that eminence, he suggests, involves cultivating a supportive attitude to "every literary attempt" by an American (113). Of course, this admonition is self-serving on Murray's part, as it urges the reader not to be too highly critical of her play. But, even so, the introduction still sets out to prime the reader's nationalist sentiments and thereby tends to orient the reader's interpretation in a nationalist direction. Thus, insofar as the works treat male–female relations, they to some extent do so in the context of a rhetorical framing that makes national identifications salient at the very outset.

Virtue Triumphant (1795)

Virtue Triumphant is, for the most part, a prototypical romantic comedy. Charles Maitland wishes to marry Eliza. However, his father opposes the marriage and, despite the fact that she loves Charles, Eliza herself refuses to wed unless the couple are equal. In the end, Eliza learns that she is an heiress. Thus established as equal to Charles in economic class, she is free to marry him. Meanwhile, Augusta is behaving frivolously and mistreating her husband. Matronia, Augusta's aunt, speaks to her about this lack of sober circumspection and succeeds in reforming her. The play also includes a long-lost relative of Eliza's (Mellfont) and a backstabbing "mean girl" (Miss Scornwell), as well as a couple of offstage characters who appear only in the stories of the onstage characters.

This play is often seen as feminist, or at least as consistent with "On the Equality," because Eliza refuses to marry unless she is the "equal" of her husband (cf. 32). Taken out of context, this certainly sounds as if the play illustrates Murray's appeal published five years earlier. Moreover, Murray prepares us to think of Eliza's insistence as parallel to the affirmation of democratic equality that is at the foundation of the American self-concept (for more on the American self-concept, see Chapter 1). Specifically, Mr. Maitland—despite his opposition to his son's marriage—begins the play by asserting "the *Commonwealth of Equality*" as the highest ideal, for which he would, "were it necessary, fight and die" (16, italics in the original). There is even a possible hint of feminist criticism when Mr. Maitland identifies this affirmation of equality with "fraternity" (16), a sex-marked term that might be taken to exclude women.

However, the equality to which Eliza appeals is not equality in political status, professional opportunity, and intellectual cultivation. It is simply equality in social class. As far as she is aware, she is a penniless orphan. Thus, she tells Charles that she would marry him if he "had been born the *equal* of my *humble family and lowly fortunes*" (30, italics in the original). Of course, there is a feminist issue regarding the wealth of the spouses, in the sense that women's autonomy is largely contingent on them having control of their own finances. As Skemp (2009: 154) notes, regarding the revolutionary period, "the ideology of independence did nothing to give women economic security." However, Eliza would in effect have lost her wealth upon marriage anyway, due to the legal fiction of "coverture," which gave the wife's property over to her husband (see Skemp 2009: 146). In any case, Murray does not develop the issue of equality in class status in this way. To a great extent, Eliza seems concerned principally with avoiding the accusation of "fortune-hunting" (2018: 17)—what Mr. Maitland accuses her of in the opening pages of the play. Thus, we find her explaining that she "will never unite herself to a man, whose family detests her" (31). Insofar as this is a matter of resistance to confirming a stereotype, there might be a (somewhat distant) hint of a feminist concern here. But Eliza does not suggest that she wishes to avoid any appearance of supporting of sexism. Rather, she suggests that the antipathy of her in-laws would make her life unhappy. This is a perfectly reasonable point, of course. Moreover, it has the minimal feminist implication that a woman should give some thought to her future condition before she agrees to marry. But this is rather a far cry from the feminist demand for complete impartiality in opportunities for intellectual development put forth in the "Equality" essay.

This is not to say that there are no points of contact between the essay and the play. Certainly, Matronia Aimwell is an admirable character.[2] She is the most conscientious and acute character in the play. She handles her money well, even to the point of helping Georgia's financially distressed husband. Still more significantly, she gives solid advice to her niece, Augusta, convincing her to mend her frivolous ways. She is an exemplar of all the admirable qualities that, in Murray's view, a woman might possess. The only thematic problem here is that Murray never makes clear just why Matronia is so wise, prudent, and rational. There does not seem to be anything in the play suggesting that she came to this state by being offered possibilities for self-cultivation that were not offered to, say, her niece. In other words, she does not appear to illustrate the point that women can excel if they are given opportunities for intellectual development. Rather, her character seems simply to suggest that some women are naturally more circumspect than others. Indeed, the way Murray develops the relationship between Augusta and her husband appears consistent with Matronia's harsh judgment that Augusta suffers "strange degeneracy!" (33). When she finally convinces Augusta to mend her ways, Matronia maintains that Augusta committed a "guilty deed" in deceiving her husband about her feelings, thus doing him "a most heinous injury." In consequence, she must "let [her] husband's wishes become [her] future study" (77), selflessly devoting herself to him.

Similar points seem to apply to the slanderous Miss Scornwell. This character is consistent with the "Equality" essay only in suggesting that slander may be a female propensity. Indeed, contrary to the essay, Scornwell does not even seem to be particularly good at it. She sets out to slander Eliza, but fails abysmally. Moreover, Scornwell explains that she prefers "a ride to a book, and the ball-room to the play-house" (38). Since Murray's essay suggests the calumny-inhibiting value of literature, this may seem continuous with that argument. But the very fact that Scornwell is able to choose rides and balls over books and plays suggests that she was not denied access to the latter. Rather, she seems to have had the opportunity to read and to see plays. She simply chose not to do so.

Moreover, the libelous propensities of women are testified to by one of the offstage characters as well. This is Olivia, an "execrable female" (85), who defamed Mellfont to Eliza. This led Eliza to flee France before Mellfont could inform her of her inheritance. In short, Olivia came very close to ruining Eliza's life. In this case, we do not know what Olivia thought of the theater. However, we do not have any reason to infer that her "execrable" character would have been different had she been encouraged to read more.

Finally, it is worth noting that Eliza's biological mother seems to have been unreasonable, to say the least. In this way, she is a sort of counterbalance to the reasonable Matronia, and thus a character who indicates that we should not take Matronia to represent womankind generally. Eliza's mother bound her brother, Mellfont, to conceal Eliza's parentage from Eliza herself, deceiving her into thinking that she was "the offspring of poverty" (84). Eliza could be told the truth only after 15 years. This does produce a reflective and staid young woman. But Matronia achieves the same results with Augusta through a few minutes of rational conversation. This suggests that—at least as far as the play goes—there is no need for extensive dishonesty; moral results may be achieved by the simple application of reason. Moreover, the latter does not carry the palpable risks that attend on the former. Again, a sensible enough point, but one that is not in any clear way feminist. Indeed, in giving us yet another example of extreme and misguided thought in a woman, Eliza's mother seems to reinforce sexist views.

These apparent flaws are to some degree mitigated by the representation of men in the play. For example, Scornwell may be in some ways matched with Captain Flashet, as both are undereducated outsiders to the comic society formed by Matronia, the Maitlands—Matronia's niece and her husband—and Mellfont at the end of the play. Indeed, Flashet is the object of repeated ridicule. He continually parades his supposed learning, but makes such ludicrous errors that we either laugh at him or disdain him entirely. In contrast, despite her failure at full-fledged slander Scornwell can be sharp and witty, if in a rather mean-spirited way, as when she comments on "the antiquated dame, Arabella Worthy, whose face is a perfect antidote to every idea of conviviality" (39). When she is contrasted with the wholly unsalvageable Flashet, we see that there is some spark in Scornwell. In consequence, we might with reason apply the following comment from Murray's "Equality" essay to at least some instances of Scornwell's scorn: "Assuredly great activity of mind is thereby discovered, and was this activity properly directed, what beneficial effects would follow" (2017: 773).

More significantly, Mr. Maitland should be parallel to Matronia as the wise elder of his clan. At the start, however, he is logically inconsistent—celebrating equality, but then enforcing class-based elitism. Moreover, he is physically vain—rushing to have his hair done and calling out for his "powder and perfume-box" (19) when he learns that he is to be visited by Matronia. In the end, he does move into a sort of wise elder role when he shows himself to be very empathetic and kind after meeting Eliza. In any case, his pairing with Matronia does indeed make a feminist point. Specifically, it suggests a criticism of gender stereotypes, rather than an acceptance and explanation of them. At the start, Mr. Maitland actually exhibits stereotypically female faults—illogic and vanity—that Matronia never exhibits. Subsequently, his warm-hearted fellow feeling is stereotypically feminine—in contrast with Matronia's more principle-governed and relatively unemotional solemnity.

Indeed, this pairing of Matronia and Maitland even begins to suggest a way in which the subnational division between men and women may be resolved, and how this might in turn be connected with national identification. Specifically, men and women need to cultivate both putatively masculine and putatively feminine virtues and guard against both putatively masculine and putatively feminine vices. To achieve genuine equality, as advocated by Maitland early on in the play, one needs the sympathetic (what we would now call "empathetic") sensitivities that are stereotypically associated with women. Conversely, to make one's way through the world and guide one's children (or other young relatives, such as a niece, in Matronia's case), one needs to develop the supposedly masculine virtues of rationality and the ability to modulate emotion, as we see in Matronia.

In short, *Virtue Triumphant* does not appear to follow the arguments of Murray's "On the Equality of the Sexes." Indeed, the play often seems to support sexist stereotypes in both characterization and overt statement (e.g., when an apparently trustworthy character refers to women's "wily arts of deception" [2018: 21]). Moreover, the play does not even appear to devote much attention to patriarchy or misogyny (except in making the male and female characters comparably likeable). These points are perhaps less surprising when we recall that reasoning through abstract principles and simulating particular sequences of events involve distinct processes and therefore need not be entirely consistent in the writings of any given author.

On the other hand, once we look at the male characters in the play, we may isolate some unexpected contrasts. These contrasts suggest a sort of feminism in the play that is rather different from the one expressed in "On the Equality of the Sexes." Specifically, rather than accepting and explaining stereotypes, here Murray seems to reject them, at least in some characters. That rejection too suggests differences between abstract principles and particular simulations. On the one hand, our simulations will draw on fictions and anecdotes that embody stereotypes that we would reject if stated baldly (e.g., a white person may imagine a black man to be dangerous even if he or she would reject the abstract, general statement that black men are dangerous). On the other hand, our simulations will also draw on real cases that do not fit stereotypes—thus irrational or empathetic men and rational or emotionally distant women. Indeed, in real life we are likely to come upon comparable numbers of stereotypical and nonstereotypical cases for each putatively sex-linked trait. In these ways, then, the play does gesture toward the issue of sex-based subnational division and the possibility of egalitarianism in that area.

The Traveller Returned (1796)

Murray's 1796 comedy tells a story similar to that of her work of the year before. It concerns a poor young woman, Emily, who has been orphaned and adopted by her aunt, Mrs. Montague. Emily is in love with Major Camden, who is affianced to Mrs. Montague's daughter, Harriot. However, Camden is in love with Emily, while Harriot wishes to marry Alberto Stanhope. Stanhope, in turn, reciprocates Harriot's feelings. The Harriot–Alberto alliance is approved by Mr. Stanhope. But Mrs. Montague supports only Camden for her daughter. Being a circumspect and pious young woman, Emily shuns Camden, despite her attachment to him.

Meanwhile, the mysterious Rambleton has turned up in town with his stereotypical but endearing and comical Irish servant. Rambleton lodges with the Vansittarts. Dissatisfied with their finances, Mrs. Vansittart convinces her husband to slander Rambleton—indeed, to denounce him to a committee of the revolutionary government that operates to enforce law during the Revolutionary War, which is underway at the time of the action. (The play takes place sometime between late 1780 and early 1783.) The Vansittarts are eventually apprehended for their crime. Rambleton is revealed to be the long-estranged husband of Mrs. Montague. Disheartened by his wife's frivolity and emotional (though not physical) infidelity, Rambleton—that is, Mr. Montague—left with his son some 19 years earlier. The son, raised by a foster parent, turns out to be Camden, which makes Harriot his sister and thus an inappropriate spouse. Kneeling, Mrs. Montague begs forgiveness from her spouse. All the lovers are united; the frivolous tendencies of the wayward women are curbed; Rambleton-Montague is exonerated on the accusation of treason; the Vansittarts are in custody; and the nation is on its way to independence.

There are some obvious points of connection between this play and Murray's "Equality" essay. For example, Mrs. Vansittart shows the supposedly feminine affinity for the creative use of slander in suggesting that she and her husband "inform against" Rambleton "to the Committee of Safety" (2018: 139). Murray has her rationalize this slander by calling it "patrolitical" (139)—a combination of "patriotic" and "political," presumably in the derogatory sense of the latter. Thus, the coinage would appear to suggest invoking patriotism for self-interest. The way that Mrs. Vansittart corrupts Mr. Vansittart may also remind readers of the Adam and Eve myth, discussed in Murray's essay. In both cases, however, the feminist element of Murray's essay is not evident. Mrs. Vansittart probably has not developed her intellectual capacities, but that is not foregrounded or suggested as a reason for her slander. Moreover, Murray's clever reinterpretation of the Adam and Eve events does not appear to have any parallel in the tale of the Vansittarts. There is no obvious way in which Mrs. Vansittart's fault is more elevated or justifiable than her husband's.

Similar points apply to the other characters. Emily (like Eliza in the earlier play) is admirably serious and sober. However, there is no reason to believe that this results from intellectual training, such as reading about phlogiston (the central example of intellectual pursuit in the play). Indeed, Harriot cites the theory of phlogiston to her mother. However, unlike Emily, she is excessively lighthearted, "resolve[d] to enjoy the present moment," even when that involves consorting with the misguided and misguiding Mrs. Fallacy, with her prodigious "talents at ridicule" (126). She even goes so far as to judge the admirable Major Camden "a perfect antidote to every mirthful idea" (127).

The issue of self-cultivation does arise in the play, in that the largely admirable Mrs. Montague does spend a good deal of time reading about phlogiston. But this seems mostly comical, if innocuous. Certainly, her intellectual interests do not appear to do her any harm. But it is far from clear that her abstention from frivolity and cruel gossip results from poring over texts on combustion. The main link between Mrs. Montague and the "Equality" essay concerns her own frivolity, her susceptibility to the allure of "sexual ... amusements" (to quote from the essay, (2017: 774). She was, in her husband's words, "grossly wanting, both to herself and me" (125). But we do not have to take his word for her deficiency. She herself confesses to "dissipation" (143) and, when Rambleton-Montague appears, she kneels before him, appealing for his forgiveness and insisting that "each day" for 19 years she went through "suffering" for what she had done (160).

Here, as in the preceding play, we see that the women exhibit the flaws that sexist ideology attributes to them. But it is not clear that these faults are explained by the patriarchal structure criticized in the "Equality" essay. Of course, sometimes wives are inadequately affectionate, as are husbands. The mere fact of Mrs. Montague's emotional infidelity does not necessarily say anything about women generally. Indeed, I myself am overwhelmingly less sympathetic with Mr. Montague for running off rather than trying to discuss and resolve any issues rationally—though I do not see much criticism of this decision in the play itself. The play seems to put Rambleton-Montague in the position of Rip van Winkle, escaping his disagreeable and unsympathetic wife almost inadvertently (for more on the latter, see the Introduction). Indeed, it would seem that the men were absent for almost exactly the same years. The main differences are that Rambleton-Montague returns a year earlier and his wife is still alive, but she is reformed. In addition, the Revolutionary War is still in progress, though evidently nearing its end.[3]

The final point draws our attention to the national concerns of the play. These are first signaled by the opening, where Rambleton, returning to America during the Revolutionary War, rejoices that his emerging nation has "given birth to such a race of heroes" (117). Not much later, Murray elaborates on the national identity issue by presenting a dialogue between Rambleton and Major Camden concerning a great national hero—unnamed but clearly George Washington. They list some of his successes, celebrating his "military talents" as "unequalled" and rejoicing in his "intrepid valour and inborn patriotism" (122). They go on to express their warm admiration and appreciation for their "matchless soldiers" who, as "FREE AMERICANS" (capitals in the original), "bear arms in defence of the invaded Rights of Man" (124).

As noted above, Rambleton left 19 years earlier. Evidence internal to the play indicates that the action takes place before the end of the Revolutionary War (in 1783) but after the execution of Major André (in October of 1780). This means that Montague-Rambleton may have left as early as late 1761 or early 1762. This would place his departure before the end of the French and Indian War and the Proclamation of 1763, which restricted the expansion of European settlements taking over territory from the Amerindians. In this way, like Rip van Winkle, Rambleton-Montague left the colonies before there was any clear national movement. (Also like Rip, his return opens him to suspicion as a Loyalist.) The passages cited to this point may seem to suggest that the nationalism of the play is entirely untroubled. But, in fact, it is as complex and ambivalent as that in Irving's story.[4]

Even in the dialogue between Rambleton and Major Camden, there is a hint of a darker side to the revolution, indeed, a darker side to General Washington. Rambleton remarks that "the ignominious death of Major André has taught some people to question his sensibility" (123). Major André was a British officer who worked with Benedict Arnold, the revolutionary officer who, from the U.S. point of view, became a traitor to his country. André was captured and executed, while Arnold escaped. André was well liked, and there was a common feeling that he was acting loyally to his own country. Many people felt that he was treated with unnecessary severity. What is most significant in the present context is that, as Skemp (2009: 86) notes, "like many Americans, [Murray] was horrified by George Washington's determination to hang Major John André." Rambleton's questioning of Washington's "sensibility" may point toward a hardness of heart that enables cruel behaviors. Indeed, faced with the violence of the Revolutionary War, Murray "began to think that bravery was not a virtue. Rather, it was a 'sickness' that led to the destruction of all she cherished" (Skemp 2009 86).

This revolutionary insensibility is suggested elsewhere in the play. For example, Mrs. Vansittart refers to the United States as "this *Freetonian* land" (Murray 2018: 139, italics in the original). Though "Freetonian" may be taken to refer to a resident of a place named Freetown, I take the suggestion here to be slightly different. The United States is *free*, but only in a *Washingtonian* way, a way allowed by the oversight of the Committees of Safety. Indeed, Mrs. Vansittart refers to "this *Freetonian* land" directly after referring to the Committee of Safety and the way that her and her husband's unsupported accusation against Rambleton will lead to his arrest and leave them free to abscond with his valuables (139).

Obviously, the entire business with the Committee of Safety is the main sequence of events that suggests Murray's ambivalence about the identity of the new nation. A tip, with no supporting evidence, provokes a certain Mr. "Vigilant" to send Officer Tipstaff to arrest the slandered individual. It is, of course, good to be vigilant, but one may be excessively vigilant (as suggested by the development of the idea of "vigilantism"). Moreover, Tipstaff's name does fit his official function—using his staff to round up those accused by someone giving a tip to the committee. However, it may also suggest that his use of his staff may be affected by tips (in effect, bribes; the *Oxford English Dictionary* attests the monetary meaning of "tip" going back to the mid-eighteenth century). The arrest involves a specific accusation, that Rambleton is a spy, this in some degree paralleling him with Major André; indeed, Major André is mentioned not only by Rambleton (as noted above), but also by Mrs. Vansittart when she is planning her slander and robbery. In the course of the arrest, the affable stage Irishman, Patrick O'Neal, tries to intervene on Rambleton's behalf, insisting that it is wrong to be "boddering"—bothering or harassing—a man "in his own country" (146). Tipstaff insists that it is his duty, but Patrick baffles at the notion that harassing citizens could be anyone's duty. Indeed, his invocation of an anticolonial group of Irish rebels (147) suggests that he implicitly sees such botheration as colonial, thus a repetition of precisely what the rebels are criticizing in the British government.

When we next see Rambleton, he has been interrogated by the safety committee for "many hours" (158), evidently as he has been assumed guilty. The only advance they have made is the discovery that Rambleton is fond of Major Camden (we will later learn that Camden is Rambleton's son). This weighty and suspicious fact leads some of them "to suspect the fidelity of that young soldier" (157). The committee only allows Rambleton to leave when the testimony of the Vansittarts is wholly undermined by their robbery of Rambleton and the committee's realization that the arrest and interrogation served precisely to provide an opportunity for this act.

Though not so extreme as that of Irving, Murray's ambivalence about U.S. national identity seems clear. But just how does this relate to sex identity and the social relations between the sexes as subnational identities? The relation is not at all straightforward or explicit. Nonetheless, I believe it is real. Rambleton-Montague abandons his wife and daughter and in effect kidnaps (and more or less abandons) his son on the suspicion of his wife's emotional disloyalty. This suspicion was based on a passing and unacted infatuation fostered by youthful lightheartedness. The Committee of Safety is similarly precipitous in taking Rambleton into custody with no evidence that any crime has been committed. In short, there is a homology here. Mr. Montague is to Mrs. Montague as the Committee of Safety is to Rambleton (or perhaps to the citizenry generally). The vigilance of the revolutionary committee is arbitrary and authoritarian, as is the vigilance of the husband. Moreover, the groveling confession and remorse of Mrs. Montague are just the sort of display required by the invigilators of national and other forms of group loyalty.

This suggests a simultaneous criticism—or suspicion—of both national identity and the standard organization of patriarchy. As to the latter, one aspect of any group hierarchy is the demand of the dominant group that the subordinated group continually demonstrate their loyalty. This is because the dominant group almost inevitably fears disloyalty—unsurprisingly, given the social hierarchy. The relevant features of patriarchy are too well known to require more than a brief mention. They include male suspicion of women's infidelity, men's association of wifely chastity with their own honor, and the brutal treatment women may receive when men believe their honor has been tarnished—that is, when they feel they have been shamed—by their wives' misbehavior.

In this case, then, we seem to find yet another form of psychological inconsistency in writers (and, by implication, in nonwriters as well). Murray explicitly criticizes women for being frivolous. But as she imagines the relations between men and women, she cannot help but be affected by her own emotional response to patriarchal suspicion and policing. Her critical attitude toward that aspect of patriarchy—largely ignored in her essay on "Equality"—to some extent manifests itself in the absurd behavior of Mr. Montague. She does not present that behavior as if she or the other characters judge it to be absurd, but it plainly is and, whatever Murray thought about it self-consciously, she must have responded to it with some degree of aversion. This aversion manifests itself quite strongly, however, in the parallel case of governmental surveillance and suspicion, the questionable "sensibility" of its military leaders, and its operation on the presumption of guilt.

Conclusion

In sum, *Virtue Triumphant* introduces the issue of equality in marriage, but it develops that idea in a way that does not really critique patriarchy, misogyny, or sexism. This suggests a discrepancy between the abstract principles accepted and advocated by Murray and her concrete imagination (or simulation) of particular actions by individual men and women. Moreover, Murray's characterization of women in the play is to some extent stereotypical. On the other hand, this stereotyping is partially counterbalanced by her treatment of men. Overall, the play appears to suggest the importance of integrating putatively masculine and putatively feminine traits to achieve an equitable society, whether national or familial.

Issues of national identity are clearer in *The Traveller Returned*. Unsurprisingly, this play too is complicated. On the one hand, Murray seems to have illustrated the sexist commonplaces that she apparently accepted (such as a female propensity to slanderous gossip). Worse still, she does not go on to explain those stereotypes in a way that would undermine their support for patriarchy and point the way toward alternative, antipatriarchal practices. Indeed, the play appears to accept the validity of the patriarchal hierarchy itself, with Mrs. Montague kneeling for forgiveness because she was fond of someone else (without acting on it), while Mr. Montague only acted within his rights by abandoning her and his daughter and kidnapping and then abandoning their son.

On the other hand, Murray's accommodation to patriarchy at the level of particular simulation is only partial. It not only contradicts her more general beliefs,[5] it also appears to have contradicted her own emotional responses. Specifically, the play is much more ambivalent than it may at first seem. It is most obviously ambivalent in its response to affirmations of national identity. But that ambivalence carries over to its implicit attitude toward the policing of women's loyalty—even down to their thoughts and feelings—that is characteristic of patriarchy. Though the play seems to accept Mr. Montague's behavior, the homology between his behavior and that of the Committee of Safety suggests that it is highly problematic in its—in this case, patriarchal—paranoia. Moreover, the explicit incorporation of the Committee of Safety suggests that intrusive suspicion has consequences not only for the home, but for the nation as well. Such suspicion contradicts the nation's aspirations to universal, democratic egalitarianism by arbitrarily restricting the exercise of individual freedom, a key American value. Finally, this relation between the authoritarian structure of the nation and that of the home may suggest that various forms of nonmeritocratic social hierarchy are not only parallel with patriarchy, but in fact derive from patriarchy as the most fundamental form of such hierarchy. In this way, *The Traveller Returned* may point toward the unique role of patriarchy as the initial and prototypical (nonmeritocratic) hierarchy of identity categories, and thus the form of identity conflict that is most determinative in undermining universal, democratic egalitarianism.

Notes

1 In fact, part of her feminism involved affirming that women and men bore the same broad relation to the nation. As Sheila Skemp (2009: 242) explains, "she insisted that a woman could declare her 'Amor patria' with as much justice as any man."
2 Skemp (2009: 262) sees Matronia as Murray's ideal for herself.
3 I do not mean to suggest an actual connection between the works, though it is in principle possible that Washington Irving was familiar with Murray's play.
4 In this respect, Murray's play contrasts with the "postrevolutionary patriotism" of U.S. theater (including its celebration of George Washington), as interpreted by Jason Shaffer (2007: 166–178).
5 This contradiction has been recognized by critics; however, they tend to explain and even describe it very differently. For example, Pauline Schloesser (2002: 159) considers why "in the end ... Murray withdraws, reverses, or denies these radical [feminist] gestures, suggesting that all she ever contended for was completely harmonious with the separate spheres of modern patriarchy." In part, she concludes (reasonably) that Murray wished to avoid persecution (185). However, she goes on to say that a full explanation would draw on psychoanalytic ideas about masochism (186). This is clearly very different from an account that stresses the complexity of cognitive structures active differently for various contexts and processes (e.g., abstract verbal assertion versus concrete simulation).

11

MOBY DICK

Interracial romance beyond the nation

Herman Melville's 1851 novel, *Moby Dick*, illustrates once again many of the main issues outlined in the preceding chapters. Though his approach and specific concerns are very different from those we have been exploring, George Shulman (2013: 3) articulates a crucial point about the novel when he writes that *Moby Dick* "exalts what [Melville] calls 'democratic dignity' while dramatizing what prevailing political rhetoric of democratic self-rule finds unspeakable: American freedom is premised on multiple forms of domination and forgetting."[1] In our terms, the novel treats a subnational racial division and elaborates on the romantic model for interracial reconciliation, though it does so in relation to same-sex rather than heterosexual love. The novel also stresses the specifically American context, including such common national motifs as the rugged individualism of the frontier. However, it takes us beyond American identity to the internationalism that is the logical outcome of universal, democratic egalitarianism. Perhaps surprisingly, it does so in part by way of satire rather than the more expected methods of romance, realism, or melodrama.

The novel may be divided into two parts. The first, introductory part comprises perhaps a fifth of the volume. It has the form of a comic novel, though a comic novel that often focuses on deeply troubling issues. It is pervaded by irony, and that at two levels. The book is almost entirely a first-person narration spoken by Ishmael to an implicit narratee. One might imagine that the narratee has just met Ishmael, since he or she needs to be informed of Ishmael's name at the start of the novel. Alternatively, they are acquainted but only now shifting from formal address to first-name intimacy. Or perhaps "Call me Ishmael" (Melville 1988: 1) suggests that this is not the sailor's name at all but a *nom de plume*, a way of concealing his identity rather than announcing it. If so, there may be a hint of the sort of authorial distancing that we found in Washington Irving's story (though, in this case, the distancing would seem to have more to do with nonnormative sexuality than with the author's attitude toward the American Revolution). The irony is only made more dense by the fact that Ishmael often represents his own thoughts and attitudes indirectly, stating one thing to mean another. And all this does not even touch on departures from first-person narration, as when Melville gives us a chapter (chapter 40) in the form of a playscript. (Are we to imagine Ishmael, after surviving the voyage, preparing himself for a late career in the theater?) Be that as it may, this first part focuses on the impoverished Ishmael, changing his career from pedagogue to whaleman, and his newfound mate, Queequeg. That is the part we will be examining in the following pages.

Briefly, the second part is still ironic, but more in the form of a classical tragedy. It concerns Ahab, with his leg made of whalebone and his *idée fixe*, the elusive white whale.[2] Both parts involve mirth and terror, satire and sublimity, but in different proportions. As we discussed in Chapter 6, even long works with many narrative threads often have a dominant story genre. That dominant genre for the bulk of Melville's book is the revenge plot. There is also commonly a dominant mode of organizing the action of the story. Here, that mode is the quest adventure, specifically a quest adventure pervaded by justified terror and genuine grief. (Ahab's revenge does not work itself out as, for example, a domestic plan of insinuating himself into the home and trust of his victim, then betraying that intimacy; of course, this is not really an option when the target is a whale.) In contrast, the dominant genre of Ishmael and Queequeg is arguably that of a love story, if one that can never quite be worked out explicitly. It too takes as it organizing mode a quest adventure, but in this case one that is pervaded by misguided terror over innocuous events and misplaced grief over disasters that never happened (again, satire and mirth).

Both parts have thematic concerns relevant to American identity.[3] Our concern here is, again, with the first part of the novel, which takes up the epical, tender, comic, and symbolic relations between Ishmael, as the white man, and Queequeg, as a Muslim Afro-Amerindian Chinese Pacific Islander. "*Wait a darned minute!*" you say? "*A Muslim, Afro-Amer-Chineseean-watchamacallit? You are skylarking with me now! I'll have none of it! I'm no greenhorn! I know Quohog or Warthog or whatever his name is can't be whatever you said he was there!*" Let me explain.

The other works we have considered focus on relations between European Americans and either Native Americans or African Americans. But Melville's book is different. At a literal level, he treats the relation between the narrator, who is presumably European American, and a Pacific Islander, a prince from the mythical land of Kokovoko, which probably derives its name from having—in Melville's mind—a superabundance of coconuts, themselves associated with what we would now call "the Global South." But Melville gives us somewhat contradictory accounts of Prince Queequeg of Kokovoko, making him a little hard to place, racially or culturally. As to the former, he has a "purplish, yellow color" (1988: 18). One might initially take this to mean that his skin is yellow while his tattoos are purplish. But Ishmael explains that "his unearthly complexion ... completely independent of the squares of tattooing" was "purplish yellow" (19). I take this to be "unearthly" quite literally, as not found on earth. The "yellow" skin suggests the stereotypical characterization of the Chinese or other East Asians. What about the purple? That seems to suggest what is sometimes called "blue black" today, a true blackness of the skin, not simply a dark brown.

So, Queequeg is from a Pacific Island, with suggestions that he is racially Chinese and/or equatorial African (a "composite racial figure," in Geoffrey Sanborn's [2005: 235] phrase, describing one standard way of understanding Queequeg). Culturally, his idol, Yojo the Hunchback, is connected with the "Congo" (20). This "deformed" idol (20) does seem to recall some African deities, including perhaps Obatala, the Yoruba shaper of human forms and patron of the disabled and "deformed" (Soyinka 1976: 159), though this moves us a bit north of the Congo. In any case, there are physical properties linking Queequeg with China and Africa, and cultural practices possibly enhancing the connection with Africa. But other cultural practices are different. Most obviously, he is closely associated with the tomahawk, which is both a weapon and a tobacco pipe. As a weapon, it is a sort of parallel to the (European) harpoon that he wields when whaling. Indeed, his facility with the tomahawk—presumably derived from his own cultural background—suggests why he came to use the harpoon so skillfully. This tomahawk would appear to identify Queequeg as Native American. Then there is the curious fact that, despite being an idol-worshipping pagan, Queequeq has what Ishmael refers to as a "Ramadan" (see, for example, the title to chapter 17), which would seem to suggest that he is Muslim, most obviously making him Middle Eastern or North African.

Here, we might reasonably ask just what Melville might be up to. I suspect that he is seeking to represent a broad range of—possibly all—outgroups in a single character. I suspect further that Melville is doing this because his purposes are the same, whatever the outgroup. We will turn to Melville's purposes shortly. But, put simply, the point here is that we are all humans and that it does not really matter whether one is European or African, Native American or Kokovokian. Conversely, if Melville had made Queequeg simply Native American or simply African, it might have seemed that his concerns bore only on that group. But these concerns are more encompassing. It does seem that the African and Native American identities are the most prominent, due to the skin color (purple), the Yojo idol, and the tomahawk. This is just what one would expect, since those were the salient and historically most consequential outgroups for European Americans at the time.[4] The point is indirectly emphasized later in the novel, when Melville introduces the three harpooneers. The first was Queequeg; the second was Tashtego, an Amerindian; and the third was Daggoo, an African (105). It is presumably no coincidence that Queequeg's two companions have precisely these ethnic identities.

As indicated above, Melville is to some extent advocating a sort of humanism, though what he represents and advocates is somewhat more complex than this suggests. Part of his project bears in a straightforward way on color prejudice. He deals with this topic explicitly in the chapter 42 the book, "The Whiteness of the Whale." My general approach in this chapter will be to introduce the main points, then turn to a more detailed interpretation of specific passages. However, in this case, it might be worth looking briefly at Melville's comments on whiteness before going on. The chapter begins with the socially commonplace celebration of whiteness. To be clear about where he is going with this, Melville has Ishmael state that the "pre-eminence" of the color "applies to the human race itself, giving the white man ideal mastership over every dusky tribe" (168). The statement bothers my students, and some critics, who take it to suggest a justification of white supremacism, on account of it not reading (for example), "*putatively* giving the white man ideal mastership." There's something to that. But I take it that Melville's purpose is different. He aims to link the blankness of whiteness with a sinister quality, and he wants the idea of white superiority front and center in order to bear the brunt of his censure. There "lurks," he writes, "an elusive something in the innermost idea of this hue, which strikes more of panic to the soul than that redness which affrights in blood" (169). He instances different cases, perhaps most forcefully the "pallor" of "the dead" (171). White "stabs us from behind with the thought of annihilation" and is "the intensifying agent in all things the most appalling to mankind" (175). The point is not, of course, that whiteness is necessarily evil, and thus that black or "red" supremacism would be a valid social program. The point would seem, rather, to be that either whiteness or blackness or redness can be recruited to symbolize evil and thereby to rationalize a hierarchy of humans ranked by gradations of tint.

So, Melville pairs up a white man with a man of all nonwhite races to challenge the subnational divisions, most particularly those into white against black and red. But what does he think about the nation? Many early American authors are enthusiastic about the (still relatively new) nation. As we have seen, some set out to overcome subnational conflict and to reaffirm national unity. This is not precisely the case with Melville. Indeed, at various points in the novel he appears to favor either isolated individualism or internationalism, and thus to reject national belonging. And yet this rejection takes place in a broader ideological context where he in effect affirms key features of the American self-concept (for more on the American self-concept, see Chapter 1).

The novel begins with a legion of epigraphs. One of these reads as follows: "By art is created that great Leviathan, called a Commonwealth or State—(in Latin, Civitas)." This epigraph (from Thomas Hobbes's *Leviathan* [1651]) at least gestures toward the possibility that, what seems to be a mere whale on the horizon, what the crew seeks to slay and dissect—the enemy that has deprived Ahab of his bodily integrity and driven him half-mad—is intended to suggest (among other things) the state.

There are other hints of national—or antinational—concerns as well. One follows the epigraphs. Again, the narrator addresses his narratee in the book's first sentence: "Call me Ishmael" (1). Presumably, that is his name. But, again, maybe not. If nothing else, this suggests that he should be labeled "Ishmael" for his condition. The reference is to the biblical character, the son of a slave, exiled from family and community and in effect disenfranchised by his father, sent into the wilderness, replaced by a better-born half-brother (see Genesis 16–21), though later recuperated by Islamic tradition (which is subsequently linked with Queequeg, as we have seen above). There may also be an indirect allusion to the Puritan identification of Puritan New England with Israel (see, for example, Simpson 1955: 23), marking Melville's as an alternative, non-Puritan tradition from an alternative, non-Puritan lineage (that of Ishmael rather than that of Isaac).

As the opening chapter shows, our Ishmael is lowly, cast into the wilderness even among crowds, impoverished—and a sort of slave to boot: he asks, rhetorically, "Who ain't a slave?" and orders us: "Tell me that" (4). Whatever answer might be correct, we know that answer is not "Ishmael." A misfit, a pariah, he links himself, not with the whiteness of American society, but with Africans in chains. All the nation's repudiated outgroups are amalgamated in his loving bedfellow, the head-pedaling cannibal. Queequeg is not only his mate and *semblable* (as Charles Baudelaire might put it), but also his good angel, freeing him from want (though in this case by giving him money, rather than, say, causing a well to spring up in the desert, as is famously recounted in Ishmael's case [see Genesis 21:17–19]). Indeed, Ishmael has in effect hit bottom at the start of the story. He is contemplating direct suicide or, more indirectly, recklessness that would lead to death at someone else's hands. He presents it all in a comic way, confessing an impulse toward giddy aggressions to provoke a duel. But, instead of "pistol and ball," he plumps for a whaling voyage. The dangers are salient, both literal or real (cf. the memorials to the whaling dead in Father Mapple's chapel) and figurative or superstitious (as when he rests for his voyage in the room of a Coffin, the ominously named proprietor of The Spouter-Inn).

But what does all this have to do with nations and states? Ishmael compares himself to the younger Cato, explaining that "with a philosophical flourish Cato throws himself upon his sword; I quietly take to the ship" (1). Cato made his quietus in defiance of a Roman state ruled by Julius Caesar (see Harvey 1984: 94). This may suggest that Ishmael's taking ship is parallel—and, indeed, it is a sort of escape from the state. It is a flight from the laws of the land, a flight away from the state into "the watery part of the world" (1). If this is correct, it is not without irony, for in the eighteenth century the story of Cato was popular as a representation of Republicans rejecting tyranny, as with the American revolutionaries rejecting British monarchy. Indeed, George Washington was particularly fond of the story and drew repeatedly on Joseph Addison's version of it (see Meer 2016: 77; on the American reception of Addison's play, see Dillon 2005). Washington would have been dismayed at Melville's invocation of the story against the (putatively antityrannical) United States.

Moreover, in heading to the watery part and thereby escaping the state (rather than the sorts of domesticity stressed by Leslie Fiedler), Ishmael chooses a vessel named for "a celebrated tribe of Massachusetts Indians, now extinct" (61). Though Ishmael overestimates the genocidal effectiveness of the European settlers and their subsequent government, his claim could at least be read as intimating something sinister about the nation and its practices regarding racial outgroups. There are adumbrations of Africans too. Later, reflecting on the aloof and enigmatic Bulkington, Ishmael draws our attention to "the intrepid effort of the soul to keep the open independence of her sea; while the wildest winds of heaven and earth conspire to cast her on the treacherous, slavish shore" (95). Thus, he sets up a sharp contrast between the free watery world—the place that is truly independent—and the lands, which are defined by genocidal settlers and their slavery-supporting states. The slaves here are in part the slaves like Ishmael ("Who ain't a slave?"), men including Ishmael who are seeking independence. But, in a book published only 13 months following the Fugitive Slave Act and in a country embroiled in conflict over "the peculiar institution," the mention of slaves and the hint of nations could not avoid a connection with actual slavery as well.

Yet, there is more still. Melville sets the sea, presided over by the whalers of Nantucket and their counterparts from elsewhere, in contrast with the land with its colonial conquests. He singles out two of the latter for special mention—England "overswarm[ing] all India" and "America add[ing] Mexico to Texas" (56). The sea is not conquered in this way, with the place parceled out to invaders, the native inhabitants murdered, and slaves made to work the expanse. There are, of course, some similarities. For example, on the sea customary law tells us that "a Loose-Fish is fair game for anybody who can first catch it" (354). The difference, of course, is that in the sea a Loose-Fish is actually a fish. In the world of terrene politics, a Loose-Fish may be an entire society with all its people: "What was America in 1492 but a Loose-Fish, in which Columbus struck the Spanish standard … What at last will Mexico be to the United States?" (356–357).

The contrast is also represented in Ishmael's satiric depiction of the way the newspapers would treat his decision. He presents us with three titles. The first concerns a "contested election" for the presidency of the United States. The third is bound to the nation-state as well, announcing a "BLOODY BATTLE IN AFGHANISTAN." Sandwiched between these world events is the implausible headline, "Whaling Voyage by One Ishmael" (5). Ishmael's decision is not only apparently inconsequential in contrast with the world-historical events signaled by the other headlines, it also indicates that Ishmael is escaping the nation-state system and its depredations.

On the other hand, the "one" (in "One Ishmael") may serve to remind us of something. Ishmael's flight from civilization is an affirmation of his own particular choice, his own autonomy and independence. In consequence, it is in a sense deeply American. Part of the American self-concept is that we are a nation of rugged individualists who stake out new spaces on the frontier, leaving behind the constraints and impositions of the state. The only difference from the usual version of this escape is that Ishmael travels east to the sea, rather than west to new land. (Of course, that difference is not inconsequential, since Ishmael's choice does not lead him to genocidal conflict with the native population—at least if we consider only humans, not whales, as comprising the native population.) This is the "independence of [the] sea" (94), an intensified version of the independence that formed the initial rationale for the new nation of the United States.

Of course, Ishmael does not set out in a solitary canoe. He joins an entire group of individuals on the Pequod. But they are oddballs, misfits—"Isolatoes," he calls them. This may suggest that they are prototypically American individualists. But the crew is not simply American. They form "an Anacharsis Clootz deputation from all sides of the sea" (106). As Tony Tanner explains, Clootz "led a multinational crowd of foreigners into the French National Assembly in 1790 to represent the Human Race" (in Melville 1988: 519). The Pequod in this way is a sort of cosmopolitan alternative to the nation that is riven by subnational divisions. This all suggests that the novel is deeply concerned with—and no less deeply critical of—nations as both systems of administrative control and objects of group identification.

From pseudospeciation to practical identity: Reconciling races and cultures

As mentioned above, one of Melville's main concerns in the first part of this novel—the Ishmael–Queequeg story—is to address key subnational divisions based on race or ethnicity and the cultures that were associated with racial divisions. This is less of a concern in the second part of the novel, the Ahab–Moby Dick story. Given Melville's evident attitude toward the nation-state, this is unsurprising. Subnational reconciliation is needed in the terrestrial plot, but not, or not so much, in the aquatic narrative. On sea, the sailors on the Pequod to a great extent escape from the ethnocentric and racial supremacist ideas and practices that rive the nation. Rather, the sailors are integrated in concrete networks of practical identity that unite them in ways that are much more fundamental than the pseudo-unities of categorial identity, whether of nation or of race. The antidivisive consequences of shared work, the unifying effects of cooperative labor across racial or other identity divisions, are well-established empirically (see Duckitt 1992: 98, 252, 256; see also Varshney 2001, 2002–2003). Indeed, early work by Edwin Hutchins (1995) treating "distributed cognition"—a paradigm case of integrated practical identities manifest in cooperative activity—focused precisely on the interconnected labor of crew members on a ship.

More exactly, we are dealing with distributed cognition whenever information is processed to achieve goals not within individual brains alone, but across many individual brains and bodies. To subdue a whale, the Pequod (or any ship) needs someone perched high to spy the leviathan, others to loose the boats or row, others to man the harpoons, and so on. Each person is observing certain aspects of the situation—the whale's location and movements, the position of the ship, and so forth; they are each making calculations, such as how to orient the different boats or what force and direction to use with the harpoon. The crew members are like performers in a symphony orchestra, each coordinating an individual part with other parts that, all together, constitute the whole. On the sea, then, at least in the conditions of a whaling vessel, practical identity is foregrounded and categorial identities tend to recede. This tendency is reinforced by the development of personal relations among the crew members. The sailors on the Pequod would tend to see one another as individuals—as Ahab, Queequeg, Fedallah, and so on—rather than as, say, an amputee, a cannibal, and a Parsee, respectively. (As noted in Chapter 1, individuating information tends to displace group stereotypes [Holland et al. 1986: 215].)

This is not to say that outgrouping disappears in such contexts. Indeed, Melville depicts racism among the crew of the Pequod (see Melville 1988: 157; on the other hand, since one of the combatants refers to an "old grudge," it could be argued that this fight is not the result of racial antagonisms, but rather involves combatants who, angered by something else entirely, make racist comments because they know such comments will be hurtful). Again, it is distressingly easy to trigger outgrouping. Moreover, we have a cognitive tendency to insulate our generalizations against disconfirmation. Thus, if I begin to see Jones (an African American) as an individual, rather than as a stereotype, I am unlikely to take Jones as evidence that my stereotype of African Americans is wrong. I am more likely to class Jones as an exception and maintain the stereotype (on such "confirmation bias," see Nisbett and Ross 1980: 238–242; see also Mynatt et al. 1977). That stereotype, therefore, remains a viable cognitive structure for me, perhaps even with regard to Jones, should circumstances change (as they often do). The point is not that the Pequod is utopian. It is far from utopian. Indeed, the rule of Ahab is to a degree statelike, and not even democratic. But it is not actually a state. In this way, Melville may connect a relative interracial harmony with internationalism and with the mutual engagement of coordinated practical identities through cooperative work toward shared goals.

Yet the practical identities of—and thus relations among—people on the Pequod serve only as a general background to the antiracism of the Ishmael–Queequeg story. Melville develops this antiracism by several of the usual means, such as criticizing stereotypes and shifting perspective from ingroup to outgroup. But, again, his main technique is the development of an interracial love between Ishmael and Queequeg.

The homoerotic romance

There is a chapter well into the Ahab–Moby Dick story, where Melville returns to Ishmael and Queequeg. It concerns a safety precaution—thus a part of practical identity—in which one sailor tries to remain stable for work on the whale's shifting corpse, while another undertakes to secure him from the deck with a rope. The security and insecurity of the former then become the security and insecurity of the latter, for a good roll of the wave-rocked, slippery, half-sunken monster could drag both of them to a watery grave. Referring to this relation, but suggesting something far more general, Ishmael asserts that "Queequeg was my own inseparable twin brother" (287). They are the same—except for the matter of Ishmael having the terrifying pallor of a corpse (due to his whiteness), while Queequeg was somehow a purple yellow. The twinning comes, rather, in the less superficial parallels that Ishmael uncovers in the course of the first part of the novel.

The mention of brothers may seem to suggest that the main narrative structure of *Moby Dick*, the main story type through which Melville organizes this thematic criticism of racial division, is that of familial separation and reunion (for more on this structure, see Chapter 6). However, the main narrative structure is in fact romantic. Moreover, the sexual component of romance is important to this reconciliation (this structure is introduced in Chapter 2). However, the romance is not the usual one, between a man and a woman. It is, rather, between two men.[5] Indeed, we catch a glimpse of this even in the chapter where Ishmael characterizes himself and Queequeg as twin brothers. Specifically, Ishmael expresses appreciation for Queequeg's good looks, explaining that Queequeg was wearing "a shirt and socks," an outfit "in which to my eyes, at least, he appeared to uncommon advantage; and no one had a better chance to observe him" (287).

But surely (some already discontented readers may respond querulously) *a man can appreciate a male friend's good looks without lust or romance muddying the waters. We need grounds more relative than this, as Hamlet would say* (II.ii.615–616). *After all, there is never any explicit sexuality.* Never any explicit sexuality? Of course, not! Melville is not trying his hand at gay pornography (though he probably could have made a go of it if he had). To the contrary, he requires plausible deniability.⁶ Moreover, Melville pretty clearly indicates that sailors, alone with men only on a three-year tour of the watery world (where the state law of Alabama or anywhere else does not put handcuffs on their genitalia, though they might do so themselves, if they like that sort of thing)—these sailors, he informs us, are happy practitioners of what some literary theorists delicately term the *sodomitical*. So, the year before, he had written in *White Jacket* that "the sins for which the cities of the plain were overthrown still linger in some of these wooden-walled Gomorrahs of the deep" (1983: 744). More strikingly, very early in *Moby Dick*, Ishmael is looking for a place to stay before he has signed on to a ship. He passes two establishments that seem too expensive. Finally, he sees a door "invitingly open." When he encounters ashes in the entryway, he immediately wonders if they are "ashes from that destroyed city, Gomorrah" (7). There seems little reason to anticipate Gomorrah, unless one is anticipating the customs of its brother city, as well. Sodomitical, indeed.

Then, of course, there is the well-known chapter in which Ishmael—and Melville—dwell on the magnificence of a whale's penis. More important for our purposes, when looking at the organ Ishmael is reminded of Queequeg's idol (375). Ostensibly, this is due simply to its color. But the association is clearly suggestive of Ishmael's unmentionable interest in some property of Queequeg's that is more obviously parallel to the whale's member. If the point were not clear enough, Ishmael refers cryptically to a biblical passage (1 Kings 15), which it turns out involves a link between idol worship and sodomy, as Fiedler explains (1992: 372). Finally, there is the chapter in which Ishmael joins with his mates to squeeze whale sperm. He squeezes the fingers of his mates in the "gentle globules," with a "loving feeling," "looking … into their eyes sentimentally," then wishing that they could "squeeze ourselves into each other" (373). I know: whale sperm is not sexual fluid. But, please, Melville could not possibly have missed the implication of the word "sperm" here.

One more general point before turning to the text of the Ishmael–Queequeg story itself. The chapter devoted to the whale penis is entitled "The Cassock," as the skin of that organ (it seems) resembles that item of clerical garb. As this less-than-reverential comparison suggests, in treating both European and non-European custom, Ishmael—and Melville—appear to be quite skeptical of religion. This is part of what allows Melville to oppose racism and ethnocentrism, since he is not committed to his own religion being the one true faith. (This distinguishes him from some other writers we have considered, such as Catharine Maria Sedgwick [Chapter 3] and Harriet Beecher Stowe [Chapter 5].)

Ishmael and Queequeg

We may now turn to the main narrative of the first story sequence. As noted above, the novel begins with Ishmael's suicidal thoughts and their indirect connection with the American national state (in part via the parallel with the Roman senator Cato). The first chapter also introduces the idea that we are all slaves in one way or another. Thus, there is no superior class of the elect and, rather than affirming hierarchies, "all hands should rub each other's shoulder-blades, and be content" (Melville 1988: 4). None of this is explicitly addressing interracial relations. But the simple reference to "slaves," in the United States in 1851, would necessarily have called to mind European–African relations for virtually every American reader at the time.

The second chapter turns to Ishmael's poverty, his "patched boots" in a "miserable plight" against the "congealed frost ten inches thick" (7). The only lodging he can afford is at an inn run by Mr. Coffin—an unwelcoming name for a place to shelter. This may seem entirely irrelevant to our interests, but it is not. Ishmael's condition is a sharp, if implicit, criticism of American "Christian" society. We see this when the chapter ends with a discussion of Jesus's parable concerning Lazarus and the rich man. Because the rich man would not help the impoverished Lazarus when alive, he is condemned to eternal punishment while Lazarus is taken up to Heaven. Ishmael explains who the rich man is today (i.e., in 1851). He is the exemplar of Christian virtue, the "president of a temperance society," who drinks no alcohol, but quenches his thirst with "the tepid tears of orphans" (9). Cato had only Caesar to fret over. Imagine how he would respond to tear-swilling sobriety invigilators, reverenced preachers squeezing the lacrimal ducts of motherless toddlers to moisten their throats before ascending the pulpit.

Given all this, it is little wonder that Ishmael later takes up with Queequeg, thinking "I'll try a pagan friend … since Christian kindness has proved but hollow courtesy" (45). Christians talk about charity, but when Ishmael is in need it is Queequeg who gives him money (46). Not that we should idealize Kokovokians, mind you. Indeed, Queequeg first sets sail with the Christians to learn how to improve his own people, whose faults he finds quite evident. "But, alas!", Ishmael explains, "the practices of whalemen soon convinced [Queequeg] that even Christians could be both miserable and wicked." Indeed, they were worse "than all his father's heathens." All in all, he concludes, "it's a wicked world" (50).

The third chapter brings us to the interracial relations. Ishmael enters the inn and speaks with Coffin about lodging. The latter offers Ishmael the half of a mattress to be shared with a harpooneer. Perhaps because the harpooneer is described as "dark complexioned" (12), Ishmael suffers qualms. But he decides that these are "unwarrantable prejudices" (15). All this time, Ishmael (perhaps the reader too) is unaware that the complexion is a signal of racial difference. He does not even catch on when he is informed that this fellow is out trying to sell an embalmed head. Head-shrinking was a stereotype about a broad range of "savages." In fact, the practice of miniaturizing human skulls was very limited, though Gordon Campbell (2012) explains that it did have "a long history in South-east Asia (especially Borneo and New Guinea) and in South America (especially among the Shuar (or Jívaro) people of Brazil, Ecuador and Peru)." (This point may extend Queequeg's global, non-European representativeness.) When Ishmael realizes that Queequeg is not European, his "unwarrantable prejudices" revive with far greater force, in part to suggest the absurdity of such prejudices. Indeed, just in case we might miss the point, Ishmael explains that "ignorance is the parent of fear."[7] In consequence of his ignorance, Ishmael fears Queequeg as if he were "the devil himself" (19). Melville engages in a clever shifting of perspectives when this fear of his "infernal" (21) bedmate leads Ishmael to cry out and the unprepared Queequeg replies: "Who-e debel you?" (21). When confronted by an unknown man in his bed, Queequeg too takes up the demonic model in evaluating the stranger.

When innkeeper Coffin first introduced the prospect of Ishmael bunking with a harpooneer, he explained that the two would be sleeping in his own matrimonial bed (17). This—and Ishmael's observation on Queequeg's "comely" appearance (22)—partially prepare us for the start of the next chapter, in which Queequeg, asleep, embraces Ishmael in a "most loving and affectionate manner," as if Ishmael were "his wife" (22). This, in turn, sets the stage for subsequent developments. But before further, now conscious, intimacies, Melville presents us with some reflections bearing on racial and cultural differences. Surely, if there are no other differences between the barbarians and our civilized selves, there are differences in the manners of polite society—not just in the superficial matters (e.g., when to put on or take off one's hat—a convention that Queequeg does appear to find troublesome), but in the underlying forms of consideration as well. And yet the behavior of the two mates that morning suggests otherwise. Indeed, fearing that we might not follow the implications, Melville makes Ishmael explicit on the point. He characterizes Queequeg as "very civilized," then goes on to generalize, stating that "savages have an innate sense of delicacy" and are "essentially polite" (24). This is particularly well illustrated by Queequeg's abundance of "civility and consideration" (24–25). In contrast, Ishmael judges himself "guilty of great rudeness" (25) in their morning interactions.

Chapters 6 and 7 continue this critical treatment of outgrouping, largely through fostering a shift in perspective by the reader. A small case of this occurs when we find Queequeg observing the goings-on in a Christian church. As Europeans might behave in a Kokovokian ceremony, he looks about with "incredulous curiosity" (31). More significantly, Ishmael sets out to give the reader a sense of the strange characters who people New Bedford, CT, at the time. There are, of course, exotics from the Fiji Islands and elsewhere around the globe. But these are far less comical than the rural visitors from the northern farmlands of Vermont and New Hampshire, such as the "bumpkin dandy—a fellow that, in the dog-days, will mow his two acres in buckskin gloves for fear of tanning his hands" (29).

In chapter 10, Melville develops these techniques further. Looking at Queequeg with knowledge of him as an individual person, Ishmael no longer confuses him with the devil, but rather thinks that Queequeg had a "spirit" that could "dare a thousand devils" (44). As to the place of non-Europeans in the nation, Ishmael goes so far as to discern a striking resemblance between Queequeg and George Washington. In a remarkable passage, Ishmael tries to imagine what it is like for Queequeg to be thrust into an alien society. He finds Queequeg's equanimity in such difficult circumstances to be "sublime" (45).

Perhaps most importantly, the love theme returns—and this interracial love serves as a sort of healing medicine for the outcast and embittered Ishmael. "I began to be sensible of strange feelings," he explains; "I felt a melting in me. No more my splintered heart and maddened hand were turned against the wolfish world" (45). He and his cannibal decide that they will share a mattress once more. Queequeg embraces Ishmael and proclaimers that "henceforth we were married" (46). Queequeg immediately divides his fortune in two, giving half to his mate. Note that this makes Queequeg into the provider, not the recipient of beneficence, a straightforward reversal of the colonial ideology of the white man's burden—or of more recent ideas about social welfare. That night, Queequeg and Ishmael have their "honeymoon" as a "loving pair," lying in bed, their legs intertwining (47).

One of the most effective and affecting passages in the novel occurs at the end of this chapter. Queequeg invites Ishmael to join him in worship. Ishmael is at first uncertain—"How," he wonders, "could I unite with this wild idolator in worshipping his piece of wood?" But he reflects that worship must be "to do the will of God" and that doing the will of god must be doing "to my fellow man what I would have my fellow man to do to me" (46). This leads to only one possible conclusion. Just as Ishmael would wish for Queequeg to share in his (Ishmael's) devotions, Ishmael must honor Queequeg's desire to share his (Queequeg's) devotions. The idol Yojo, that Ishmael previously thought a "devil" (20), is now "innocent" (47). The next chapter in effect summarizes the point of invoking interracial romantic love, not only in connection with worship, but broadly. Though the immediate reference is particular, Ishmael is clearly making a general claim when he observes "how elastic our stiff prejudices grow when once love comes to bend them" (48).

I should perhaps say something at this point about the homoeroticism of this relationship. In part, I take it that Melville is expressing a progressive view of same-sex sexuality, as well as some of his own (perhaps partially denied) longings. Non-normative sexual preference—as well as other sex-related concerns, such as gender identification—are themselves deeply consequential for the implementation or violation of universal, democratic egalitarianism. This becomes particularly clear in the literature and social movements of the twentieth century. In this respect, as well as in its internationalism, Melville's novel is prescient.

But the focus on same-sex romantic love has other benefits in this context also. Indeed, the choice of a same-sex relation here is actually more effective in some ways than a heterosexual bond would have been. First of all, despite Ishmael's thought about Gomorrah, there is no reason to think that he is seeking a sexual partner among the men he encounters. If this were a standard, heterosexual romance, there would always be the possibility that the relation developed due to sexual pursuit, particularly by the man. This leads to the second advantage of a homoerotic bond—the relation of the two parties to sexuality is symmetrical. In a heterosexual relation, there are always added burdens on the woman, as the social stigma for sexual activity is very different and of course men do not risk pregnancy. In contrast, as they are both men, Ishmael and Queequeg share the same general relation to sexuality and its possible consequences.

The techniques of paralleling cultures and shifting perspectives are reprised in chapter 13. Melville has Queequeg tell an outlandish tale of intercultural incompetence. Faced with a wheelbarrow, Queequeg places his trunk in the bed of the contraption, then heaves the trunk-laden barrow up on his shoulders and carries the whole lot. He pairs that with a tale of a European visiting Kokovoko who washes his hands in the punch bowl (52). Both show cultural ignorance. But the story of the wheelbarrow also testifies to Queequeg's prodigious muscle, which is almost awe-inspiring. In contrast, the tale of the punchbowl shows the European to be unselfconsciously self-important, and his act is likely to make us gag with disgust.

These techniques also surface in the events of the chapter itself. Queequeg and Ishmael are going to the dock and find that they are the object of considerable public dismay. The problem, it seems, is that the "companionable" mates are not of the same hue. (Though the disapproving attention is likely to remind some readers of homophobia as well.) Ishmael makes an interesting comment on their epidermal difference, asserting that "a white man" is nothing more than "a whitewashed negro" (53). This is interesting not for the relatively banal (but still important) point that we are all essentially just human "under the skin." It is interesting because it suggests that we are all "negroes," that the African is our true nature and Europeans only appear different due to concealment. In any case, Queequeg is the object of some "bumpkin's" mocking mimicry (53). Queequeg lifts him up in the air, causing the bumpkin considerable fright, but no injury. The fellow immediately pulls out the all-purpose demonic model and calls for the captain, exclaiming that Queequeg is "the devil" (53). Shortly thereafter, the bumpkin is thrown overboard by a sweeping boom. After securing the renegade equipment, Queequeg dives into the sea and rescues his erstwhile nemesis. All those present cheer Queequeg's valiant act. But the hero himself displays no inordinate pride, recognizing rather that "we cannibals must help these Christians" (55). I imagine none of my readers needs reminding that—except for the reversal of perspectives—this is the standard, patronizing view of (colonizing) Christians toward (colonized) "cannibals," represented for example by the ideology of the white man's burden. Nor need I recall that, in the case of colonialism, the colonizers were in fact exploiting the colonized, not helping them. (I will therefore not mention either point.)

Chapter 17 begins with Ishmael's reflections on Queequeg's "Ramadan." Ishmael—and, I assume, Melville—find the ritual and its associated beliefs "comical" and "absurd," even "half-crazy" (73). Nonetheless, he urges respect for others' religious obligations and a self-critical recognition that "we are all somehow dreadfully cracked about the head, and sadly need mending" (73). Ishmael does draw the line at practices he considers imprudent. In consequence, he argues with Queequeg about the virtues of fasting, and cautions him against bringing on dyspepsia. The chapter ends with Ishmael's reflections on Queequeg's own attitudes toward other religions. As it turns out, he outgroups in a way directly parallel with Ishmael. Queequeg "thought he knew a good deal more about the true religion" than Ishmael did. In consequence, he expresses "condescending concern and compassion" (78). The point is to encourage the reader to recognize that he or she is not the only one to assume the superiority of his or her ingroup and its beliefs and practices. Everyone shares this bias. Moreover, given the ubiquity of this attitude, it becomes difficult to claim genuine superiority, at least insofar as this relies on our intuitions about ingroup and outgroup value.

Finally, in chapter 18, Melville takes up a sort of nonsectarian religious view that encompasses both Christians and "pagans" and that arguably expresses the fundamental principles of Christianity, rather than stressing its superficial manifestations. Specifically, Captain Bildad is insisting that Queequeg must be a Christian if he is going to serve on the Pequod. He is particularly concerned that Queequeg attend meetings led by a certain Deacon Deuteronomy. The ludicrous name of the good deacon presumably derives from an attentiveness to the rigid—and, it seems, spiritually irrelevant—legalism of some Old Testament law books. Ishmael, in contrast, characterizes Queequeg as a member of the universal church "to which you and I, and Captain Peleg there ... and all of us, and every mother's son and soul of us belong." What kind of a denomination is that? you reasonably ask (no doubt wondering about the dimensions of its meeting house). It is "the great and everlasting First Congregation of this whole worshipping world" (79).

Conclusion

Melville's novel neatly illustrates many of the main theoretical ideas introduced in Chapter 1 of this book and developed in the subsequent literary analyses. Through the Ishmael–Queequeg narrative, Melville addresses both racial-ethnic and religious-cultural outgrouping.[8] Specifically, through the development of an only slightly muted interracial romance, Melville fosters a sense that cognitive and affective biases—including the emotions of fear and disgust, often linked with demonic modeling—are not only wrong, but ludicrous as well; thus, they are fitting objects of satire. In connection with this, he also humanizes and normalizes same-sex sexuality as well as interracial bonding. The novel's antiracism is furthered by Melville's development of cultural parallels between European and non-European practices and his work to guide the reader in taking up the perspective of outgroup members. Melville extends the novel's purposes through his portrayal of distributed cognition and cooperation in coordinated practical identities on the ship, practical identities that largely (though not entirely) displace divisive categorial identities. However, the localized, communal quality of the ship—its isolation from any nation-state (despite the tyranny of Ahab) makes it unclear just how these points might be extended to and implemented within the nation. Indeed, Melville's novel is highly skeptical about state authority, apparently affirming a sort of individualism that is not clearly compatible with broad national unity or identity—even though that individualism is a key part of the predominant American self-concept. Melville's characters in effect demonstrate the value of abandoning subnational racial (and religious) identity divisions. But by the same token, Melville's development of these characters and their interrelations indicates that the cognitive and emotional errors that underlie subnational divisions recur in national divisions as well. In this way, the novel suggests the necessity of extending universal, democratic egalitarianism beyond the nation into a form of internationalism. In this way, Melville's novel leads beyond American identity. But it does so by taking the ideal principles of that identity—at least its universal egalitarianism—to their logical, and global, conclusion.

Notes

1 In noting my differences from Shulman, I do not mean to suggest that his particular interpretations are necessarily incompatible with those of the present chapter. Often, our analyses appear complementary, especially as they focus on different aspects of the novel.
2 In fact, it would probably be more accurate to say that the novel has three parts: the introductory story of Ishmael and Queequeg, the subsequent story of Ahab and the whale, and the information about whales and whaling vessels. Though the third does sometimes include short story sequences, it is not a narrative as such. Thus, it is of limited concern here.
3 For example, regarding the second part, Sacvan Bercovitch (1980: 192) explains that "Melville affirms the democratic ideal by contrast with the actual tyranny that Ahab manages to enforce."
4 East Asians and Muslims became salient outgroups only later—though not much later, in the case of the former (see, for example, Geoffrey Ward [1996: 147] on Chinese immigration at the time just before and just after *Moby Dick* was published). Melville was prescient in including them here.
5 The importance of same-sex desire in the novel has, of course, been recognized and explored by a wide range of critics, often drawing on psychoanalysis and/or post-structuralism, as in Person's (2006: 235) discussion of how Melville "deconstructs" a "phallic symbol." These analyses clearly begin from very different premises than the present analysis; their precise conclusions are correspondingly different as well. More generally, however, critics often agree that "Melville celebrates the possibilities of homosocial and homoerotic communion" (Person 2006: 235).
6 It is probably clear from my overall theoretical approach that I do not take apparent contradictions in the text as contributing to poststructuralist destabilizations or anything of that sort. Of course, some critics do. For example, Michael Snediker (2013: 156) observes that "Melville's characters seem oblivious to erotic contexts that strike readers as flagrantly sexual" and takes this to be "queer-theoretically resonant." I take it to be something more like commonsense caution. (On the other hand, we clearly agree on the presence of sexuality.)
7 The issue of politically consequential, misguided fear is a recurring one in U.S. society, and everywhere else. To take examples more directly relevant to our own time, the harm caused by terrorists is tiny when compared to the harm caused by events that we consider ordinary or normal, such as automobile accidents (see, for example, Gardner 2008: 3). Moreover, even the fear of terrorism is absurdly focused on nonwhites, despite statistics indicating that there is more terrorism by whites than by nonwhites. As Adam Serwer (2019) explains, "most deaths from terrorist attacks, are caused by white extremists."
8 Critics have noticed the general point, though they have not explored it in terms of the research on ingroup and outgroup formation and related research in cognitive psychology and affective science. For example, Dennis Berthold (2006: 149) notes that "unquestionably, Ishmael believes in a 'just Spirit of Equality' ... that demands toleration and respect for people of all races, nationalities, creeds, and classes, from the Pequod's black cabin-boy Pip through its Polynesian, Native American, and African harpooners to its multi-lingual, international crew," noting that this is a common view among Melville scholars. Similarly, Jennifer Greiman (2013: 37) explains that "democracy is fundamental to Melville's art." But she goes on to add that "it is also elusive, its meaning and function changing." Specifically, "democracy can be linked with Melville's most robust afirmations of freedom, equality, and right, and yet it can also coexist with the suspension of all of these under conditions of war and the persistence of inequality" (38). In our terms, this is in part the reason that "democracy" must be qualified as "universal" and "egalitarian"— with the last made fundamental—to establish the ideal of unalienable rights.

AFTERWORD

In place of a premature conclusion

In 1970, Rebecca Grumer wrote:

> American nationalism in the early nineteenth century was comprised of the glorious vision of a land with political and economic equality and freedom for all men. It was marred by the fact that everyone was not included in the application of this ideal. It set the problem of America's development, for the same dilemma has persisted throughout the history of the republic into the last third of the twentieth century. These limitations on the realization of the vision can be removed. It is not a question of whether the American people can do it; it is a question of whether we will. If we do so, we will realize the promise of our nationhood and the task which the first years of the republic bequeathed as part of its legacy.
>
> *(Grumer 1970: 315)*

At around the same time, responding in part to the massive destruction of the Vietnam War, historian Gabriel Kolko (1976: vii) wrote that the United States had suffered from "pervasive self-satisfied chauvinism" and that it had "been a nation blind to itself." From Kolko's comments, we might expect the United States to be largely oblivious to the democratic failures noted by Grumer. There is certainly some of that, a great deal in fact. Societies form ingroups and outgroups; the in-groups tend to adopt a generous view of themselves. Even their most sensitive authors are not immune to the fantasies of self-aggrandizing ideologies. I do not know if Americans have been more prone to chauvinism than others; I suspect that most groups are pretty similar in this regard. In any case, despite its universal, democratic, egalitarian ideal, the United States has not escaped the general trend.

And yet, as we have seen, chauvinistic blindness is not so pervasive when American authors work through the process of simulating social relations in the United States, when they concretely imagine the connections and disconnections between European

Americans and African Americans or Native Americans, or between men and women. In such simulations, they recognize the problems, the profound contradictions, and their great human cost. Sometimes the recognition is explicit; more often it is implicit—unstated, but visible to any reader who considers the text with care.

The criticism of these contradictions, whether articulated or only implied, is most often variable, changing with context, itself inconsistent (like the social system that is its target). Even so, as should be clear by this point, there is a deeply important strain of American literature that affirms the ideal of universal, democratic egalitarianism while leading us to recognize the very great discrepancies between this ideal and the actual practices of U.S. society, whether these discrepancies are articulated by members of the oppressing group or the oppressed group. Exploring literary works from that tradition of social criticism should help us to more fully understand our actual social practices and what underlies and rationalizes them—our destructive imaginations of putatively essential group identities. Such study should even point to ways in which we might work toward implementing the ideals more consistently, rather than invoking them ideologically in order to rationalize cruelty, whether such cruelty be violence against Native Americans or violence against the Vietnamese or Iraqis.

In the course of the preceding chapters, we have examined two key parameters in the social imagination of group formation—race and sex. We have touched on a third parameter, sexual orientation, as well. In each case, we find universal, democratic egalitarianism foundering on identity-group particularism, social exclusion, and hierarchization. We have examined this imagination through the rich and detailed depictions of novels, plays, and other literary works, with their complex—though also at times reductive—simulations of the ideas, feelings, experiences, and conditions of ingroup and outgroup characters active in diverse and variable social interactions.

As noted in the Introduction, my hope is that I have accomplished three things through this examination. Most basically, I have tried to advance our understanding of the particular works we have considered. I have sought to do this principally by considering these works in relation to issues of social group definition as treated in current empirical research in social psychology and cognitive and affective science. Second, and more importantly, I hope to have synthesized the literary analyses and the scientific research in such a way as to enrich our descriptions of American national identification, making them more systematic and nuanced, and explaining them more rigorously at the level of psychology. Finally, I hope to have contributed to a still broader account of nationalist forms of ingroup–outgroup definition, prominently the ways in which subnational divisions are developed and contested in national and subnational imagination and activism.

With respect to individual literary works, I have repeatedly argued that these works are more complex than one might initially expect. The complexity is a matter of both cognition (e.g., belief) and emotion, and it extends to out-and-out inconsistency and self-contradiction. Indeed, most (perhaps all) of us have partially contradictory ideas about any important and complicated topic, and most (probably all) of us have a significant degree of ambivalence over those topics, even when we do not admit that ambivalence to others (or even to ourselves). Most often, that complexity is patterned; our contradictory ideas and mutually incompatible feelings are not brought out together but separately in different contexts.

The different contexts that guide and explain our thought and emotion include abstract reasoning and concrete imagination or simulation. Thus, we may advocate certain general ethical principles or have fairly consistent emotional responses to the general idea of a group (e.g., African Americans). But we may respond very differently when we imagine specific situations, as when writing a work of fiction. The obvious case of this involves having antiracist views in the abstract but imagining individuals in stereotypical ways or feeling antipathy toward them. On the other hand, the reverse can occur as well and our concrete imaginations can be antiracist even as we think abstractly in racist terms. This is related to our categorization processes, thus the degree to which we categorize a target as an individual (e.g., "Uma"), as a member of a particular identity group (e.g., "woman" or "African"), or as a human person. In addition, we reason and respond emotionally in different ways, depending on the details of context (sometimes apparently trivial details), whether our thought is abstract or concrete, and other factors. These points apply to great creative writers no less than to the rest of us.

Divergence in ideas and feelings bears not only on racial or sex-based ingroups and outgroups, but on national identity as well. Thus, we find authors responding to the nation not only in ways that are different from one another, but also in ways that are different from their own responses in other contexts. Broadly speaking, the responses of individual novelists or playwrights to American identity are variations on recurring themes. We could think of these variations as parameter settings on shared principles. This idea will seem less surprising when we recall that the general principles are simply abstractions from individual responses; thus, they necessarily reflect patterns in those responses.

The human mind categorizes. Categories are typically activated by superficial features (readily recognizable properties) of the target. But they add to those superficial features a range of underlying, putatively definitive or essential qualities, with particular emphasis on the ways in which and the degree to which the target provides opportunities or threats. For example, we see an outsized, bulky, furry, lumbering quadruped and, on the basis of those apparent features label it a bear. The category, *bear*, supplies us with further information about the creature's essence, with particular attention to those features that provide opportunities or pose threats. In this case, that information would include the fact that bears can maul and eat people (such as myself). Though this process is entirely reasonable in the case of, say, animal species, the human mind extends it to human identity groups, where the supposed essences are largely imaginary and the threats and opportunities are created by the categorization itself (e.g., outgrouping does not *recognize* a set of people as mortal enemies; it *creates* the animosity that makes them mortal enemies).

One result of this difference between species and the pseudospeciation created by identity categorization is that identity categories involve greater discrepancies between the putative essence and the actual inclinations and capacities of individuals sharing an identity category. In technical terms, there is a dissociation between categorial identity and individual practical identity or, alternatively, the practical culture that is the complex, partial, and distinctive set of overlapping practical identities within an identity group. With regard to the ingroup, this necessitates the development of ingroup norms or ideals, which are always to some extent inconsistent with the actual facts about the group as a whole and the individuals who make up the group.

Different individuals, including different political leaders, will diverge in precisely how they define U.S. identity and in what they see as the most important norms governing that identity. Some writers might stress the importance of continually expanding across a frontier—first, the literal, geographical frontier in the west, then perhaps different sorts of metaphorical frontiers. Others might emphasize a particular Christian heritage. I have stressed other aspects of a recurring national identity ideal. First, there is the formal idea of America as a "city upon a hill," a model society to be scrutinized and imitated by the rest of the world. Second, there is the substance of that society, what makes it exemplary. Drawing in part on the Declaration of Independence, I have stressed the universal, democratic egalitarianism of the new nation. I have also argued that this conception of America is more fundamental than alternative accounts in that it tends to be presupposed by those alternatives, even if they qualify or limit what we might mean by *universal, democratic,* and *egalitarian.*

Again, all identity-group norms are likely to diverge in some degree from the actual practices of group members. But the founding principle of the independent United States presented its citizens with particularly sharp contradictions. How could one claim universal, democratic egalitarianism while enslaving Africans, dispossessing Native Americans, and disenfranchising women? Faced with these blatant contradictions, Americans may respond in a number of ways. First, they may rationalize the contradiction by excluding the outgroup in question from the scope of universality. This may seem too duplicitous to be at all plausible, but in fact we all restrict the scope of universality in construing American egalitarianism. Most obviously, we do not generally extend the principle of equality to animals, but restrict the degree to which we protect their "pursuit of happiness." Moreover, we do not even extend the principle to all humans, but offer only limited freedoms to, for example, children or to those suffering from senile dementia. More precisely, we allow hierarchies of *animacy* (roughly, hierarchies of self-aware personhood) and hierarchies of *age grades* to qualify our application of putatively general principles. In keeping with these literal restrictions, a standard way of rationalizing the blatant contradiction between U.S. norms and U.S. practices is by either explicit or implicit metaphorical appeal to the models of animacy and age grading. In such an appeal, the dominant ingroup is mapped onto the normative center of the model (human in animacy, adult in age), while the dominated outgroup is assimilated to a disenfranchised extreme (e.g., animal in animacy or child in age). This sort of modeling is pervasive in racism and sexism in the United States and elsewhere. To a great extent, stereotypes develop and specify the models that are standard for a particular dominated outgroup (e.g., African Americans).

Another option for dealing with such contradictions is to try to reconcile the groups. This involves changing the ideas, attitudes, and behaviors of Americans, perhaps especially those in the dominant group. Some techniques for changing ideas are fairly self-evident, such as the critique of stereotypes. Authors may undertake such a critique through, for example, the development of counterstereotypical characters. In order to oppose biased interpretations of such characters, authors may resort to idealization. Unfortunately, in both realistic and idealized cases, a biased reader is likely to maintain his or her prejudice by distorting the character in his or her reading or by classing the character as a rare exception to a general pattern (see Nisbett and Ross 1980: 238–242). Another common technique is not contradicting but explaining stereotypes—for example, showing why blacks might reasonably develop a duplicitous persona in dealing with whites. Here, too, there are problems though, as the explanation may function principally to reinforce the stereotype rather than to cultivate the reader's empathy and self-criticism.

A less immediately obvious technique for changing readers' ideas involves challenging standard ways of modeling the outgroup. Such challenges cover a range of possibilities. One author may merely shift to a less demeaning model (e.g., from animal to child) or limit the scope of the model (e.g., confining the demonic model to a particular subgroup of Native Americans). These approaches are ultimately at least in part a form of rationalizing the contradiction, but they move in the direction of reconciliation by lessening the contrast between the groups. Other authors may criticize the model more fully (e.g., rejecting the idea that there is anything particularly childish about Africans) or may reverse it, thereby criticizing the dominant group.

Change in intergroup attitudes is partially a function of such modeling and related cognitive processes. But it is also a matter of altering *interpersonal stance*, one's attitude of sympathy or antipathy toward the emotions of another person. One's interpersonal stance may be parallel, thus sympathetic (inclined to share the sufferings or joys of the other person); alternatively, it may be contrary or antipathetic (where one does not share those sufferings or joys, but may even rejoice in the former and regret the latter). Common techniques for altering interpersonal stance include simulating the perspective of outgroup members as well as other methods for fostering empathy. Antipathy commonly takes the form of anger, fear, and/or disgust. In keeping with this, authors may seek to cultivate emotions that contradict such antipathetic attitudes. For example, authors may seek to foster a feeling of trust in opposition to fear and a feeling of intimacy in opposition to disgust. The emotion that is most clearly and directly inhibitory of fear and disgust, and even to some extent anger, is attachment. Insofar as we feel a secure attachment bond with another person, we are very likely to feel trust for them and to be comfortable with—indeed, desirous of—intimacy with them. For this reason, writers aiming to reconcile opposed identity groups are particularly likely to represent that reconciliation through an intimate attachment bond between individuals, thus through deep friendship or romantic love or both.

There is, however, a problem with such resolutions—the reconciliation occurs between individuals. It may be good as far as the individuals are concerned (though it may also be tragic, depending on the precise development of the story). But it leaves the larger society untroubled. Of course, the authors in these cases are not setting out to depict a utopia. They are concerned, rather, to represent a bonding relation with which the reader might identify and which will provide a model for his or her own relations with outgroups. Even so, this response remains very limited. It addresses personal relations, but not broader patterns across practical identities (thus, culture) and not institutional structures.

This brings us to a third type of response to the discrepancies between the normative American identity and actual practices in the United States. This is the response of seeking to liberate the dominated group. A liberatory response focuses less on personal relations and more on broader patterns in cultural practice and on legal and other institutional concerns. Thus, we find Harriet Jacobs (Chapter 6) dwelling not on idealized romantic bonding but on the culture of harassment and rape, and we find Harriet Beecher Stowe (Chapter 5) repeatedly addressing the Fugitive Slave Act. This liberatory concern may or may not involve reconciliation. For example, it is perfectly possible to adopt a black separatist approach to the liberation of Africans, as Stowe in effect does.

This last point reminds us that there are different attitudes that one may have toward the nation as well. The nation may be supported by patriotic writers as an end in itself, such that the resolution of identity contradictions has instrumental value in securing the well-being of the nation. A writer such as Cooper (Chapter 2) or Sedgwick (Chapter 3) undoubtedly supports the humane treatment of Native Americans as an intrinsic good. But they also seem to support it as a means toward achieving a better nation. In the case of Apess (Chapter 4), however, it is not at all clear that he has any concern for the United States as a nation, except insofar as it affects the lives of Native Americans. On the other hand, he does at times appear to have some interest in the national status of Native Americans, independent of European Americans. To some extent, this difference in U.S. patriotism may seem to coincide with whether or not the author is part of the dominant or dominated identity group. But things do not work out that simply, as we see from the antinationalism of Stowe's novel and the patriotism of Douglass's (Chapter 7) final autobiography.

Just as the attitudes and ideas of individual authors are to a great extent specifications of broader American patterns in national identification, so too are those American patterns specifications of cross-cultural principles. I have already pointed to many of these patterns as discussed in the preceding pages—the nature of categorization and the pseudospeciation of identity categories, the general distinction between categorial and practical identity, the nature of conflicts between a group's norms and its actual culture (as defined by the practical identities of its members), the broad tendency to hold contradictory views in context-specific ways, the near ubiquity of ambivalence, the use of cognitive models—particularly animacy and age-grade models—to rationalize social hierarchization, the difference between a parallel and an antipathetic interpersonal stance, the bearing of specific emotions (anger, fear, and disgust) on the latter, and so on. I could add other principles outlined in the preceding chapters, such as the recurring use of cross-cultural narrative structures (romantic, heroic, family separation, and so on) to emplot the nation and its subnational divisions, or the distinction between nonmeritocratic social hierarchization, dominant ideology, and affective bias. This latter distinction is perhaps most familiar in the area of sex-based identity divisions, where it is roughly equivalent to patriarchy (social hierarchization), sexism (understood in a somewhat restricted, cognitive sense, thus as dominant ideology), and misogyny (understood not as hatred alone but as general antipathy, including fear, anger, and disgust—thus affective bias).

Despite the range of cognitive and affective principles and patterns set out in the preceding chapters, I should emphasize that none of this implies anything even distantly suggesting completeness. In the case of the individual works examined, in the case of understanding U.S. national identification, in the case of the general features of national identification, the best I can claim for the preceding analyses is that they might take their place as parts of ongoing research programs, programs that are always incomplete. Most obviously, the present work is incomplete in that it covers only a small number of works. These works have, for the most part, been important and influential. Not all works of American literature have had the same number of readers, or the same influence on culture. But even the most widely read works with the greatest social impact do not represent the whole. Another obvious way in which this study is incomplete is that it covers only a bit over a century of the new nation's literary history. (It therefore points toward a subsequent volume treating the next century or so—a period in which the proliferation of works and diverse imaginations increases greatly, making the first problem of completeness even more daunting.)

I will not bore the reader with an attempt to list all the ways in which this study is incomplete. However, I will mention one more. This concerns the precise group divisions explored in the course of the book, most significantly the absence of any treatment of class. It should be abundantly clear that I have no affinity for "identity politics." Identity categories, in my view, have no validity. They appear to be justified in some cases because they create the very antagonisms and social incompatibilities that they pretend merely to name. They serve primarily to organize our social lives, as well as our thought and emotion, in inegalitarian, nonuniversal, and undemocratic ways. But there are two important points to make here. First, as Melville's (Chapter 11) novel suggests, the problems with subnational identity politics are found equally in the identity politics of nationalism. Thus, I am an ardent internationalist. Second, there is a common criticism of identity politics that is, in my view, far more misguided than identity politics itself. I am referring to the view that the aims of identity politics no longer need to be pursued. For example, sometimes people claim that we are in a postracial age. If the impetus behind, say, African American identity politics is to oppose racism (race-based discrimination and bias), then—in this "postracial" view—there is no need to continue such identity politics, since we have already left racism behind. Certainly, there have been improvements in American racial inequality. But, no less certainly, discrimination and cognitive and affective bias based on race continue. Put differently, it is abundantly clear that racial problems still prevent the United States from being a universal, egalitarian democracy. Thus, the important aims of African American identity politics—and Native American and women's or feminist identity politics—remain pressing and deeply consequential.

However, this returns us to class. At least with regard to race, the fundamental division that undermines the validity of the American egalitarian self-concept is the division of socioeconomic classes. As Walter Benn Michaels (2007) has argued, to a great extent the pernicious effects of racism—in my terms, the pernicious effects of a discriminatory sociopolitical system—work their way out through socioeconomic stratification. As Michaels puts it, some people are disturbed that a disproportionate percentage of the poor are nonwhite. But the real problem is that there are lots of poor people. If we did not have poor people at all, we would not have too many poor black people. The point becomes clearer if we put it in terms of slavery. If Southern plantation owners had been able to own white slaves in proportion to their presence in the general population, would that have made slavery alright? This is not to say that eliminating poverty would solve all racial issues. It would not. Moreover, it would do little to establish equality of men and women. Nonetheless, socioeconomic class hierarchies are crucial to America's violation of its own identity norms. Socioeconomic class provides the structure of social hierarchization that is taken up in racial hierarchization. Moreover, class issues are far from irrelevant to patriarchy, as sex-based hierarchies are inseparable from the limitations on women's access to (indeed, their historical exclusion from) dominant positions in the ownership and management of the national economy.

Unfortunately, I have not been able to treat economic class in the preceding pages. Economic class is, I believe, much more difficult to discuss in the context of national self-concept and practical identity. This is in part due precisely to its fundamental character. Class underlies a great deal of the way we think about and act regarding identity. Yet Americans do not most often conceive of class as an identity category. It has been politely ignored by most Americans, rather than addressed explicitly, as is the case with race and sex. This makes the task of working out the relation of class to identity almost archeological. The point here is simply that my nearly complete silence on socioeconomic class should not be taken to suggest its unimportance. Though race- and sex-based discriminatory systems are not reducible to class, they work through class. Class is important for fully understanding racial and (to a lesser extent) sex-based cognitive and affective bias as well. But, then again, one cannot treat everything in a single book. Indeed, it seems clear that we in the United States need to respond systematically to class hierarchies if we wish even to begin to overcome the discrepancies between our (idealized) self-concept, on the one hand, and our cultural and political reality, on the other. But that is a topic for future work, work advancing a larger research program, of which the present book is necessarily only one, limited part.

REFERENCES

Akhtar, Salman. *Shame: Developmental, Cultural, and Clinical Realms.* London: Karnac, 2016.
Aldama, Frederick Luis. *Your Brain on Latino Comics: From Gus Arriola to Los Bros Hernandez.* Austin: University of Texas Press, 2009.
Alderdice, Lord. "The Individual, the Group and the Psychology of Terrorism." *International Review of Psychiatry* 19 (3) (2007): 201–209.
Althusser, Louis. *For Marx.* Trans. Ben Brewster. New York: Verso, 2005.
Althusser, Louis. *Lenin and Philosophy and Other Essays.* Trans. Ben Brewster. New York: Monthly Review Press, 1971.
Ammons, Elizabeth. "*Uncle Tom's Cabin*, Empire, and Africa." In Ammons and Belasco, *Approaches to Teaching Stowe's "Uncle Tom's Cabin,"* 2000, 68–76.
Ammons, Elizabeth and Susan Belasco, eds. *Approaches to Teaching Stowe's "Uncle Tom's Cabin."* New York: Modern Language Association of America, 2000.
Anderson, Donald R. "Freedom's Lullaby: Rip Van Winkle and the Framings of Self-Deception." *ESQ* 46 (4) (2000): 255–283.
Andrews, Evan. "How Ping-Pong Diplomacy Thawed the Cold War." *History.com*, 8 April 2016. Available at https://www.history.com/news/ping-pong-diplomacy.
Apess, William. *On Our Own Ground: The Complete Writings of William Apess, a Pequot.* Ed. Barry O'Connell. Amherst, MA: University of Massachusetts Press, 1992.
Ashcroft, Bill, Gareth Griffiths, and Helen Tiffin. *The Empire Writes Back: Theory and Practice in Post-Colonial Literatures.* 2nd ed. New York: Routledge, 2002.
Axtell, James. "The White Indians of Colonial America." In Frazier, *The Underside of American History, Volume I: To 1877*, 1987, 57–82.
Ayeres, Harry. "The English Language in America." In Trent et al., *The Cambridge History of American Literature*, 1921, 554–571.
Baker, Houston A. "Autobiographical Acts and the Voice of the Southern Slave." In Davis and Gates, *The Slave's Narrative*, 1985, 242–261.
Baldwin, James. *Notes of a Native Son.* Boston: Beacon Press, 1955.
Baptist, Edward E. *The Half Has Never Been Told: Slavery and the Making of American Capitalism.* New York: Basic Books, 2016.

Barry, John. *Roger Williams and the Creation of the American Soul: Church, State, and the Birth of Liberty*. New York: Penguin, 2012.
Baudelaire, Charles. "Au Lecteur." In *Les Fleurs du Mal*. Paris: Auguste Poulet-Malassis, 1857. Available at https://fleursdumal.org/poem/099 (accessed 15 December 2019).
Baym, Nina. "How Men and Women Wrote Indian Stories." In Peck, *New Essays on The Last of the Mohicans*, 1992, 67–86.
Baym, Nina. "Nathaniel Hawthorne and His Mother: A Biographical Speculation." *American Literature* 54 (1982): 1–27.
Benstock, Shari. "The Scarlet Letter (a)dorée, or the Female Body Embroidered." In Murfin, *The Scarlet Letter*, 1991, 288–303.
Bercovitch, Sacvan. *American Jeremiad*. Madison: University of Wisconsin Press, 1980.
Bercovitch, Sacvan. "Hawthorne's A-Morality of Compromise." In Murfin, *The Scarlet Letter*, 1991, 344–358.
Bercovitch, Sacvan. *The Puritan Origins of the American Self*. New Haven, CT: Yale University Press, 1970.
Berlant, Lauren. "The Queen of America Goes to Washington City: Harriet Jacobs, Frances Harper, Anita Hill." In Moon and Davidson, *Subjects and Citizens: Nation, Race, and Gender from Oroonoko to Anita Hill*, 1995, 455–480.
Berthold, Dennis. "Democracy and Its Discontents." In Kelley, *A Companion to Herman Melville*, 2006, 149–164.
Blight, David. *Frederick Douglass: Prophet of Freedom*. New York: Simon & Schuster, 2018.
Bracher, Mark. *Literature and Social Justice: Protest Novels, Cognitive Politics and Schema Criticism*. Austin: University of Texas Press, 2013.
Bradford, William. *Of Plymouth Plantation*. Ed. Harvey Wish. New York: Capricorn, 1962. Available at https://babel.hathitrust.org/ (accessed 18 May 2019).
Branscombe, Nyla and Bertjan Doosje. *Collective Guilt: International Perspectives*. Cambridge: Cambridge UP, 2004.
Brewer, Marilynn. "Intergroup Discrimination: Ingroup Love or Outgroup Hate?" In Sibley and Barlow, *The Cambridge Handbook of the Psychology of Prejudice*, 2017, 90–110.
Brinton, Howard. *The Religious Philosophy of Quakerism: The Beliefs of Fox, Barcla, and Penn as Based on the Gospel of John*. Wallingford, PA: Pendle Hill Publications, 1973.
Britton-Purdy, Jedediah. "Infinite Frontier: The Eternal Return of American Expansionism." *The Nation* (1 April 2019): 27–32.
Bronski, Michael. *A Queer History of the United States*. Boston, MA: Beacon Press, 2011.
Brown, Harry. "'The Horrid Alternative': Miscegenation and Madness in the Frontier Romance." *Journal of American and Comparative Cultures* 24 (3–4) (2008): 137–151.
Bush, Doug. *Capturing Mariposas: Reading Cultural Schema in Gay Chicano Literature*. Columbus: Ohio State University Press, 2019.
Campbell, Gordon. "Shrunken Head." *Grove Art Online* (6 February 2012). https://www.oxfordartonline.com/groveart (accessed 17 May 2019).
Cashin, Sheryll. *Loving: Interracial Intimacy in America and the Threat to White Supremacy*. Boston: Beacon Press, 2017.
Castillo, Susan, and Ivy Schweitzer, eds. *A Companion to the Literatures of Colonial America*. Malden, MA: Blackwell, 2005.
Chase, Richard. *The American Novel and Its Tradition*. London: G. Bell and Sons, 1957.
Chester, Stephen. "Paul and the Introspective Conscience of Martin Luther: The Impact of Luther's Anfechtungen on His Interpretation of Paul." *Biblical Interpretation* 14(5) (2006): 508–536.

Child, Lydia Maria. "The Quadroons." In *The Liberty Bell*. Boston, MA: Anti-Slavery Fair, 1842, 115–141. Available at http://utc.iath.virginia.edu/abolitn/abfilmcat.html (accessed 5 May 2019).

Citrin, Jack and David O. Sears. *American Identity and the Politics of Multiculturalism*. Cambridge: Cambridge University Press, 2014.

Clore, Gerald L. and Andrew Ortony. "Cognition in Emotion: Always, Sometimes, or Never?" In *Cognitive Neuroscience of Emotion*. Ed. Richard Land and Lynn Nadel with Geoffrey Ahern, John Allen, Alfred Kaszniak, Steven Rapcsak, and Gary Schwartz. Oxford: Oxford University Press, 2000, 24–61.

Colacurcio, Michael. "Footsteps of Ann Hutchinson: The Context of *The Scarlet Letter*." *ELH* 39 (1972): 459–494.

Cooper, James Fenimore. *The Last of the Mohicans*. New York: Penguin, 2014.

Cooper, James Fenimore. "Preface." In *The Last of the Mohicans: A Narrative of 1757*. New York: Hurd and Houghton, 1870, iii–viii.

Crane, Gregg. "Stowe and the Law." In Weinstein, *The Cambridge Companion to Harriet Beecher Stowe*, 2004, 154–170.

Cronon, William. "Indians, Colonists, and Property Rights." In Frazier, *The Underside of American History, Volume I: To 1877*, 1987, 11–33.

Davis, Charles and Henry Louis Gates, eds. *The Slave's Narrative*. Oxford: Oxford University Press, 1985.

Dayan, Joan. "Amorous Bondage: Poe, Ladies, and Slaves." In Moon and Davidson, *Subjects and Citizens: Nation, Race, and Gender from Oroonoko to Anita Hill*, 1995, 109–143.

Declaration of Independence, The. In *The Declaration of Independence and the Constitution of the United States*. Washington, D.C.: U.S. Citizenship and Immigration Services, n.d., 1–7. Available at https://www.uscis.gov/sites/default/files/USCIS/Office%20of%20Citizenship/Citizenship%20Resource%20Center%20Site/Publications/PDFs/M-654.pdf (accessed 16 June 2019).

De Crèvecoeur, J. Hector St. John. *Letters from an American Farmer and Sketches of Eighteenth-Century America*. Ed. Albert Stone. New York: Penguin, 1981.

Degler, Carl. *Out of Our Past*. New York: Harper & Row, 1970.

Dekker, George and John McWilliams. "Introduction." In *Fenomore Cooper: The Critical Heritage*. Ed. George Dekker and John McWilliams. London: Routledge, 1973.

De Tocqueville, Alexis. *Democracy in America*. Trans. Henry Reeve. State College, PA: Pennsylvania State University Press, 2002. Available at http://seas3.elte.hu/coursematerial/LojkoMiklos/Alexis-de-Tocqueville-Democracy-in-America.pdf (accessed 6 May 2019).

Dickson-Carr, Darryl. "Now You Shall See How a Slave Was Made a Man: Gendering Frederick Douglass's Struggles with Christianity." In Fessenden et al., *The Puritan Origins of American Sex: Religion, Sexuality, and National Identity in American Literature*, 2001, 127–144.

Dillon, Elizabeth Maddock. "Republican Theatricality and Transatlantic Empire." In Castillo and Schweitzer, *A Companion to the Literatures of Colonial America*, 2005, 551–565.

Donovan, Josephine. *"Uncle Tom's Cabin": Evil, Affliction, and Redemptive Love*. Boston, MA: Twayne, 1991.

Douglass, Frederick. *The Complete Autobiographies of Frederick Douglass*. New York: Start Publishing, 2012a. Unpaginated Kindle edition.

Douglass, Frederick. *Life and Times of Frederick Douglass*. In Douglass, *The Complete Autobiographies of Frederick Douglass*, 2012b.

Douglass, Frederick. *My Bondage and My Freedom*. In Douglass, *The Complete Autobiographies of Frederick Douglass*, 2012c.

Douglass, Frederick. *Narrative of the Life of Frederick Douglass, An American Slave, Written by Himself*. In Levine, *The Norton Anthology of American Literature: 1820–1865*, 2017, 1163–1228.

Dovidio, John, Samuel Gaertner, and Adam Pearson. "Aversive Racism and Contemporary Bias." In Sibley and Barlow, *The Cambridge Handbook of the Psychology of Prejudice*, 2017, 267–294.
Duckitt, John H. *The Social Psychology of Prejudice*. New York: Praeger, 1992.
Dunbar-Ortiz, Roxanne. *An Indigenous Peoples' History of the United States*. Boston: Beacon Press, 2014.
Easton, Alison. "Hawthorne and the Question of Women." In Millington, *The Cambridge Companion to Nathaniel Hawthorne*, 2004, 79–98.
Edwards, Jonathan. "One Cause of Errors Attending a Great Revival of Religion, is Undiscerned Spiritual Pride." In *Works of Jonathan Edwards, Volume I*. Ed. Edward Hickman. The Christian Classics Etherial Library, 1995. Available at https://www.ccel.org/ccel/edwards/works1 (accessed 4 May 2019).
Elliott, Emory. "Foreword." In Fessenden et al., *The Puritan Origins of American Sex: Religion, Sexuality, and National Identity in American Literature*, 2001, ix–xi.
Erskine, John. "Hawthorne." In Trent et al., *The Cambridge History of American Literature*, 1918, 16–31.
Fairbanks, Henry. "Hawthorne and Confession." *The Catholic Historical Review* 43(1) (1957): 38–45.
Fan, Hong and Lu Zhouxiang. *The Politicization of Sport in Modern China: Communists and Champions*. New York: Routledge, 2013.
Fessenden, Tracy, Nicholas Radel, and Magdalena Zaborowska, eds. *The Puritan Origins of American Sex: Religion, Sexuality, and National Identity in American Literature*. New York: Routledge, 2001.
Fetta, Stephanie. *Shaming into Brown: Somatic Transactions of Race in Latina/o Literature*. Columbus: Ohio State University Press, 2018.
Fiedler, Leslie. *Love and Death in the American Novel*. New York: Anchor Books, 1992.
Foner, Eric. "The Double Battle: Frederick Douglass's Moral Crusade." *The Nation*, 26 November 2018, 24–28.
Foreman, Gabrielle. "Manifest in Signs: The Politics of Sex and Representation in Incidents in the Life of a Slave Girl." In Garfield and Zafar, *Harriet Jacobs and Incidents in the Life of a Slave Girl*, 1996, 76–99.
Forgas, Joseph, ed. *Feeling and Thinking: The Role of Affect in Social Cognition*. Cambridge: Cambridge University Press, 2000.
Foster, Charles. *The Rungless Ladder: Harriet Beecher Stowe and New England Puritanism*. Durham, NC: Duke UP, 1954.
Foster, Edward. *Catharine Maria Sedgwick*. New York: Twayne, 1974.
Frank, Jason, ed. *A Political Companion to Herman Melville*. Lexington: University Press of Kentucky, 2013.
Franklin, Benjamin. *Franklin's Autobiography*. Ed. O. Leon Reid. New York: American Book Company, 1910. Unpaginated Kindle edition.
Franklin, Benjamin. "The Speech of Miss Polly Baker." In Gustafson, *The Norton Anthology of American Literature: Beginnings to 1820*, 2017, 449–451.
Franklin, Wayne. *James Fenimore Cooper: The Early Years*. New Haven, CT: Yale University Press, 2007.
Frazier, Thomas, ed. *The Underside of American History, Volume I: To 1877*. 5th ed. New York: Harcourt Brace Jovanovich, 1987.
Frederickson, George. *The Black Image in the White Mind*. New York: HarperCollins, 1971.
Gardner, Daniel. *The Science of Fear*. London: Dutton, 2008.
Garfield, Deborah. "Vexed Alliances: Race and Female Collaborations in the Life of Harriet Jacobs." In Garfield and Zafar, *Harriet Jacobs and Incidents in the Life of a Slave Girl*, 1996, 275–291.

Garfield, Deborah and Rafia Zafar, eds. *Harriet Jacobs and Incidents in the Life of a Slave Girl.* Cambridge: Cambridge UP, 1996.

Gazzaniga, Michael. *Who's in Charge? Free Will and the Science of the Brain.* New York: Ecco, 2011.

Gilbert, Daniel T., and Timothy D. Wilson. "Miswanting: Some Problems in the Forecasting of Future Affective States." In Forgas, *Feeling and Thinking: The Role of Affect in Social Cognition*, 2000, 178–197.

Gilligan, James. *Preventing Violence.* New York: Thames & Hudson, 2001.

Gilmore, Michael. "Uncle Tom's Cabin and the American Renaissance: The Sacramental Aesthetic of Harriet Beecher Stowe." In Weinstein, *The Cambridge Companion to Harriet Beecher Stowe*, 2004, 58–76.

Ginsberg, Allen. "America." *Poetry Foundation*, n. d. Available at https://www.poetryfoundation.org/poems/49305/america-56d22b41f119f.

Godard, Jean-Luc, dir. *Vivre Sa Vie.* Written by Marcel Sacotte and Jean-Luc Godard. Paris: Les Films de la Pléiade, 1962.

González, Christopher. *Permissible Narratives: The Promise of Latino/a Literature.* Columbus: Ohio State University Press, 2017.

Grandin, Greg. *The End of the Myth: From the Frontier to the Border Wall in the Mind of America.* New York: Metropolitan Books, 2019.

Greiman, Jennifer. "Democracy and Melville's Aesthetics." In Levine, *The New Cambridge Companion to Herman Melville*, 2013, 37–50.

Grumer, Rebecca. *American Nationalism: 1783–1830.* New York: Capricorn, 1970.

Gustafson, Sandra, ed. *The Norton Anthology of American Literature: Beginnings to 1820.* 9th ed. New York: Norton, 2017.

Hamilton, Patrick. *Of Space and Mind: Cognitive Mappings of Contemporary Chicano/a Fiction.* Austin: University of Texas Press, 2011.

Harvey, Paul. *The Oxford Companion to Classical Literature.* Oxford: Oxford University Press, 1984.

Hawthorne, Nathaniel. *The Scarlet Letter.* In Levine, *The Norton Anthology of American Literature: 1820–1865*, 2017, 425–569.

Hein, G., G. Silani, K. Preuschoff, C. D. De Batson, and T. Singer. "Neural Responses to Ingroup and Outgroup Members' Suffering Predict Individual Differences in Costly Helping." *Neuron* 68 (1) (2010): 149–160.

Herbert, T. Walter. "Hawthorne and American Masculinity." In Millington, *The Cambridge Companion to Nathaniel Hawthorne*, 2004, 60–78.

Herman, Edward and Noam Chomsky. *Manufacturing Consent: The Political Economy of the Mass Media.* New York: Random House, 2002.

Hess, Ursula. "Mimicry (Psychological Perspectives)." In Sander and Scherer, *Oxford Companion to Emotion and the Affective Sciences*, 2009, 253–254.

Higonnet, Margaret. "Comparative Reading: Catharine M. Sedgwick's Hope Leslie." *Legacy* 15 (1) (1998): 17–22.

Hirschfeld, Lawrence A. *Race in the Making: Cognition, Culture, and the Child's Construction of Human Kinds.* Cambridge, MA: MIT Press, 1996.

Hogan, Patrick Colm. *Affective Narratology: The Emotional Structure of Stories.* Lincoln: University of Nebraska Press, 2011a.

Hogan, Patrick Colm. *Colonialism and Cultural Identity: Crises of Tradition in the Anglophone Literatures of India, Africa, and the Caribbean.* Albany: State University of New York Press, 2000.

Hogan, Patrick Colm. *The Culture of Conformism: Understanding Social Consent.* Durham, NC: Duke University Press, 2001.

Hogan, Patrick Colm. *Literature and Emotion*. New York: Routledge, 2018a.
Hogan, Patrick Colm. *The Mind and Its Stories: Narrative Universals and Human Emotion*. Cambridge: Cambridge University Press, 2003.
Hogan, Patrick Colm. *Narrative Discourse: Authors and Narrators in Literature, Film. And Art*. Columbus: Ohio State University Press, 2013.
Hogan, Patrick Colm. *Sexual Identities: A Cognitive Literary Study*. New York: Oxford UP, 2018b.
Hogan, Patrick Colm. *Understanding Nationalism: On Narrative, Cognitive Science, and Identity*. Columbus: Ohio State University Press, 2009c.
Hogan, Patrick Colm. *What Literature Teaches Us about Emotion*. Cambridge: Cambridge University Press, 2011b.
Holland, John, Keith Holyoak, Richard Nisbett, and Paul Thagard. *Induction: Processes of Inference, Learning, and Discovery*. Cambridge, MA: MIT Press, 1986.
Huntington, Samuel. *Who Are We? The Challenges to America's National Identity*. New York: Simon and Schuster, 2004.
Hutchins, Edwin. *Cognition in the Wild*. Cambridge, MA: MIT Press, 1995.
Hutson, Richard. "Introduction." In Cooper, *The Last of the Mohicans*. New York: Penguin, 2014. Unpaginated Kindle edition.
Irving, Washington. "Rip Van Winkle." In Levine, *The Norton Anthology of American Literature: 1820–1865*, 2017, 29–41.
Isenberg, Nancy. *White Trash: The 400-Year Untold History of Class in America*. New York: Penguin, 2016.
Jacobs, Harriet. *Incidents in the Life of a Slave Girl*. Ed. Lydia Maria Child. Overland Park, KS: Digireads.com, 2016.
Jameson, Fredric. "Third World Literature in the Era of Multinational Capital." *Social Text* 15 (1986): 65–88.
Jansen, Jan. "Flucht und Exil im Zeitalter der Revolutionen: Perspektiven einer atlantischen Flüchtlingsgeschichte (1770er – 1820er Jahre)." *Geschichte und Gesellschaft* 44(4) (2018): 495–525.
Kant, Immanuel. *Groundwork of the Metaphysic of Morals*. Trans. H. J. Paton. New York: Harper and Row, 1956.
Karcher, Carolyn. "Stowe and the Literature of Social Change." In Weinstein, *The Cambridge Companion to Harriet Beecher Stowe*, 2004, 203–218.
Kazin, Alfred. "Introduction." In Stowe, *Uncle Tom's Cabin*, 2003, vii–xvi.
Kelley, Wyn. *A Companion to Herman Melville*. Malden, MA: Wiley-Blackwell, 2006.
Kerkering, John. *The Poetics of National and Racial Identity in Nineteenth-Century American Literature*. Cambridge: Cambridge University Press, 2003.
King James Bible (KJV). *King James Bible Online* (2019). Available at https://www.kingjamesbibleonline.org (accessed 15 April 2019.)
Kolko, Gabriel. *Main Currents in Modern American History*. New York: Pantheon, 1976.
Korsgaard, Christine. *The Sources of Normativity*. Cambridge: Cambridge University Press, 1996.
Kövecses, Zoltán. *Metaphor and Emotion: Language, Culture, and Body in Human Feeling*. Cambridge: Cambridge University Press, 2000.
Kringelbach, Morten and Helen Phillips. *Emotion: Pleasure and Pain in the Brain*. Oxford: Oxford University Press, 2014.
Kunda, Ziva. *Social Cognition: Making Sense of People*. Cambridge, MA: MIT Press, 1999.
Lakoff, George and Mark Turner. *More than Cool Reason: A Field Guide to Poetic Metaphor*. Chicago: University of Chicago Press, 1989.

Leary, Mark and June Tangney, eds. *Handbook of Self and Identity*. 2nd ed. New York: Guilford Press, 2012.
Leonard, Ira and Robert Parmet. *American Nativism, 1830–1860*. New York: Van Nostrand Reinhold, 1971.
Leverenz, David. "Mrs. Hawthorne's Headache: Reading *The Scarlet Letter*." In Murfin, *The Scarlet Letter*, 1991, 263–274.
Levine, Robert, ed. *The New Cambridge Companion to Herman Melville*. Cambridge: Cambridge University Press, 2013.
Levine, Robert, gen. ed. *The Norton Anthology of American Literature: 1820–1865*. 9th ed. New York: Norton, 2017.
Levine, Robert. "Reading Slavery and 'Classic' American Literature." In Tawil, *The Cambridge Companion to Slavery in American Literature*, 2016, 137–152.
Lukács, Georg. *Essays on Realism*. Ed. Rodney Livingstone. Trans. David Fernbach. Cambridge, MA: MIT Press, 1981.
Lukianoff, Greg and Jonathan Haidt. *The Coddling of the American Mind*. New York: Penguin, 2018.
MacDougall, Hugh. "Afterword." In Cooper, *The Last of the Mohicans*. New York: Penguin, 2014. Unpaginated Kindle edition.
Maddux, James and Jennifer Gosselin. "Self-Efficacy." In Leary and Tangney, *Handbook of Self and Identity*, 2012, 198–224.
Madsen, Deborah, ed. *Beyond the Borders: American Literature and Post-Colonial Theory*. London: Pluto Press, 2015.
Maitner, Angela, Eliot Smith, and Diane Mackie. "Intergroup Emotions Theory: Prejudice and Differentiated Emotional Reactions Toward Outgroups." In Sibley and Barlow, *The Cambridge Handbook of the Psychology of Prejudice*, 2017, 111–130.
Mancall, Peter. *Deadly Medicine: Indians and Alcohol in Early America*. Ithaca, NY: Cornell University Press, 1995.
Mann, Barbara Alice. "Race Traitor: Cooper, His Critics, and Nineteenth-Century Literary Politics." In Person, *A Historical Guide to James Fenimore Cooper*, 2007, 155–185.
Massari, Paul. "God and Money." *Harvard Divinity School*, 7 October2014. Available at https://hds.harvard.edu/news/2014/10/07/god-and-money# (accessed 4 September 2019).
Mather, Cotton. *The Wonders of the Invisible World*. London: John Russell Smith, 1862. Available at http://www.gutenberg.org/ebooks/28513#download (accessed 18 May 2019).
McFarland, Sam. "Identification with All Humanity: The Antithesis of Prejudice, and More." In Sibley and Barlow, *The Cambridge Handbook of the Psychology of Prejudice*, 2017, 632–654.
McLeod, John, ed. *The Routledge Companion to Postcolonial Studies*. London: Routledge, 2007.
McWilliams, John. "'More than a Woman's Enterprise': Cooper's Revolutionary Heroines and the Source of Liberty." In Person, *A Historical Guide to James Fenimore Cooper*, 2007, 61–90.
Meer, Sarah. "Slave Narratives as Literature." In Tawil, *The Cambridge Companion to Slavery in American Literature*, 2016, 70–85.
Melville, Herman. *Moby Dick*. Ed. Tony Tanner. Oxford: Oxford University Press, 1988.
Melville, Herman. *White-Jacket or The World in a Man-of-War*. In Tanselle, *Melville: Redburn, White-Jacket, Moby-Dick*, 1983, 341–770.
Michael, John. *Identity and the Failure of America: From Thomas Jefferson to the War on Terror*. Minneapolis: University of Minnesota Press, 2008.

Michaels, Walter Benn. *The Trouble with Diversity: How We Learned to Love Identity and Ignore Inequality.* New York: Metropolitan Books, 2007.
Millington, Richard, ed. *The Cambridge Companion to Nathaniel Hawthorne.* Cambridge: Cambridge UP, 2004.
Mitchell, Thomas. *Hawthorne's Fuller Mystery.* Amherst: University of Massachusetts Press, 1998.
Moon, Michael and Cathy Davidson, eds. *Subjects and Citizens: Nation, Race, and Gender from Oroonoko to Anita Hill.* Durham, NC: Duke University Press, 1995.
Morgan, Edmund. "The Puritans and Sex." *The New England Quarterly* 15 (4) (1942): 591–607.
Murfin, Ross. "Introduction: The Biographical and Historical Background." In Murfin, *The Scarlet Letter*, 1991, 3–19.
Murfin, Ross, ed. *The Scarlet Letter.* By Nathaniel Hawthorne. Boston, MA: Bedford Books, 1991.
Murray, Judith Sargent. *The Gleaner: A Miscellaneous Production.* London: Forgotten Books, 2018.
Murray, Judith Sargent. "On the Equality of the Sexes." In Gustafson, *The Norton Anthology of American Literature: Beginnings to 1820*, 2017, 772–779.
Murrin, John. "A Roof without Walls: The Dilemma of American National Identity." In *Beyond Confederation: Origins of the Constitution and American Identity.* Ed. Richard Beemen, Stephen Botein, and Edward Carter. Chapel Hill: University of North Carolina Press, 1987, 333–348.
Mynatt, Clifford, Michael Doherty, and Ryan Tweney. "Confirmation Bias in a Simulated Research Environment: An Experimental Study of Scientific Inference." In *Thinking: Readings in Cognitive Science.* Ed. P. N. Johnson-Laird and P. C. Wason. Cambridge: Cambridge University Press, 1977, 315–325.
Nandy, Ashis. *The Intimate Enemy: Loss and Recovery of Self under Colonialism.* Delhi: Oxford University Press, 1983.
Nandy, Ashis, Shikha Trivedy, Shail Mayaram, and Achyut Yagnik. *Creating a Nationality: The Ramjanmabhumi Movement and Fear of the Self.* Delhi: Oxford University Press, 1998.
Nelson, Diana. "Cooper's Leatherstocking Conversations: Identity, Friendship, and Democracy in the New Nation." In Person, *A Historical Guide to James Fenimore Cooper*, 2007, 123–154.
Newtown, George. "From Bottom to Top: Frederick Douglass Glimpses Male Identity from the Closet." *a/b: Auto/Biography Studies* 20 (2) (2005): 246–267.
Nielsen, Kim. *A Disability History of the United States.* Boston: Beacon Press, 2013.
Nietzsche, Friedrich. *The Birth of Tragedy.* In *Basic Writings of Nietzsche.* Ed. and Trans. Walter Kaufmann. New York: Modern Library, 1968.
Nisbett, Richard and Lee Ross. *Human Inference: Strategies and Shortcomings of Social Judgment.* Englewood Cliffs, NJ: Prentice-Hall, 1980.
Noble, Marianne. *The Masochistic Pleasures of Sentimental Literature.* Princeton, NJ: Princeton University Press, 2000.
Nussbaum, Martha. *Anger and Forgiveness: Resentment, Generosity, Justice.* Oxford: Oxford University Press, 2016.
Nussbaum, Martha. *From Disgust to Humanity: Sexual Orientation and Constitutional Law.* Oxford: Oxford University Press, 2010.
Nussbaum, Martha. *Hiding from Humanity: Disgust, Shame, and the Law.* Princeton, NJ: Princeton University Press, 2004.
Nussbaum, Martha. *The Monarchy of Fear: A Philosopher Looks at Our Political Crisis.* New York: Simon and Schuster, 2018. Unpaginated Kindle edition.

Nussbaum, Martha. *Upheavals of Thought: The Intelligence of Emotions.* Cambridge: Cambridge University Press, 2001.

Oatley, Keith, Dacher Keltner, and Jennifer Jenkins. *Understanding Emotions.* 2nd ed. Malden, MA: Blackwell, 2007.

Olney, James. "'I Was Born': Slave Narratives, Their Status as Autobiography and as Literature." In Davis and Gates, *The Slave's Narrative*, 1985, 148–175.

Ortiz, Paul. *An African American and Latinx History of the United States.* Boston: Beacon Press, 2018.

Oshiek, Carolyn. "Mary 3." In *Women in Scripture.* Ed. Carol Meyers. Boston, MA: Houghton Mifflin, 2000.

Otter, Samuel. "Stowe and Race." In Weinstein, *The Cambridge Companion to Harriet Beecher Stowe*, 2004, 15–38.

Oxford English Dictionary: OED Online. Oxford: Oxford University Press, 2019. Available at www.oed.com (accessed 6 May 2019).

Paine, Thomas. *The Essential Thomas Paine.* New York: New American Library, 1969.

Panksepp, Jaak. *Affective Neuroscience: The Foundations of Human and Animal Emotions.* New York: Oxford University Press, 1998.

Peck, Daniel, ed. *New Essays on The Last of the Mohicans.* Cambridge: Cambridge UP, 1992.

Person, Leland. "Gender and Sexuality." In Kelley, *A Companion to Herman Melville*, 2006, 231–246.

Person, Leland, ed. *A Historical Guide to James Fenimore Cooper.* Oxford: Oxford University Press, 2007.

Person, Leland. "Introduction: Fenimore Cooper's Literary Achievements." In Person, *A Historical Guide to James Fenimore Cooper*, 2007, 3–26.

Poe, Edgar Allan. "The Black Cat." In Levine, *The Norton Anthology of American Literature: 1820–1865*, 2017a, 670–676.

Poe, Edgar Allan. "The Tell-Tale Heart." In Levine, *The Norton Anthology of American Literature: 1820–1865*, 2017b, 666–670.

Poteat, V. Paul and Michelle Birkett. "Sexual Prejudice: Advances in Conceptual and Empirical Models." In Sibley and Barlow, *The Cambridge Handbook of the Psychology of Prejudice*, 2017, 371–391.

Putnam, George. "Irving." In Trent et al., *The Cambridge History of American Literature*, vol. 1, 1917, 245–259.

Ray, Larry, David Smith, and Liz Wastell. "Shame, Rage and Racist Violence." *British Journal of Criminology* 44 (3) (2004): 350–368.

Reynolds, Larry. *Devils and Rebels: The Making of Hawthorne's Damned Politics.* Ann Arbor: University of Michigan Press, 2008.

Rodgers, Daniel T. *As a City on a Hill: The Story of America's Most Famous Lay Sermon.* Princeton, NJ: Princeton University Press, 2018.

Rothermund, Dietmar. *The Routledge Companion to Decolonization.* London: Routledge, 2006.

Rowlandson, Mary. *A Narrative of the Captivity, Sufferings, and Removes of Mrs. Mary Rowlandson.* Boston: Thomas and John Fleet, 1791. Available at https://www.free-ebooks.net/fiction-classics/Narrative-of-the-Captivity-and-Restoration-of-Mrs-Mary-Rowlandson/pdf/preview. (Accessed 1 May 2019.)

Russell, Bertrand. *The Autobiography of Bertrand Russell: 1914–1944.* Boston, MA: Little, Brown and Company, 1968.

Said, Edward. *Culture and Imperialism.* New York: Vintage, 2012.

Samuels, Shirley. "Generation through Violence: Cooper and the Making of Americans." In Peck, *New Essays on The Last of the Mohicans*, 1992, 87–114.

Sanborn, Geoffrey. "Whence come you, Queequeg?" *American Literature* 77 (2) (2005): 227–257.
Sander, David and Klaus Scherer, eds. *Oxford Companion to Emotion and the Affective Sciences.* Oxford: Oxford UP, 2009.
Sapolsky, Robert. *Behave: The Biology of Humans at Our Best and Worst.* New York: Penguin, 2017.
Scheff, Thomas. "Social-Emotional Origins of Violence: A Theory of Multiple Killing." *Aggression and Violent Behavior* 16 (6) (2011): 453–460.
Scheff, Thomas and Suzanne Retzinger. *Emotions and Violence: Shame and Rage in Destructive Conflicts.* Lexington, MA: Lexington Books, 1991.
Schlenker, Barry. "Self-Presentation." In Leary and Tangney, *Handbook of Self and Identity,* 2012, 542–570.
Schloesser, Pauline E. *The Fair Sex: White Women and Racial Patriarchy in the Early American Republic.* New York: New York University Press, 2002.
Schwartz, Andrew. "In Person: Abigail Echo-Hawk." *In These Times,* November 2018, 7.
Sedgwick, Catharine Maria. *Hope Leslie: or, Early Times in the Massachusetts.* Overland Park, KS: Digireads.com, 2012.
Serwer, Adam. "The Terrorism that Doesn't Spark a Panic." *The Atlantic,* 28 January 2019. Available online at https://www.theatlantic.com/ideas/archive/2019/01/homegrown-terrorists-2018-were-almost-all-right-wing/581284/ (accessed 22 July 2019).
Shaffer, Jason. *Performing Patriotism: National Identity in the Colonial and Revolutionary American Theater.* Philadelphia: University of Pennsylvania Press, 2007.
Shah, Apurva. "The Cultural Faces of Shame." In Akhtar, *Shame: Developmental, Cultural, and Clinical Realms,* 2016, 49–70.
Shakespeare, William. *The Tragedy of Hamlet Prince of Denmark.* Ed. Edward Hubler. New York: Signet, 1987.
Shakespeare, William. *The Tragedy of Julius Caesar.* In *The Norton Shakespeare.* Gen. Ed. Stephen Greenblatt. New York: W.W. Norton, 1997, 1525–1589.
Shulman, George. "Chasing the Whale: Moby Dick as Political Theory." In Frank, *A Political Companion to Herman Melville,* 2013: 70–108.
Sibley, Chris and Fiona Barlow, eds. *The Cambridge Handbook of the Psychology of Prejudice.* Cambridge: Cambridge University Press, 2017.
Simpson, Alan. *Puritanism in Old and New England.* Chicago: University of Chicago Press, 1955.
Skemp, Sheila. *First Lady of Letters: Judith Sargent Murray and the Struggle for Female Independence.* Philadelphia, PA: University of Pennsylvania Press, 2009.
Slotkin, Richard. *The Fatal Environment: The Myth of the Frontier in the Age of Industrialization, 1800–1890.* New York: HarperPerennial, 1994.
Smith-Rosenberg, Carroll. *This Violent Empire: The Birth of an American National Identity.* Chapel Hill: University of North Carolina Press, 2010.
Snediker, Michael D. "Melville and Queerness without Character." In Levine, *The New Cambridge Companion to Herman Melville,* 2013, 155–168.
Soyinka, Wole. *Myth, Literature and the African World.* Cambridge: Cambridge University Press, 1976.
Stern, Jessica. *Terror in the Name of God: Why Religious Militants Kill.* New York: HarperCollins, 2003.
Stowe, Harriet Beecher. *Uncle Tom's Cabin.* New York: Bantam, 2003.
Sundquist, Eric. "The Frontier and American Indians." In *The Cambridge History of American Literature.* Ed. Sacvan Bercovitch. Cambridge: Cambridge University Press, 1995, 175–238.
Tanselle, G. Thomas, ed. *Melville: Redburn, White-Jacket, Moby-Dick.* New York: Library of America, 1983.

Tawil, Ezra, ed. *The Cambridge Companion to Slavery in American Literature*. Cambridge: Cambridge University Press, 2016a.

Tawil, Ezra. "Introduction." In Tawil, *The Cambridge Companion to Slavery in American Literature*, 2016b, 1–15.

Tawil, Ezra. *The Making of Racial Sentiment: Slavery and the Birth of the Frontier Romance*. Cambridge: Cambridge University Press, 2006.

Taylor, Olivia. "Cultural Confessions: Penance and Penitence in Nathaniel Hawthorne's *The Scarlet Letter* and *The Marble Faun*." *Renascence: Essays on Values in Literature* 58 (2) (2005): 135–152.

Thoreau, Henry David. *The Writings of Henry David Thoreau (II): Walden*. Boston: Houghton Mifflin, 1906. Available at https://www.walden.org/work/walden/ (accessed 6 May 2019).

Tompkins, Jane. *Sensational Designs: The Cultural Work of American Fiction, 1790–1860*. New York: Oxford University Press, 1985.

Trent, William, John Erskine, Stuart Sherman, and Carl Van Doren. "Preface." In Trent, et al., *The Cambridge History of American Literature*, 1917, iii–xi.

Trent, William, John Erskine, Stuart Sherman, and Carl Van Doren, eds. *The Cambridge History of American Literature*. 3 vols. (published in one text). Cambridge: Cambridge University Press, 1917, 1918 and 1921.

Varshney, Ashutosh. "Ethnic Conflict and Civil Society: India and Beyond." *World Politics* 53 (3) (2001): 362–398.

Varshney, Ashutosh. "Understanding Gujarat Violence." *Items and Issues* 4 (*1*) (2002–2003). Available at http://conconflicts.ssrc.org/archives/gujarat/varshney/ (accessed 25 May 2013).

Walker, Julian and Victoria Knauer. "Humiliation, Self-Esteem, and Violence." *Journal of Forensic Psychiatry and Psychology* 22(5) (2011): 724–741.

Wallace, Maurice. "Constructing the Black Masculine: Frederick Douglass, Booker T. Washington, and the Sublimits of African American Autobiography." In Moon and Davidson, *Subjects and Citizens: Nation, Race, and Gender from Oroonoko to Anita Hill*, 1995, 246–270.

Waller, Bruce. *Against Moral Responsibility*. Cambridge, MA: MIT P, 2011.

Ward, Abigail. "Psychological Formulations." In McLeod, *The Routledge Companion to Postcolonial Studies*, 2007, 190–201.

Ward, Geoff. *The Writing of America: Literature and Cultural Identity from the Puritans to the Present*. Cambridge: Polity Press, 2002.

Ward, Geoffrey. *The West: An Illustrated History*. Boston, MA: Little, Brown, and Co., 1996.

Warhol, Robyn. "'Ain't I De One Everybody Come to See?!': Popular Memories of Uncle Tom's Cabin." In *Hop on Pop: The Politics and Pleasures of Popular Culture*. Ed. Henry Jenkins, Tara McPherson, and Jane Shattuc. Durham, NC: Duke University Press, 2002, 650–669.

Weekes, Karen. "Poe's Feminine Ideal." *The Cambridge Companion to Edgar Allan Poe*. Ed. Kevin J. Hayes. Cambridge: Cambridge University Press, 2002, 148–162.

Weik von Mossner, Alexa. *Affective Ecologies: Empathy, Emotion, and Environmental Narrative*. Columbus: Ohio State University Press, 2017.

Weik von Mossner, Alexa. *Cosmopolitan Minds: Literature, Emotion, and the Transnational Imagination*. Austin: University of Texas Press, 2014.

Weinstein, Cindy, ed. *The Cambridge Companion to Harriet Beecher Stowe*. Cambridge: Cambridge University Press, 2004.

Welter, Barbara. *Dimity Convictions: The American Woman in the Nineteenth Century*. Athens, OH: Ohio University Press, 1976.

Winthrop, John. "A Modell of Christian Charity (1630)." Hanover Historical Texts Project, Hanover College. Available at https://history.hanover.edu/texts/winthmod.html (accessed 18 May 2019).
Wyman, Sarah. "Washington Irving's Rip Van Winkle: A Dangerous Critique of a New Nation." *ANQ: A Quarterly Journal of Short Articles, Notes, and Reviews* 23(4) (2010): 216–222.
Yellin, Jean Fagan. *Harriet Jacobs: A Life*. New York: Basic Civitas Books, 2004.
Zajonc, Robert B. "Feeling and Thinking: Closing the Debate over the Independence of Affect." In Forgas, *Feeling and Thinking: The Role of Affect in Social Cognition*, 2000, 31–58.
Zinn, Howard. *A People's History of the United States*. New York: HarperCollins, 2015.

INDEX

Page numbers in italics refer to figures.

Adams, Abigail 123, 127
Adams, John 123
adultery 130, 133
affective bias 33, 36, 38–39, 123, 174;
    see also bias
affectivity 21
African Americans: antipathy toward racial
    outgroups 38; biases of reasoning towards
    87–88; childhood models for
    understanding 46, 89–93; defiance 67;
    emotions of 98; issue of national identity
    among 93–95; men, denial of manhood
    to 114; nature of, men 44; racial
    discrimination towards 32; right to pursue
    happiness 28; and slavery 29, 35;
    subnational identity biases 35–38, 44;
    sufferings of 35; women, dangers of
    slavery for 99; see also Jacobs, Harriet, on
    slave African American women
age grades 33
ageism 139
aging 47, 132
alcoholism, in Native Americans 35, 49–50,
    75
Algers, Horatio 12
American dialect/speech 24, 29, 46; see also
    language
American exceptionalism 24
American identity 158; alternative
    formulations 29–30; and American
    literature 150–151; democratic

egalitarianism 27–30, 86, 93, 159, 161,
    172, 177, 179; derived from 28–29;
    ingroup definition 23–24; male–female
    relations 151; overlapping 22; practical
    identity 8, 19, 27, 30–31; among Russian
    Americans 21; self-concepts 19, 26–28,
    31, 164, 166; see also identity
American literary distinctiveness 24–25
American Novel and Its Tradition, The
    (Richard Chase) 24
American society, attitudes toward
    outgroups 31–35
Amerindians: association with demonic
    model 48, 63; customs 30–31;
    disappearance 45–46; emotions of 36, 38;
    outgrouping of 67
anger 50, 67; against discriminatory practices
    36; intergroup 67; and interpersonal
    stance 59
Anglo-Protestantism 30
animacy 33–34, 48, 62–68
animal and demonic models 47–48; see also
    demonic modeling
Annals of Salem, The 133
antiracism 168; see also racism
Apess, William, writings of 73–82; emotions
    in 79–81; empathy and modeling
    outgroups in 77–79; overview 73–75;
    spirituality and empathy in 76–77
Apollonian concept 25
aristocracy 27, 28, 53

attachment bonding 37, 81, 86; centrality of 103–105, 125; between Europeans and Amerindians 52–55; interracial 44–45; nonsexual 105; and religion 80–81; and sexual desire 144–145
attachment insecurity 80, 86

Baldwin, James 36
Baptist, Edward 3
Baym, Nina 133
bias: affective 33, 36; cognitive 20, 32, 33, 38, 78; emotional 36; evaluative 20; ideological 65; race-based cognitive 34; sex-based 34, 38–39
Bible, the 51, 87–88, 136
biblical conception of Israel 128
biblical legalism 126
black nationalism 95, 121; see also identity
black people see African Americans
black readership, awareness of see Douglass, Frederick
black–white racial opposition 20; see also racism
Brackenridge, Hugh 42
Bradford, William 65
British-American ingroup 47; see also ingroups
British imperialism 34
British violence, against Native Americans 70
Britton-Purdy, Jedediah 25
Brown, Charles Brockden 42
Brown, John 115

Calvinism 129
Canada 95
captivity narratives 35, 61–62
Cashin, Sheryll 37
categorial identity 54; emotions in 34; formation 20; meaning 8–9, 19; pseudospeciation of 20
Catholicism 134
Chase, Richard 24
Child, Lydia Maria 102, 114
childhood, model for African Americans 77, 89–93; see also African Americans
child–parent attachment 117–118
Chosen People of the Old Testament 128
Christians: European 76; principles of 60–61, 76
citizenship 22, 23, 120
Citrin, Jack 9, 29–30
class, as identity division 11–12; see also identity

cognitive biases 20, 32, 33, 38, 78; see also bias
Colacurcio, Michael 136
Cold War 24
collective punishment, based on race 69; see also racism
collective society 28
colonial hierarchy 81
compassion 36, 38
contempt 34, 36
Cooper, James Fenimore see Last of the Mohicans (James Fenimore Cooper)
Coquette, The (Hannah Webster Foster) 149
cosmopolitan liberalism 29–30
Cox, Harvey 129
Crayon, Geoffrey 1
cross-group friendships 37
cultural degradation 64–65, 80
cultural identity 64–65; see also identity
cultural mixing 26
Culture of Conformism, The (Hogan) 33

"death," of group 46
de Buffon, Georges-Louis Leclerc 25
Declaration of Independence (1776) 28–29
de Crèvecoeur, J. Hector St. John 2, 26, 28
defiance 67–69
Degler, Carl 4
dehumanization 49–50
Delawares 46, 47
demeaning 33, 36
democratic dignity 161
democratic egalitarianism 27–30, 86, 93, 159, 161, 172, 177, 179
demonic modeling 33, 48, 51, 63–64, 78–79, 134, 171, 173
demon slavery 101; see also slavery
deniability 169
despair 34–35, 38, 54, 86, 111, 131, 136–137
destigmatizing adult women 125, 132; see also women
de Tocqueville, Alexis 27
"devil," the (Chillingworth) 139
discriminatory sociopolitical systems 34, 35
disgust 34, 36, 37, 59–60, 64, 124–125
distrust 37–38, 104, 112, 115, 118
Douglass, Frederick 98, 99, 110, 111; see also Life and Times of Frederick Douglass (Frederick Douglass)
Dovidio, John 36, 37
Dunbar-Ortiz, Roxanne 8, 45, 65, 126
durability 12, 21
Dionysian concept 25

economic self-reliance 30
Edgar Huntly (Charles Brockden Brown) 42
egalitarianism: democratic 27–30, 86, 93, 159, 161, 172, 177, 179; socioeconomic 127
emotions: of African Americans 98; of Amerindians 36; Apess's appeals to 79–81; in categorial identity 34; emotional attitudes toward outgroups 33; emotional biases 36; emotional orientation 20; reader's 52–55; for self-presentation 112–114; of women 156
empathy 33, 99, 130–131
empowerment 38
English identity 51, 106
English literary traditions 24–25
envy 33
epigraphs 164
ethnic diversity 24, 26–27; *see also* multiethnicity
ethnic identity 78, 163; *see also* identity
European Americans 25–26, 28; adult attitudes of 36; anger towards Amerindians 35; antipathy toward racial outgroups 38; human sympathy in 35; Jacobs on distrust of 104; parallelism with Native Americans 61–62; racial discrimination by 32
European subcultures 26–27
evaluative biases 20; *see also* cognitive biases
expansive inclusiveness 23

fear 37, 59
feminism 151, 154
Fiedler, Leslie 11, 34–35, 37–38, 42, 45
Fletcher, William 60–62, 68–69
Flint, Timothy 44
Foster, Hannah Webster 149
Franklin, Benjamin 30–31
Frontier Thesis 26
Fugitive Slave Act 37, 85, 88, 113
Fuller, Margaret 127

Gandhi, Mahatma 98–99
gays 67; in Melville's *Moby Dick* 169; in Poe's "The Black Cat" 142, 145–146
gender: deviance 137; identification 113–115, 172; *see also* males; women
genderqueer activism 9
Gilligan, James 12
Grandin, Greg 26
Grumer, Rebecca 25, 42, 44, 46
guilt 34–35, 38, 100, 159

Harris, George 95, 114
Hawthorne, Nathaniel: attitude toward Hutchinson 136–137; on national and familial tradition 132–133; themes 127–132; *see also Scarlet Letter, The* (Nathaniel Hawthorne)
helplessness 38, 77
history distinctiveness 24
homoerotic romance 168
honor killings 123
Hope Leslie (Catharine Maria Sedgwick) 58–71; animacy modeling 62–64; critique 60–61; defiance 67–69; explaining stereotypes 66–67; ideological retreat 70–71; irony regarding characters' ideological blindness 65; overview 58–60; parallelism of European American and Native American 61–62; romantic love and friendship 64–65; spirituality 69–70
humanism 163
humiliation 49, 50, 123
Huntington, Samuel 30
Hurons 47–48
Hutchinson, Ann 135, 136–137
Hutson, Richard 45, 50–51

identity: categories 31–32; class as identity division 11–12; concept of 19–23; cultural 64–65; definition 25; ethnic 78, 163; identity-group conflict 102; identity-group opposition 36; meaning 19–23; national 7–9, 23, 31, 44, 106, 119–120, 128, 151, 154; oppositions 20; *see also* American identity; English identity
ideological biases 65; *see also* bias
ideology: meritocratic 32; racial 45–50, 63, 84; sexist 33
immigrants, from Catholic Europe 26
implicated authors 84
implied authors 84
inclusion criteria 22
India, states and religions of 7
Indian Wars of the West (Timothy Flint) 44
individualism 26, 29–30, 161, 164
ingroups: British-American 47; distinctiveness 24; identifications 20–21; inferiority 34; ingroup–outgroup relations 32–33; national 25; *see also* outgrouping/outgroups
insensibility 157
interpersonal stances 20, 33, 36, 52, 59, 77
interracial bonding 53–55, 54, 76, 104, 118
interracial reconciliation 101–102, 105–106

interracial romance 37–38, 79, 101–103; see also romance
intersectionality 132
Irving, Washington 34
Isenberg, Nancy 4, 28

Jacobs, Harriet, on slave African American women 98–107; emplotment 105; on moral feelings 100; nationalism 106–107; overview 98–99; on romantic love and racism 101–103; on sexual vulnerability of female slaves 99–100; standard techniques 100–101; suffering due to attachment 103–105
Jefferson, Thomas 25
Jews 22–23, 33, 59, 78–79, 128
Johnson, Samuel 29
just-world thinking 129–130

Kant, Immanuel 101
Kashmiri Hindus 45
kinship 118
Know-Nothings 22
Kunda, Ziva 143–144

language: distinctiveness and identity 24; fluency 60; and identity 8; Native American 46; transnational issues of 7
Last of the Mohicans (James Fenimore Cooper) 42–56; age and ethnic trajectory 45–47; changing readers' emotions 52–55; critique 50–52; interracial attachment bonding in 44–45; nonstandard stereotyping 47–48; stereotype explanation 48–50
legal exclusion 79
lesbians 67
Letters from an American Farmer (J. Hector St. John de Crèvecoeur) 24
Liberia 90, 94, 95, 120
Life and Times of Frederick Douglass (Frederick Douglass) 110–122; dominant narrative structure 114–115; emotions for self-presentation 112–114; experiences and inclinations of his personal identity 115–118; Frederick Douglass and attachment to the national home 118–121; overview 110–112
Life of a Slave Girl (Harriet Jacobs) 114
Lincoln, Abraham 93, 113, 118, 120
Lukács, Georg 83

Macbeth, Weird Sisters in 124
MacDougall, Hugh 45, 47, 49
Maitner, Angela 59

males: antipathy toward women 142–146; bonding 115; see also women
male–female identity categorization 32–33
male–female outgrouping 34
Mancall, Peter 35
Mann, Michael 44
Marxist internationalism 23
material well-being 129
maternal women 104; see also women
Mather, Cotton 125–126
Melville, Herman 45, 161–183; see also *Moby Dick* (Herman Melville)
"*Men of Color, to Arms*" 114–115
meritocratic ideology 32; see also ideology
meritocratic system 27–28
Milton, John 44
misogyny 32–33, 123, 132, 138; disgust and desire 124, 143–145; and sexism 142–146
Moby Dick (Herman Melville) 37–38; American identity 162; antiracism 168; companionable mates 173; epigraphs 164; European American 162; homoerotic romance 168, 172; humanism 163; interracial romance in 105; justification of white supremacism 164; main narrative structure of 168; national/antinational concerns 164; paralleling cultures, techniques of 172; from pseudospeciation to practical identity 167–168; racism and ethnocentrism 169; religious obligations 173–174; sexual component of romance 168–169; subnational racial division 161
Mohicans 47; see also *Last of the Mohicans* (James Fenimore Cooper)
moral/morality 127–128; guilt 100; and intellectual maturity 90; self-improvement 28; sufferings of slaves 100
Morton, Thomas 127
multiethnicity 26–27, 30
Murray, Judith Sargent 31; on American identity and American literature 150–151; "On the Equality of the Sexes" (essay) 149–150; literary works of, overview 148–149; *The Traveller Returned* (1796) 155–159; *Virtue Triumphant* (1795) 151–155
Murrin, John 27, 65
Muslims 7, 8, 22–23, 26
My Bondage, My Freedom (Frederick Douglass) 111

Nandy, Ashis 33–34, 46
Narrative of the Captivity and Restoration of Mrs. Mary Rowlandson (Mary Rowlandson) 66–67

Narrative of the Life of Frederick Douglass (Frederick Douglass) 99, 110
national delegitimation 93, 95
national ingroups 25; *see also* ingroups
national unity 23
nation-building 5–7, 10–11, 23, 31
Native Americans 30–31, 32, 35, 36; alcoholism 35; animal and demonic models 47–48; antipathy toward racial outgroups 38; defiance 67; dominant ideological identification of 43; egalitarian understanding of 60; ethnicities 47; parallelism with European Americans 61–62; religion 51; *see also Last of the Mohicans* (James Fenimore Cooper)
Native Son (Richard Wright) 36, 44
nativism 29–30
negros 29, 89–90, 103, 112, 114; *see also* African Americans
Nietzsche, Friedrich 25
nonsexual attachment bonds 105; *see also* attachment bonding
Notes on the State of Virginia (Thomas Jefferson) 25
Nussbaum, Martha 59, 124, 135, 143

"On the Equality of the Sexes" (essay) 31; intellectual talents of women 150; psychology 149; shifting tastes of women 150; unmarried woman 150; *see also* Murray, Judith Sargent
opposability 21
outgrouping/outgroups 20; of Amerindians 67; attitudes toward 31–35; in hierarchical societies 129; by sex 124; of women 131; *see also* ingroups

Paine, Thomas 3, 28, 29, 127
Pakistan 7
patriarchy, defined 32
"patrolitical" slander 155
Pequot War 61
"Philo Americanus" (Lover of America) 151
physical well-being 80
place distinctiveness 24
Poe, Edgar Allan 142–146
political enfranchisement 36, 85
political participation 30
political structure distinctiveness 24
practical identity 8, 30–31; development in women 148; meaning 19; in *Moby Dick* (Herman Melville) 167–168
pre–Civil War 112, 119
pride 15, 34, 38, 52, 68, 98, 102, 112, 115, 119, 129–131

prosperity theology 129–130
Protestants 22–23
pseudospeciation 20, 167–168
public whipping 50
Puritans 27, 125–127

"Quadroons, The" (Lydia Maria Child) 102, 105, 114
Quakerism 87, 127

race-based cognitive bias 34; *see also* bias
racial and cultural prejudices, criticism of 55
racial antipathy 37, 78, 123
racial hierarchies 42
racial ideology 45–50, 63, 84; *see also* ideology
racially discriminatory sociopolitical system 32
racial slavery 93; *see also* slavery
racism 32, 36, 49, 51–53, 79–80, 81, 169, 182
radical divergence 24–25
rage *see* anger
religion 21; and attachment bonding 80–81; distinctiveness 24; religious belief and practice 27; religious devotion 80–81; religious diversity 28; religious groups, rationalization of 30; religious obligations 173–174; religious quality of the U.S. national self-concept 27
Revolutionary War 156–157
romance: interracial 37–38, 79, 101–103; romantic love and friendship 64–65; romantic sympathy 44; same-sex romantic love 172; sexual component of 168–169
Romantic Satanism 44; *see also* Satan
Rosaldo, Renato 45
Rowlandson, Mary 61, 65–67
Russell, Bertrand 99

Said, Edward 67
salience 11–12, 21, 125
Samaritans 78
same-sex romantic love 172; sexual desire 146; *see also* romance; sexual desire
Sapolsky, Robert 145
Satan: invocation of 101; Satanic seduction 124; sin of 131; worship 63–64
Scarlet Letter, The (Nathaniel Hawthorne) 123–139; malleable children, wrinkled witches, and demonic old men 138–139; in national and familial tradition 132–133; New England, Puritan and Victorian 125–127; sex and national identity 123–125; sexuality, and the

moral goodness of sin 133–136; themes 127–132; women and spiritual independence 136–138
Schadenfreude 20, 33, 52, 59
Schoolcraft, Henry 48
Sears, David O. 9, 29–30
self-aggrandizement 74, 129
self-criticism 89, 94, 128–132
self-cultivation 148, 150, 156
self-disgust 135–136, *144*
self-doubt 74
self-efficacy 77
self-esteem 98
self-pity 112, 121
self-respect 98, 114–115
separation anxiety 86, 120
settler colonialism 8, 11
sex: categorization 21, 127; gratification 101–102; identity, subnational division created by 142–146; liberation 127; and national identity 123–125; opposition 139; purity 127; sex-based antipathy 123, 125; sex-based bias 34, 38–39, 123; sex-based outgrouping 32, 124–125, 139; shame 127, 144–145
sexism 32, 33
sexual desire 37–38, 105; and attachment 144–145; motivations of *144*; same-sex 146
Sexual Identities 70
sexuality 27, 124, 133–136
sexual violence 142–146
shame 34, 38, 49–50, 127, 135, 144–145
Sheridan, Philip (General) 47
sinfulness 15, 128–131, 133–134, 138–139
Skemp, Sheila 10
skin color 76–77, 79, 99
slaveholding society 29
slavery 53, 101; and African Americans 29, 35; demon 101; racial 93; Stowe on 85–88; women, dangers for 99; *see also* Jacobs, Harriet, on slave African American women
Smith-Rosenberg, Carroll 30
social attributions 22, 23
social class 20, 152
social definition, of identity groups 23
social hierarchy 78, 84, 113, 158
social mobility 12
social structure 12, 24, 31, 101
social well-being 84
socioeconomic egalitarianism 127; *see also* egalitarianism
sociopolitical distinctiveness 27
sodomitical, the 169
Sommer, Doris 45

Son of the Forest, A (William Apess) 74, 77
spirituality: Apess on 76–77; Cooper's view on 51; Hawthorne on 127–128, 133–134; *Hope Leslie* (Catharine Maria Sedgwick) 69–70; and ideological blindness 65–66; Stowe on 92–93
stereotype 44; Apess on 75–76; *Hope Leslie* (Catharine Maria Sedgwick) 66–67; *Last of the Mohicans* (James Fenimore Cooper) 48–50; reversal 100
Stowe, Harriet Beecher 36–37, 46, 83, 114; *see also Uncle Tom's Cabin* (Harriet Beecher Stowe)
subcultures, European 26–27
subnational division 7–9, 161
subnational identity/identification 9–11, 35–39, 38

taboos 38, 53
Tallmadge, James 29
Thoreau, Henry David 27
Tompkins, Jane 89
transgendering 23
Traveller Returned, The (Murray, Judith Sargent): American identity 158; comedy 155; connection with "Equality" essay 155; darker side to revolution 157; emotions of women 156; issue of self-cultivation 156; national concerns of 156; psychological inconsistency in writers 158–159; revolutionary insensibility 157; and Revolutionary War 156–157; safety issues 157–158
trust 103–104
Twain, Mark 24

unalienable rights 29
Uncle Tom's Cabin (Harriet Beecher Stowe): childhood model 89–93; implied readers 88–89; overview 83–85; race and nation 93–95; on slavery and empathy 85–88
Understanding Nationalism (Hogan) 21
universalism 18, 23

Victorians 125–127
Vietnam War 34, 43, 93
Virtue Triumphant (Judith Sargent Murray) 151–155; application of reason 153; equality in social class 152; feminism 151, 154; financial management by women 152–153; libelous propensities of women 153; representation of men 153–154; romantic comedy 151; sensitivities of women 154; subnational division between men/women 154

Ward, Geoff 29
Washington, George 94
well-being: of black people 93; material 129; physical, of Native Americans 80; social 84; of nation 181
White Jacket 169
white supremacism 35–36, 164
Whitman, Walt 24
Williams, Roger 60, 63
Wilson, John 135
Winthrop, John 65, 128
witchcraft 126; and sexual violence 142–146; victims of 136, 138
women 36; black, dangers of slavery for 99; defiance 67; "On the Equality of the Sexes" (essay) 150; feeling of exclusion among 35; financial management by 152–153; inferior to men in reason and judgment 150; intellectual talents of 150; maternal 104; outgrouping of 32; practical identity development 148; quest for self-cultivation 148; sensitivities of 154; and spiritual independence 136–138; white men exploiting 80; *see also* Jacobs, Harriet, on slave African American women
Wonders of the Invisible World, The 125–126
Wright, Richard 36, 44

Yellin, Jean 106

Zinn, Howard 4, 127, 136

For Product Safety Concerns and Information please contact our EU representative GPSR@taylorandfrancis.com
Taylor & Francis Verlag GmbH, Kaufingerstraße 24, 80331 München, Germany

www.ingramcontent.com/pod-product-compliance
Lightning Source LLC
Chambersburg PA
CBHW052113300426
44116CB00010B/1649